Getting to the

CRE

of **Literacy** for
History/
Social Studies,
Science, and
Technical Subjects

Grades 6–12

This book is dedicated to my Greek parents—for all their sacrifices and for teaching me that with hard work and dedication all my dreams can come true; and to the memory of my grandmother (my namesake), an exceptional woman, who was orphaned and then later on widowed at a young age, who experienced hardship, war, and poverty in her lifetime—for teaching me, by example, to live life to the fullest and to be strong and independent.

—Vicky

This book is dedicated to Dr. O. Paul Wielan who taught me about literacy at St. John's University and has continued to be my teacher long after my graduation. I am forever grateful for your presence in my life as a friend and mentor.

—Maureen

Getting to the C⬤RE

of **Literacy** for
History/
Social Studies,
Science, and
Technical Subjects

Grades 6–12

Vicky Giouroukakis
Maureen Connolly

CORWIN
A SAGE Company

FOR INFORMATION:

Corwin

A SAGE Company

2455 Teller Road

Thousand Oaks, California 91320

(800) 233-9936

www.corwin.com

SAGE Publications Ltd.

1 Oliver's Yard

55 City Road

London EC1Y 1SP

United Kingdom

SAGE Publications India Pvt. Ltd.

B 1/I 1 Mohan Cooperative Industrial Area

Mathura Road, New Delhi 110 044

India

SAGE Publications Asia-Pacific Pte. Ltd.

3 Church Street

#10-04 Samsung Hub

Singapore 049483

Copyright © 2013 by Corwin

Printed in the United States of America

A catalog record of this book is available from the Library of Congress.

ISBN 978-1-4522-5544-6

Acquisitions Editor: Carol Collins

Associate Editor: Kimberly Greenberg

Editorial Assistant: Francesca Dutra Africano

Production Editor: Amy Schroller

Copy Editor: Linda Gray

Typesetter: C&M Digitals (P) Ltd.

Proofreader: Susan Schon

Indexer: Judy Hunt

Cover Designer: Gail Buschman

Permissions Editor: Jennifer Baron

This book is printed on acid-free paper.

SUSTAINABLE FORESTRY INITIATIVE

Certified Chain of Custody
Promoting Sustainable Forestry
www.sfiprogram.org
SFI-01268

SFI label applies to text stock

13 14 15 16 17 10 9 8 7 6 5 4 3 2 1

Contents

Acknowledgments

We wish to acknowledge Carol Chambers Collins, Lisa Luedeke, and the entire Corwin staff, Francesca Dutra Africano, Amy Schroller, and Linda Gray, for their belief in our vision for this book and for their continued support of this product from start to finish. We would also like to thank our colleagues at our respective institutions of education—Molloy College and Mineola High School—for their sustained encouragement of our work, especially the English Language Arts professionals with whom we have worked over the years who have inspired us. In addition, we wish to express our gratitude to the students (both high school students and prospective teachers) we have taught in the past and will teach in the future for motivating us to become better teachers. Finally, we would like to sincerely thank those who work tirelessly to ensure quality education for all students.

A very special acknowledgment goes to our core families:

Vicky's core family: husband, John—my saint, for your uncommon and unwavering love, patience, and encouragement (you make me a better person every day); Emanuel, Anna, and Paul—for showing me the true meaning of life and for your unconditional love and understanding; dad Polychronis and mom Constantina—for all the sacrifices you have made and still make for me and for fostering in me the values of family, education, and hard work; mom-in-law, Anna—for all your help and support; Steve, Elaine, Tina, Stephanie, Paul, and Peter; George, Margie, Tina, and Catherine—for your constant love. My co-author, Maureen, who, in many ways, has become a part of my family—for being an exceptional friend and colleague with whom to work.

Maureen's core family: mom, Elizabeth "Rose"—for always being eager to help; dad, John—for always being supportive of my education; Katie—for always being willing to listen; James—for always making me laugh; Rob—for always keeping me safe; Megan and Melissa—for always being eager to share a love of Pinkalicious reading and silly storytelling. Daniel Paul—for making me smile with your smile. My chosen family, my friends—for celebrating all of life's successes with me and supporting me through thick and thin. My writing "sister," Vicky—for your enthusiasm, your patience, and your ability to keep us on track even in the midst of our chaotic lives; it is an honor and a pleasure to work with you. And, of course, for my husband, Andrew and stepson, Ben—for turning my world around and filling it with more love and joy than I could ever have imagined. BAM!

About the Authors

Vicky Giouroukakis, PhD (née Vasiliki Menexas), is an Associate Professor in the Division of Education at Molloy College, Rockville Centre, New York. She teaches graduate courses to prospective and practicing secondary English teachers and English as a Second Language (ESL) teachers. Prior to her tenure at Molloy, Vicky taught English at a public high school in Queens, New York, and ESL to adolescents and adults. She also taught at Manhattanville College and Queens College, CUNY. Her research interests include adolescent literacy, standards and assessment, teacher education, and cultural and linguistic diversity. Her work has been featured in books and scholarly journals, and she frequently presents at regional, national, and international conferences. In 2010, Vicky was the recipient of the Educator of Excellence Award by the New York State English Council. She has been interested in standards and assessment and how they affect teaching and learning ever since she began teaching. Moreover, her dissertation work was on the impact of state assessments in English on instructional practice. Vicky received a master's degree in English Education from Teachers College, Columbia University. She also earned a master's degree in TESOL and a doctorate in Reading/Writing/Literacy at the University of Pennsylvania. Vicky resides in New York with her supportive husband and three loving children. She can be reached by e-mail at vgiouroukakis@molloy.edu.

Maureen Connolly, EdD, has been an English teacher at Mineola High School on Long Island, New York, and has worked as a professor of Education at Molloy College, Adelphi University, and Queens College. In addition, as a grant coordinator for the New York Metropolitan Area, she has developed many standards-based, service-learning experiences that link community outreach, character education, and reading. She has also collaborated on several publications related to service learning. While Maureen credits her passion for service to her mother, a music teacher who often coordinated trips for her pupils to perform at a local nursing home, she credits her love of literature and teaching to her grandmother, a professor of English at Hunter College, and her grandfather, a salesman for Macmillan. Maureen earned her master's degree in Reading and her doctorate in Educational Leadership at St. John's University. She has been awarded the title of Honoree for the ASCD Outstanding Young Educator of the Year and granted the St. John's University LEAD Award. Maureen has presented workshops at regional, national, and international conferences, and volunteered to teach in India, Ghana, Peru, and Spain. Maureen was recently part of the Teachers for Global Classrooms Program which promotes global education. She believes that at the core of her profession is the need to develop purposeful learning that opens students' eyes to the potential for positive change in themselves and in their local, national, and global communities. Maureen resides in Princeton, New Jersey, and can be reached at mocomac25@hotmail.com.

Introduction

How to Use This Book

The Common Core State Standards (CCSS) for Literacy in History/Social Studies, Science, and Technical Subjects were designed to allow teachers and students to vary their approaches to learning while maintaining a strong level of academic rigor. With the advent of the CCSS, now more than ever, teachers are working to infuse reading and writing across the curriculum in purposeful and meaningful ways. This book focuses on the literacy standards for Grades 6–12, which include two strands: Reading and Writing. It is important to note that according to the CCSS, the Reading and Writing standards are meant to complement the specific content demands of the disciplines, not replace them. Within this book, we refer to the Anchor Standards by strand and number; in other words, *R. 3* means *Reading Anchor Standard 3*.

The Reading Standards reflect the CCSS' great emphasis on reading of informational texts aligned with the **National Assessment of Educational Progress** (NAEP) Reading Framework. Reading Standard 10 requires the reading of high-quality texts in a range of genres of increasing complexity.

The Writing Standards consist of two different types of writing: argument and explanatory. If instruction is to be aligned with the NAEP Writing Framework, the major focus of writing throughout high school should be on arguments and informative/explanatory texts (National Governors Association Center for Best Practices [NGA Center]/Council of Chief State School Officers [CCSSO], 2010b). It is our hope that this book will help content-area teachers better understand and address the CCSS.

OVERVIEW OF CHAPTERS

We based the structure of this book on our first book, *Getting to the Core of English Language Arts, Grades 6–12: How to Meet the Common Core State Standards With Lessons From the Classroom* (Giouroukakis & Connolly, 2012). In the first chapter of this book, we provide an overview of the CCSS for Literacy in the Content Areas and a rationale for their creation. Also, we include a discussion of best practices regarding lesson design. Our experiences as high school teachers and as graduate education professors for preservice teachers have led us to value the Backward Design framework of Grant Wiggins and Jay McTighe. We make clear the connection between the CCSS and the development of students' skills and knowledge by highlighting common verbs used (a) in the analysis of students' career and college readiness, (b) in the CCSS, and (c) by Bloom to designate higher-order thinking. In addition, we discuss Gardner's theory of Multiple Intelligences as a guide for your reflection on how meeting the CCSS helps you to address the needs of your students. We also discuss Dewey's concept of the productive citizen and the greater purpose that this concept can give to students' efforts to meet and exceed the standards.

In Chapter 1, we focus on the Reading Standards for Literacy in History/Social Studies, Science, and Technical Subjects. In Chapter 2, we discuss the benefits of the CCSS for the teaching of reading in the content areas. Chapter 3 includes three reading lessons in History/Social Studies for Grades 6–12. Chapter 4 includes three reading lessons in Science and Technical Subjects for Grades 6–12; each reading lesson is based on one of the three strands of the Reading College and Career Readiness (CCR) Anchor Standards:

- Key Ideas and Details
- Craft and Structure
- Integration of Knowledge and Ideas

To streamline the language in our book, we consistently refer to the CCR Anchor Standards simply as *Anchor Standards.*

In Part II, we focus on the Writing Standards for Literacy in History/Social Studies, Science, and Technical Subjects. In Chapter 5, we discuss the benefits of the CCSS for the teaching of writing in the content areas. Chapter 6 includes three argument writing lessons, one in each content area—History/Social Studies, Science, and Technical Subjects. Chapter 7 includes informative/explanatory writing lessons in each of the three content areas.

LESSON FORMAT

In Chapters 3, 4, 6, and 7 we provide sample lessons that are meant to serve as examples of CCSS-based lesson design. An introduction at the start of each applications chapter provides, for your consideration, some questions that we hope will make your reflection on lessons for that strand more meaningful.

Before each lesson narrative, we include a template that outlines the workings of the lesson. This template includes the following:

1. Topic and Grade Level—Content-area topic and grade levels 6–8, 9–10, or 11–12

2. CCSS Strand—Reading or writing

3. Text Types and Purposes—Argument or informative/explanatory

4. Timing—The expected number of class periods in which the lesson takes place, although this will vary from class to class

5. Backward Design Components of the Lesson—Include Desired Results/ CCSS Addressed, Acceptable Evidence, and Learning Experiences and Instruction

6. Teaching Strategies Utilized—Include guidance and monitoring, modeling, cooperative learning, discussion, and writing process

7. Supplemental Resources—Additional resources for teachers to adapt and revise the lesson to best fit their students' needs

8. Technology/Media Opportunities—Ways of incorporating technology and media into the lesson

9. Service Learning Links—Ways to tie student learning with outreach to the school, local, or global community

10. Variations—Ways to modify or extend the lesson to meet the diverse needs of the student population, including variations such as opportunities for making interdisciplinary connections and incorporating additional or varied texts, skills, and instructional strategies

This template is meant to serve as a preview of the lesson narrative and as a model for the analysis of your own lessons. We provide a blank copy of the same template in the Appendix to serve as an organizer or checklist when you create new lessons.

Following the template is a lesson narrative. In each lesson narrative, we indicate, in brackets, the major CCSS for Literacy that are addressed. Here is an example:

> The purpose of the activity is to encourage students to analyze how the symbols in the story might have had an influence on German society [R.4, R.5, R.6].

Other CCSS are covered as well, but the major standards are those that the lesson addresses most fully. These lessons are not prescribed instruction; they are meant to be used as models and to be adapted to suit your particular students' needs.

If you think your students need to better develop their writing skills, please do not overlook the reading chapters. (The reverse also applies.) The skills within each lesson in this book are intertwined. For example, students' analysis of strong writing in the chapters "Reading Lessons in . . ." can help them develop as writers. Conversely, students' understanding of the structure of good writing can improve their skills as readers.

Throughout the lesson narratives, you will note the following marginal sidebars:

Tech Connection

Theory Link

Differentiation Tip

Cultural/Linguistic Highlight

Tech Connection indicates how technology is incorporated into the lesson. Theory Link shows how we believe the major, enduring theorists in education (Dewey, Bloom, and Gardner) relate to the lesson. Differentiation Tip helps you to adapt the lesson based on your student population. Cultural/Linguistic Highlight emphasizes supports specifically for culturally and linguistically diverse students.

Our purpose in presenting the lessons this way is to make your experience of reading through the lesson narratives similar to the experience of reading through a used book that has already been annotated. Some of the basic thinking is already done for you. We make the connections between the lessons and the CCSS overt by noting the standards in brackets. The marginal sidebars make technology infusion, differentiation, and theoretical and cultural linguistic connections explicit as well.

LESSON SELECTION

Collecting lessons for this book was an inspiring process. We are so grateful to all who contributed. We sought to vary the types of history/social studies lessons by including U.S., and world/global history. We chose a range of science lessons as well, including earth science, chemistry, and biology. As we sought out technical lessons, we found that our eyes were opened to the creative thinking of computer applications, sports-marketing teachers, and math teachers. Some might question the inclusion of math within the technical subjects, since there is a separate set of CCSS for math. Why should math teachers be concerned with two sets of standards? Literacy skills are needed in all subject areas—including math!

In addition to varying the subject areas covered in this book, we sought to include both literary readings and informational readings. Also, we wanted to present lessons that have clear opportunities for students to work independently to show what they have learned. According to the NGA Center/CCSSO

(2010b), "Students must be able to read complex informational texts in these fields with independence and confidence because the vast majority of reading in college and workforce training programs will be sophisticated nonfiction" (p. 60).

The CCSS call for us to align with the NAEP requirement that a total of 70% of reading completed by secondary students be informational rather than literary by the time they reach 12th grade. This happens fairly naturally since the content areas outside English include mainly informational reading. The majority of the readings in the lessons for this book are informational. However, given that this balance of 70/30 is applicable throughout the subject areas, we include some related fictional readings.

The skills developed through these lessons are intertwined within the literacy strands that are being met as well as across the strands. For example, students need a variety of reading skills to navigate the components of nonfiction or informational texts (higher-order thinking, sophisticated vocabulary, an understanding of universal themes). The skills are intertwined among literacy strands as well. Developing reading skills will also help students improve their writing skills. By reading well-written nonfiction or informational texts, students will gain an understanding of how to best structure their own expository writing.

The lessons in this book are organized according to the Anchor Standards that are most prevalent. For example, the reading lessons are categorized according to the topics of the Anchor Standards for reading (i.e., "Key Ideas and Details," "Craft and Structure," "Integration of Knowledge and Ideas") (see Figure I.1). The writing lessons are organized according to "Text Types and Purposes" (see Figure I.2). Of course, each lesson includes varied types of thinking, so you can expect some overlap within the specified set of Anchor Standards. For example, a reading lesson categorized under "Craft and Structure" still requires students to understand "Key Ideas and Details." Similarly, a writing lesson may involve explanatory writing along with argument.

This book is designed to help you become more familiar with the CCSS and to guide you in aligning your lesson plans with the standards. We have striven to get to the core of these state standards and uncover their benefits for the teaching of reading and writing. We believe that the most powerful components of this book are the lessons from the field for literacy in the content areas that guide students in meeting these standards. Most of the examples that we include in this book are tried-and-true lessons that content teachers have taught to actual students in actual classrooms over the past several years. Although some of these lessons were not originally designed with the CCSS in mind, we worked with our contributing teachers to refine these lessons so as to enhance their effectiveness in addressing the CCSS. As we worked with our contributors in this way, we experienced firsthand the benefits of interdisciplinary collaboration in planning and reflecting on our craft. We believe that, as presented in this book, all the lessons now align with the CCSS because they include higher-order thinking skills and varied levels of text complexity. We are proud to share them with you.

Figure I.1 Reading Lessons Organized by Anchor Standard, Content Area, Grade Level, and Lesson Title

READING IN HISTORY/SOCIAL STUDIES, SCIENCE			
Reading Anchor Standard	**Content Area**	**Grade Level**	**Lesson Title**
Key Ideas and Details	History/Social Studies: U.S. Government	6–8	Nationalism: The Good, the Bad, the Ugly
Craft and Structure	History/Social Studies: World/Global History	9–10	Social Causes of New Imperialism
Integration of Knowledge and Ideas	History/Social Studies: U.S. History	11–12	Vietnam: The Human Face of an Inhumane Time
READING IN SCIENCE, AND TECHNICAL SUBJECTS			
Reading Anchor Standard	**Content Area**	**Grade Level**	**Lesson Title**
Key Ideas and Details	Science: Biology	11–12	Bonus Science Articles
Craft and Structure	Technical Subjects: Computer Apps	9–10	Vocabulary Videos
Integration of Knowledge and Ideas	Science: Earth Science	6–8	Continental Drift

Figure I.2 Writing Lessons Organized by Content Area, Grade Level, Lesson Title, and Text Types and Purposes

WRITING IN HISTORY/SOCIAL STUDIES, SCIENCE, AND TECHNICAL SUBJECTS			
Content Area	**Grade Level**	**Lesson Title**	**Text Types and Purposes**
History/Social Studies: U.S. History	6–8	Mock Trial: Native Americans and European Colonization	Argument
Science: Chemistry	9–10	Boyle's Law	Argument
Technical Subjects: Sports Marketing	11–12	Fantasy Basketball	Argument
Technical Subjects: Math	6–8	Math in Everyday Life	Informative/ Explanatory
Science: Earth Science	9–10	Earth Day	Informative/ Explanatory
History/Social Studies: U.S. History	11–12	Montgomery Bus Boycott	Informative/ Explanatory

BEST PRACTICES

Throughout the lessons that we include in this book, you will recognize best practices (strategies and activities) for ensuring success in content-area literacy instruction. In the last chapter of this book, we discuss ways you can support reading and writing in your content lessons by employing literacy strategies and activities. Technology has facilitated instruction in today's world, so we provide valuable websites for support in understanding and implementing the CCSS. The last section offers tips for getting to the heart of the common core for literacy in the content areas. We hope to inspire you and give you new ideas by also sharing success stories involving content-area teachers working together.

Our intention is that this book will help you understand the key elements in CCSS-based lessons and apply that understanding to the development of your own curriculum. We are extremely grateful to the teachers who contributed to the book, and we hope that as you read, you consider ways to share your own positive teaching experiences with others.

1 Understanding the CCSS

An Overview

WHAT ARE THE CCSS FOR LITERACY IN THE CONTENT AREAS?

The Common Core State Standards (CCSS) for Literacy in History/Social Studies, Science, and Technical Subjects are the result of an effort coordinated by U.S. state leaders, including governors and state commissioners of education, through membership in the National Governors Association Center for Best Practices (NGA Center) and the Council of Chief State School Officers (CCSSO) "to provide a clear and consistent framework to prepare our children for college and the workforce" (NGA Center/CCSSO, 2010a, p. 1). The significance of the CCSS for Literacy in the Content Areas is that for the first time in U.S. standard-making history, there are official, state-created standards that reflect the shared responsibility within the school for students' literacy development. These standards recognize that not only English Language Arts (ELA) teachers but all content teachers are charged with the unique role of promoting the literacy skills of students in order to prepare students to be college and career ready.

One definition of content literacy is the ability to use reading and writing to learn content. The concept of literacy, however, has evolved over the years. Current views of literacy present a broader perspective that includes multiple sign systems, texts, and technologies (Lesley & Mathews, 2009). Multiple literacies move beyond print and include electronic, digital, and audio texts (O'Brien, 2006). Students today need to develop literacy skills to be able to access multiple sign systems and complex texts that are content specific. Sejnost and Thiese (2007) point out that students who are literate in one content are not necessarily literate in another. According to McKenna and Robinson (1990), content literacy requires students to possess the following:

- General literacy skills
- Content-specific literacy skills (e.g., how to read a map, write a lab report, etc.)
- Prior knowledge

According to the National Assessment of Educational Progress (NAEP) results, many students can comprehend on a literal level but not on a higher, more abstract level; they cannot synthesize, analyze, integrate new ideas with what they know, or perform countless other reading-to-learn tasks (Griggs, Daane, & Campbell, 2003). The CCSS argue that it is the responsibility of all teachers to teach students how to use literacy to learn and how to think like professionals in their particular discipline. Certainly, the type of higher-order thinking as related to reading that is noted as deficient by NAEP is necessary for students to think like professionals.

Many high school graduates do not possess the necessary literacy skills to be prepared for college and the workplace (McGrath, 2005). They may not be able to read directions, office memos, or tax forms, and if they cannot access that information, they are unable to function in college and the workforce (Sejnost & Thiese, 2007). However, content-area literacy instruction, which aims to promote students' comprehension of content-area texts through the explicit instruction of strategies (e.g., predicting, inferring, questioning, summarizing), can enhance learning. Reading strategies can be tools that students use selectively and flexibly as they see fit, depending on the literacy task (Sejnost & Thiese, 2007). Specifically,

> Adolescents who engage with these multiple text types need support in making use of appropriate strategies to mine the content for meaning and understand how the different print and nonprint structures influence understanding. For example, there are different strategies needed when moving from comprehending and composing information located on the Internet to reading and writing different genres in bound books, and then moving to still and moving images for information and/or entertainment, and so on. Educators need to help adolescents learn how to link the appropriate literacy strategies with the specific text structures. (International Reading Association, 2012, p. 4)

Teaching generic strategies (e.g., summarization) is not enough. Teachers need to help students address the highly specialized literacy demands of the subject areas by teaching their students discipline-specific content strategies to help them comprehend texts (Shanahan & Shanahan, 2008). For example, students are directly taught science writing that entails writing for different purposes (e.g., to persuade) and how to use different text structures (e.g., research articles).

Although research supports the benefits of content-area literacy instruction for all students (Alvermann & Moore, 1991; McGrath, 2005; Pressley, 2002), most teachers do not typically engage in intensive and prolonged strategic instruction (Dieker & Little, 2005; Neufeld, 2005; Pressley, 2004). According to Lesley and Mathews (2009), content-area literacy is "often perceived as teacher-directed study skills and textbook-based reading strategies . . . that constitute little more than busy work and drain the amount of time available for content area instruction" (p. 523). Many reasons may account for this. First, as is the case with many subject-area teachers, we consider ourselves content experts and not necessarily teachers of reading; second, if we do not perceive advanced reading levels as necessary for achievement in the content areas, then we do not see ourselves as responsible for teaching literacy (Lesley, Watson, & Elliot, 2007); third, the problem may lie in the expectation for teachers to broadly cover the curriculum (O'Brien, Moje, & Stewart, 2001), leaving little room for literacy instruction. The CCSS provide the expectations necessary to make literacy instruction a priority in all subjects.

HOW CAN WE USE BACKWARD DESIGN TO CREATE CURRICULUM THAT ADDRESSES THE CCSS FOR LITERACY IN THE CONTENT AREAS?

Backward Design (BD) is a curriculum design approach that was first introduced in 1998 (Wiggins & McTighe, 1998) and then revised and expanded by Grant Wiggins and Jay McTighe in 2005. Otherwise known as *Understanding by Design*, which is also the title of the book in which it is described, BD focuses first on goals that include standards and later on assessments and student learning experiences.

The authors present the analogy of the road map to describe their approach: One needs to have a destination in mind first before planning the journey to successfully reach the end. Many teachers initially think about their teaching—what they will teach and how—without considering what student outcomes they want at the end of their instruction. In other words, they are concerned with inputs rather than outputs first. For example, they select a topic (civil rights), then the text (Martin Luther King's *Letter From Birmingham Jail*), followed by instructional methods (discussion and cooperative learning) and learning experiences (close reading and analysis of text, identification of rhetorical devices, and argument writing), to help students meet the state standard. In contrast, BD ensures that teachers identify first the standards that they want their students to meet, followed by student results called for by the standards, and then learning activities that will lead to the desired results. "These standards provide a framework to help us identify teaching and learning priorities and guide our design of curriculum and assessments" (Wiggins & McTighe, 2001, pp. 7–8).

BD is appropriate to use as you take steps to create standards-based literacy lessons in the content areas because it relies on essential ideas, such as the standards, to serve as guiding principles for teaching and learning. It reflects the centrality of standards and demonstrates how understanding is derived from and frames standards so that students can learn how to think and develop content knowledge and skills. BD also addresses the vastness of standards by considering the "big ideas" in the content framed around "essential questions" to focus curriculum and instruction (Tomlinson & McTighe, 2006).

Specifically, BD helps teachers make choices regarding what standards and standards-based ideas to teach in order for students to gain *enduring understandings;* such choices are essential because the content that needs to be covered is great. Enduring understandings go to the heart of the discipline and are the big ideas that we want students to retain in long-term memory (Wiggins & McTighe, 2005). In *What's the Big Idea? Question-Driven Units to Motivate Reading, Writing, and Thinking,* Jim Burke (2010) pondered the use of the essential question to create enduring understandings:

> Perhaps my favorite and most useful question of all is, "What is the problem for which x is the solution?" This is a question that clarifies even as it challenges, helping me cut through the rationalizations that come so easily to so many of us as we are planning our classes. (pp. 23–24)

As we use BD, Wiggins and McTighe (2001, 2005), along with Burke (2010), encourage us to examine the value of our lessons by asking the following "big" questions:

> To what extent does the idea, topic, or process require uncovering and offer the potential for engaging students?
>
> Are these big ideas applicable beyond the classroom to real life?
>
> Are they fruitful to examine and uncover?
>
> Do they provide opportunities to motivate students to learn? (Wiggins & McTighe, 2005)

Why Backward Design?

Although most traditional curriculum planning relies on a linear process that is activity and coverage oriented without thoughtful consideration of student achievement, BD works the other way around; it is standards and goals oriented and focuses on student-learning outcomes and achievement (Wiggins & McTighe, 2005). BD requires educators to first identify the end results (standards, goals), decide on what assessments will provide evidence of student learning called for by the standards, and then develop learning experiences and instruction that will enable students to achieve the desired results.

Stages of Backward Design

To recap, BD advocates a sequential planning in three stages:

1. Identify desired results.

2. Determine acceptable evidence.

3. Plan learning experiences and instruction.

In this section, we examine these three stages.

Stage 1: Identify Desired Results

In this first stage, educators consider their goals and establish curricular priorities. They ask themselves the following questions:

- What should students know and be able to do?
- What do I want them to understand as a result of my curriculum?
- What 21st-century skills do I want them to acquire so that they may be successful in college, their careers, the world?

This stage requires teachers to make choices about the following that will be taught in the course or unit:

- Content (topics)
- Important knowledge (facts, concepts)
- Skills (processes, strategies)

In addition, teachers must determine what "enduring understandings" or "big ideas" they want students to retain in the long term.

Stage 2: Determine Acceptable Evidence

The second stage focuses on evidence:

- What evidence will demonstrate that students have met the standards and desired results?

The purpose of this stage is to ensure that students do not learn just content (facts and principles) but also that they represent their learning through varied means (projects, research presentations, multimedia representations, and so forth).

Stage 3: Plan Learning Experiences and Instruction

Once you determine the desired results and acceptable evidence, you are ready to plan for learning experiences that will help students meet the standards and assessments. The planning will entail how to teach—what methods and resource materials to use—in a way that will provide students with the necessary knowledge and skills to achieve the desired results.

Application of Backward Design to Content Area Literacy Unit Design

In this section, we demonstrate the application of the three stages of BD with an example of a mini-unit on the Vietnam War that aligns standards with curriculum and instruction.

Stage 1: Identify Desired Results.

We focus on the following Reading Standards in this unit:

Key Ideas and Details

R.1. Read closely to determine what the text says explicitly and to make logical inferences from it; cite specific textual evidence when writing or speaking to support conclusions drawn from the text.

Craft and Structure

R.4. Interpret words and phrases as they are used in a text, including determining technical, connotative, and figurative meanings, and analyze how specific word choices shape meaning or tone.

R.5. Analyze the structure of texts, including how specific sentences, paragraphs, and larger portions of the text (e.g., a section, chapter, scene, or stanza) relate to each other and the whole.

R.6. Assess how point of view or purpose shapes the content and style of a text.

Integration of Knowledge and Ideas

R.7. Integrate and evaluate content presented in diverse formats and media, including visually and quantitatively, as well as in words.

R.8. Delineate and evaluate the argument and specific claims in a text, including the validity of the reasoning as well as the relevance and sufficiency of the evidence.

Range of Reading and Level of Text Complexity

R.10. Read and comprehend complex literary and informational texts independently and proficiently.

We focus on the following Writing Standards in this unit:

Research to Build and Present Knowledge

W.8. Gather relevant information from multiple print and digital sources, assess the credibility and accuracy of each source, and integrate the information while avoiding plagiarism.

W.9. Draw evidence from literary or informational texts to support analysis, reflection, and research.

Using the above standards as a foundation, we develop the following enduring understandings that we want our students to take away from this unit:

Through a close examination of literary and informational texts in various formats, students will understand a historical time period and appreciate the varied points of view regarding the cost of war and the lasting effects of war on the human psyche.

These understandings are enduring because they are applied to real life, advance understanding beyond facts, and promote lifelong learning. Students will reflect on and examine the background, events, and causes and effects of the Vietnam War. They will put a human face on the war and empathize with those affected by it. We want them to know different perspectives on the Vietnam War, factual information and events about the war, and how it has influenced American history.

In terms of skills, we want students to be able to analyze, synthesize, and evaluate multiple sources of information presented in diverse formats and media in order to develop an understanding of varied points of view regarding a period in history. They reflect on their analysis of writers' narrative techniques in order to write their own personal narratives about the things they literally and metaphorically carry and later narrative works in which they represent the voices of people affected by war.

In this stage, we need to examine the verbs in the standards that provide guidance for identifying knowledge and skills that students must acquire and for helping teachers develop assessments that measure student learning (Tomlinson & McTighe, 2006). For example, the verbs *integrate* and *evaluate* suggest that students synthesize information and form an opinion based on textual evidence. These standards also assist teachers with determining, for example, whether a Discussion Chart on which students record their thoughts and provide textual evidence is an appropriate assessment measure.

Stage 2: Determine Acceptable Evidence

Guiding questions, a Writing Organizer, a Discussion Chart, and the Conversation Between Two Characters are assignments used to demonstrate that students have acquired the necessary understandings, knowledge, and skills. The guiding questions require students to read the text *The Things They Carried* (O'Brien, 2009) closely and strategically in order to answer the questions in writing. After students analyze the content and writing structure of the novel, they use the Writing Organizer to respond personally to the literary work by writing about the things they carry—both physical and emotional—adopting the writing style of Tim O'Brien (2009) with personal facts, historical information, sophisticated vocabulary, and appeal to emotion. In addition, students analyze and evaluate songs about the Vietnam War by using a Discussion Chart.

A cumulative assessment requires students to engage in creative writing that is appropriate to topic, task, and audience and that is drawn from sources studied in the course. Specifically, they select two people, either fictional or real, from the readings, songs, poems, and excerpts in the unit. Then they write a conversation between the two.

Stage 3: Plan Learning Experiences and Instruction

According to Wiggins and McTighe (2005), in this stage, we ask ourselves, "What learning experiences and instruction will enable students to achieve the desired results?" The instructional activities and experiences in this unit will include reading literary and informational works in multiple modes that examine the Vietnam War through common themes. For example:

> Students read an excerpt from the novel *The Things They Carried* (O'Brien, 2009) and view the *Time* (2006) magazine photo story "The Things They Carry." Then they analyze the two works and compose their own essay titled "The Things I Carry" based on the style of the two works and a reflective Writing Organizer in which they consider the meaning of the physical and metaphorical things that they carry. They also analyze songs of the Vietnam War and home front protest era by using a chart to gather their ideas about the information presented, the attitude of the speaker, and the purpose of the writer.

Students further examine the human cost by viewing the *Dateline* documentary "A Few Good Men," and reading an excerpt from *Born on the Fourth of July* (1976). They also read nonfiction accounts from combat nurses from *A Piece of My Heart: The Stories of 26 American Women Who Served in Vietnam* (Walker, 1985). Students examine the Vietnamese voices of the war through a poem by Duc Thanh and an excerpt from *When Heaven and Earth Changed Places* by Le Ly Hayslip (1989). (More information on the materials in this lesson is found in Chapter 3.) The students engage in a writing activity that requires them to write a conversation between two characters selected from any of the sources discussed in the course. They practice reading these conversations aloud and present them to the class. Through an analysis and evaluation of diverse and multimodal sources (print, digital, audio, video, etc.), students connect with the time period and understand more fully the historical significance of the Vietnam War. Technology and multimodal approaches serve as effective tools that enhance and motivate student learning.

The instructional activities answer the oft-heard student question, "Why do we have to read this?" by helping students personally connect with the class readings, thereby creating relevance. To foster positive learning experiences for students, teachers support them with methods such as guidance and monitoring, modeling, discussion, and cooperative learning.

BD is a curriculum design model that lends itself to the implementation of the CCSS. Teachers can focus on the desired outcomes outlined in the standards when they identify desired results in their BD planning and as they complete the following:

- Determine the goals of curricular units
- Specify what knowledge and skills are important
- Identify acceptable evidence of understanding

In addition, BD addresses the "how" and "why"—critical elements in promoting student success. Table 1.1 outlines the BD approach using the CCSS.

Table 1.1 Applying the Backward Design Approach Using the CCSS

Key Design Questions	*Responses*
Stage 1. What are the desired results?	
(a) What CCSS for Literacy in History/Social Studies does the unit address?	**Reading Standards** • Key Ideas and Details [R.1] • Craft and Structure [R.4, R.5, R.6] • Integration of Knowledge and Ideas [R.7, R.8] • Range of Reading and Level of Text Complexity [R.10] **Writing Standards** Research to Build Knowledge [W.8, W.9]
(b) What enduring understandings are desired?	• Through a close examination of literary and informational texts in various formats, students will understand a historical time period and appreciate the varied points of view regarding the cost of war and the lasting effects of war on the human psyche.
(c) What key knowledge and skills will students acquire as a result of this unit?	• Students will be able to analyze, synthesize, and evaluate multiple sources of information presented in diverse formats and media in order to develop an understanding of varied points of view regarding a period in history. • Students will be able to reflect on their analysis of writers' narrative techniques in order to write their own personal narratives of things they literally and metaphorically carry and, later, narrative works in which they represent the voices of people affected by war.
Stage 2. What is the evidence of understanding?	
(a) Through what performance-based task will students demonstrate achievement of the desired results?	• Students will create a Conversation Between Two Characters based on two different works studied during the unit. The conversation will include historical information and capture the style of each character. Students will practice reading these conversations aloud and present them to the class.
(b) Through what other evidence will students demonstrate achievement of the desired results?	• Observations • Answers to guiding questions for *The Things They Carried* • Writing Organizer for items students literally and metaphorically carry with them, like the soldiers do in *The Things They Carried* and the resulting essay • Discussion Chart for song lyrics and poetry on which students note and provide evidence of their understanding and their analysis of information presented, attitude of speaker, and intent of writer
(c) How will students reflect upon and assess their learning?	• Writing Organizer • Discussion Chart

Key Design Questions	Responses
Stage 3. What learning experiences and instruction will enable students to achieve the desired results?	
(a) What learning experiences and teaching will promote student understanding, interest, and excellence?	• Review Vietnam history packet. Introduce *The Things They Carried.* • Discuss and analyze *The Things They Carried*, view *Time* magazine photo story "The Things They Carry." Compose own "The Things I Carry" essay. • Discussion Chart—Analyze songs of the Vietnam War and home front protest era. • View *Dateline:* "A Few Good Men." • Examine the human cost: excerpt from nonfiction—*Born on the Fourth of July* and accounts from combat nurses from *A Piece of My Heart: The Stories of 26 American Women Who Served in Vietnam.* • Analyze other voices: read the work of Vietnamese writers; synthesize diverse sources by composing the writing assignment, create a Conversation Between Two Characters. • Small-group sharing of completed writing assignment
(b) What sources will be used to promote student understanding, interest, and excellence?	• Literary works: novel, short stories, Photo Story, songs, poems • Informational works: historical nonfiction, documentary
(c) What teaching methods will be employed to promote understanding, interest, and excellence?	• Guidance and Monitoring • Modeling • Discussion • Cooperative Learning

Source: Lesson by Eileen Burke and Vincent Russo applied to Wiggins and McTighe (2005) Backward Design Model.

HOW DO THE CCSS AND BACKWARD DESIGN SUPPORT THE THEORIES OF DEWEY, BLOOM, AND GARDNER?

A clear connection can be made among BD, the CCSS, and the theories of John Dewey, Benjamin Bloom, and Howard Gardner. The ideas of these enduring educational theorists resonate in both the BD approach to curriculum planning and the CCSS that can guide that planning. Dewey called for students to develop through experience into productive citizens. Bloom classified the different types of thinking—from simple recall to higher-order skills such as analysis and evaluation—that are required of all people in their journey toward good citizenry. Gardner recognized that just as the type of thinking required of students varies, the paths students take on that journey—their approach to developing skills and content knowledge—may vary as well.

Close to a century ago, John Dewey (1938) called for teachers to revise a system in which teachers imposed "adult standards, subject-matter, and methods on those who are only growing slowly toward maturity" (p. 18). His progressive approach to education was based on revealing a greater purpose for learning by connecting with life experience. Dewey asked, "What is the place and meaning of subject matter and of organization within experience?" (p. 20). When students understand the purpose of learning, they value that learning. Dewey explained, "The most important attitude that can be formed is that of the desire to go on learning" (p. 48). As teachers identify the skills outlined in the CCSS, they can adopt topics to be addressed and the methods to be used to fit students' needs and to encourage students to see the value of what they are learning (e.g., service learning, college and career reading skills). This helps fuel students' desire to learn.

Certainly, the unit on the Vietnam War outlined above supports Dewey's call for education that has a clear purpose and that allows for student input. Students are learning about a topic—war—which is relevant to their lives. The assessment of their learning (Conversation Between Two Characters) is something that will help students gain a deeper understanding of war and evaluate the catastrophic consequences of war. We believe that these purposeful elements of this unit will inspire students to develop as thinkers and learners.

The types of thinking outlined in the CCSS are clearly in alignment with Benjamin Bloom's (1956) taxonomy of cognition. Verbs such as *cite, interpret, apply, analyze, synthesize,* and *evaluate* are frequently found in the CCSS (see Table 1.2.)

We can see a variety of levels of thinking in the sample unit on the Vietnam War outlined earlier. Students *analyze, synthesize,* and *evaluate* different texts presented in multiple formats to develop an understanding of the varied points of view regarding the Vietnam War. They personally identify with the soldiers by reflecting on the actual and metaphorical weight of things that they carry, just as O'Brien and *Time* magazine wrote about the weight of what soldiers carried. Students *analyze* and *evaluate* the voices of the speakers in the pieces they review in order to develop their own written pieces in the voice of one of the speakers covered. They *analyze* how two or more texts address similar themes or topics in order to build knowledge or to compare the approaches the authors take.

The CCSS for Reading (Grades 6–12) incorporate a range of sophistication in thinking. For example, "Key Ideas and Details" indicators begin at a simple level with verbs such as *read* and *cite,* but Indicators 2 and 3 include more intensive expectations, including *determine* and *analyze.* Since different types of thinking are required of us as members of a productive society, different levels of cognition and ways of assessing each level make up acceptable evidence within well-developed CCSS-based lessons and units.

Howard Gardner (1983) examined the process that would lead students to desired results regarding thinking and learning. He determined that students need both the flexibility to arrive at such results in a variety of ways and options for providing evidence of learning. Table 1.3 lists Gardner's nine intelligences.

Often, lessons naturally address several of Gardner's intelligences. In the sample unit outlined earlier, students read about and discuss the Vietnam War (verbal-linguistic intelligence). They listen to songs (musical-rhythmic), view a

Table 1.2 Bloom's Taxonomy

Knowledge

Recognizing and recalling information

Action verbs—choose, complete, cite, define, describe, identify, indicate, list, locate, match, name, outline, recall, recognize, select, state

Comprehension

Understanding the meaning of information

Action verbs—change, classify, convert, defend, discuss, estimate, expand, explain, generalize, infer, interpret, paraphrase, retell, summarize, translate

Application

Using and applying information

Action verbs—apply, calculate, demonstrate, develop, discover, exhibit, modify, operate, participate, perform, plan, predict, relate, show, simulate, solve

Analysis

Dissecting information into its component parts to comprehend the relationships

Action verbs—analyze, arrange, break down, categorize, classify, compare, contrast, debate, deduce, diagram, differentiate, discriminate, group, illustrate, inquire, organize, outline, separate, subdivide

Synthesis

Putting components together to generate new ideas

Action verbs—arrange, assemble, combine, compile, compose, constitute, create, design, develop, devise, document, explain, formulate, generate, hypothesize, imagine, invent, modify, originate, plan, produce, rearrange, reconstruct, revise, rewrite, synthesize, tell, transmit, write

Evaluation

Judging the worth of information, an idea or opinion, a theory, a thesis, or a proposition

Action verbs—appraise, argue, assess, conclude, consider, criticize, decide, discriminate, estimate, evaluate, judge, justify, rank, rate, recommend, revise, standardize, support, validate

Source: Adapted from Dalton and Smith (1986, pp. 36–37).

Photo Story and documentary (visual-spatial), reflect on their own experiences (intrapersonal intelligence), and write conversations that they practice with each other (interpersonal intelligence). With the understanding that no two students will approach their learning with the same combination of intelligences, it is wise to offer options that allow students to build their skills and knowledge based on a mode of thinking in which they feel comfortable. The expectations or end results (CCSS) are the same.

Table 1.3 Howard Gardner's Multiple Intelligences
1. **Visual-Spatial Intelligence:** The ability to think in images and represent internally the spatial world
2. **Verbal-Linguistic Intelligence:** The ability to use words and language
3. **Logical-Mathematical Intelligence:** The ability to understand and use logic and numbers
4. **Bodily-Kinesthetic Intelligence:** The ability to use one's body or control body movements to problem solve or create something
5. **Musical-Rhythmic Intelligence:** The ability to understand, appreciate, and produce music
6. **Interpersonal intelligence:** The ability to understand other people
7. **Intrapersonal Intelligence:** The ability to understand oneself
8. **Naturalist intelligence:** The ability to be sensitive to and appreciative of the natural world
9. **Existential Intelligence:** The ability to consider life's greater meaning

Part I

Reading Standards for Literacy in History/Social Studies, Science, and Technical Subjects

2 The Benefits of the CCSS for the Teaching of Reading in the Content Areas

A capacity, and taste, for reading, gives access to whatever has already been discovered by others. It is the key, or one of the keys, to the already solved problems. And not only so. It gives a relish, and facility, for success-fully pursuing the [yet] unsolved ones.

—Abraham Lincoln

When Abraham Lincoln made the statement above in his Address to the Wisconsin State Agricultural Society on September 30, 1859, he went on to say that knowledge of science is valuable: botany helps in dealing with growing crops; chemistry is important for analyzing soils and for selecting and applying manures; and the mechanical branches of natural philosophy assist in almost everything, especially implements and machinery *(Collected Works of Abraham Lincoln, 2012)*. While we appreciate Lincoln's specific application of reading to the sciences, we chose to begin our reading chapter with this quote because of its general application to successful problem solving and innovation. Developing an understanding of how great minds have solved problems of the past and applying that understanding to today's problems are—according to Lincoln—the major benefits of reading well.

Unfortunately, most middle and high schools are not set up to support the development of meaningful comprehension. As literacy expert Donna Ogle stated, subject matter learning becomes more challenging, and the demands for knowledge continually increase; however, students shift from one subject to the next very quickly throughout the school day without having the necessary discipline-specific knowledge to understand what is important and what is not and how to learn complex material (as cited in D'Arcangelo, 2002).

One might argue that students develop their reading skills before entering middle school. However, the notion that strong early reading skills develop into strong later reading skills as students progress through the grades is faulty. The fact that students learn to read does not necessarily mean that they have learned to read advanced content texts and that literacy instruction is unnecessary. Students need sustained and continued direct instruction and guidance in

Table 2.1 Anchor Standards for Reading

READING

Key Ideas and Details

1. Read closely to determine what the text says explicitly and to make logical inferences from it; cite specific textual evidence when writing or speaking to support conclusions drawn from the text.

2. Determine central ideas or themes of a text and analyze their development; summarize the key supporting details and ideas.

3. Analyze how and why individuals, events, or ideas develop and interact over the course of a text.

Craft and Structure

4. Interpret words and phrases as they are used in a text, including determining technical, connotative, and figurative meanings, and explain how specific word choices shape meaning or tone.

5. Analyze the structure of texts, including how specific sentences, paragraphs, and larger portions of the text (e.g., a section or chapter) relate to each other and the whole.

6. Assess how point of view or purpose shapes the content and style of a text.

Integration of Knowledge and Ideas

7. Integrate and evaluate content presented in diverse formats and media, including visually and quantitatively as well as in words.

8. Delineate and evaluate the argument and specific claims in a text, including the validity of the reasoning as well as the relevance and sufficiency of the evidence.

9. Analyze how two or more texts address similar themes or topics in order to build knowledge or to compare the approaches the authors take.

Range of Reading and Level of Text Complexity

10. Read and comprehend complex literary and informational texts independently and proficiently.

tackling the specialized language and reading tasks particular to each discipline (Shanahan & Shanahan, 2008).

In fact, students will not be able to master content unless they develop the reading skills necessary to comprehend discipline-specific complex text. As far back as 1944, Artley argued that the role of all classroom teachers is to develop the reading skills and abilities essential for comprehension in their particular content area as well as apply to their content field those skills and abilities being developed by teachers in other disciplines. In other words, teachers need to help students develop the abilities to learn specific content as well as general reading skills that can be transferred from one discipline to the other and generalized across the curriculum.

In this chapter, we introduce the Reading strand of the Common Core State Standards (CCSS) for Literacy in History/Social Studies, Science, and Technical Subjects, 6–12, and provide commentary on the value of each of the Anchor Standards for increasing student college and career readiness. For easy reference, the CCSS Anchor Standards for Reading that we reference throughout this chapter are listed in Table 2.1. Shaded citations within the chapter come directly from these Anchor Standards. At the end of the chapter, we go beyond the more general Anchor Standards and take a closer look at the "Key Ideas and Details" grade-specific Reading Standards for Literacy in History/Social Studies, Science, and Technical Subjects, 6–12.

KEY IDEAS AND DETAILS

ACT (2010) established a baseline against which to measure the effectiveness of the implementation of the CCSS by evaluating a quarter-million 11th-grade students in several states throughout the United States. They found that "only 31% of students are performing at a college- and career-ready level with respect to successfully understanding complex text" (p. 5). The "Key Ideas and Details" Anchor Standards for Reading address the need for the development of better skills for deciphering meaning of text, ranging from a basic understanding to a more nuanced interpretation of meaning:

1. Read closely to *determine what the text says explicitly* and to make logical *inferences* from it; *cite* specific textual evidence when writing or speaking to support conclusions drawn from the text.

2. *Determine central ideas or themes* of a text and *analyze* their development; *summarize* the key supporting details and ideas.

3. *Analyze* how and why individuals, events, or ideas develop and interact over the course of a text.

This set of Anchor Standards supports reading development for 21st-century learners through the balance of the types of thinking skills that would fall in various sections of Bloom's Taxonomy from basic understanding ("determine what the text says explicitly") to higher-order thinking ("make logical inferences"; "analyze"). This balance addresses the need for change that Grant Wiggins (2010) demanded:

> Here is our problem in a nutshell. Students are taught formulas that they learn and spit back unthinkingly—regardless of subject matter—all in the name of "meeting standards." Yet, as so many assessment results reveal, a large portion of U.S. students are so literal minded that they are incapable of solving fairly simple questions requiring interpretation and transfer—which is surely the point of the state standards. (p. 51)

According to Kamil (2003), "One in four adults cannot read well enough to identify the main idea in a passage or understand informational text" (p. 38). Therefore, "in the name of meeting standards," students need to be taught on the basic level how to extract the main ideas of a text. Additionally, as Bloom would call for, they must reach a higher level by learning how to engage in textual analysis and evaluation.

In their work on discipline literacy instruction, Shanahan and Shanahan (2008) found that the discipline experts in their study approached reading in different ways: mathematicians emphasized rereading and close reading as two of their most important strategies. Chemists, when reading prose, were trying to understand concepts by visualizing; writing down formulas; or, if a diagram or a chart were on the page, going back and forth between the graph and the chart. They continue:

> The historians, on the other hand, emphasized paying attention to the author or source when reading any text. That is, before reading, they would consider who the authors of the texts were and what their biases might be. Their purpose during the reading seemed to be to figure out what story a particular author wanted to tell; in other words, they were keenly aware that they were reading an interpretation of historical events and not "Truth." (p. 50)

In response to these findings, Shanahan and Shanahan (2008) advocated for instruction that includes discipline-specific strategies rather than general-purpose strategies. For example, in history class, students need to be taught the approaches that historians use, how to evaluate sources, and how to think more critically; science students need to be shown how to read back and forth between visuals and/or text; in math, students need to be taught strategies such as rereading and visualizing. Consequently, literacy strategy instruction should be differentiated according to the unique literacy practices particular to each discipline. The use of strategies across disciplines should also be considered. For instance, an approach that a student learns in social studies may also be valuable for science readings. The more options a student has, the more likely that student is to comprehend complex texts.

The importance of helping students become proficient in comprehending sophisticated, discipline-specific information is made clear by Adam Gamoran, an associate dean for research in the school of Education at the University of Wisconsin–Madison. In a presentation to the U.S. House of Representatives Committee on Science, Space, and Technology, Gamoran (2011) stated,

> As a nation, our goals extend beyond having a capable and competitive work force. We also need to help all students become scientifically literate. Our students are facing decisions related to science and technology, from understanding a medical diagnosis to weighing competing claims about the environment. (p. 3)

Though the CCSS are focused on college and career readiness, it is important to note that the skills students develop to meet these standards are equally important in everyday life. This would appeal to Dewey's (1916, 1938) call for schooling to be clearly purposeful for all students.

> If students are to be truly prepared for college, work, and citizenship, they cannot settle for a modest level of proficiency in reading and writing. Rather, they will need to develop the advanced literacy skills that are required in order to master the academic content areas— particularly the areas of math, science, English, and history. (Heller & Greenleaf, 2007, p. 1)

The "Key Ideas and Details" Anchor Standards address the need to help students develop the means to understand science and other content-area readings at a sophisticated level in order to carry those skills into college, career, and everyday life situations.

CRAFT AND STRUCTURE

ACT (2010) stated that we must "ensure that students gain sufficient understanding of how language varies by context; how to use language effectively for different audiences, purposes, and tasks; and how to gain and use a vocabulary adequate for college and careers" (p. 5). The "Craft and Structure" Anchor Standards for Reading address awareness of language, construct, and style:

4. *Interpret* words and phrases as they are used in a text, including determining technical, connotative, and figurative meanings, and *analyze* how specific word choices shape meaning or tone.

5. *Analyze* the structure of texts, including how specific sentences, paragraphs, and larger portions of the text (e.g., a section, chapter scene, or stanza) relate to each other and the whole.

6. *Assess* how point of view or purpose shapes the content and style of a text.

According to ACT (2010), fewer than half of students have the skills to recognize when to use varied forms of language or the ability to acquire and use new vocabulary at the college and career readiness level. The CCSS for Literacy in Science and Technical Subjects for Grades 6–12 call for students to develop subject-specific vocabulary, including "symbols, key terms, and other domain-specific scientific or technical context" (National Governors Association Center for Best Practices [NGA Center]/Council of Chief State School Officers [CCSSO], 2010b, p. 62).

Heller and Greenleaf (2007) discussed how difficult higher-level thinking might be for some students and the need for content-area teachers to recognize the challenges that subject-specific readings may present for basic comprehension:

> As a matter of basic professional preparation, all teachers should know not only how to integrate comprehension strategies into their ongoing instruction to help students access the academic content, but they should also understand what is distinct about reading and writing in their own discipline, and how to make those rules, conventions, and skills apparent to students. If students are to succeed in the content areas, teachers will need to demystify the reading and writing that go on there, putting those things on the table for everyone to see and discuss. They may need to help their students to see that such disciplinary styles exist and that each discipline uses vocabulary, text, structures, stylistic conventions, and modes of analysis and debate that are very different from the language students hear at home or among their friends, or elsewhere in school. (p. 22)

In the content areas, students are challenged by the specialized vocabulary specific to each discipline. In science, terms and symbols, such as *osmosis* and H_2O, must be learned; in history, knowledge of general vocabulary words (e.g., *economy*) as well as technical terminology (e.g., *industrialization*) are important; in math, students must rely on the memorization of precise mathematical definitions in order to understand their meaning (e.g., *odd* refers to an integer that is not a multiple of 2; it also means *strange*, but this definition does not aid in mathematical understanding) (Shanahan & Shanahan, 2008).

Bird (2006) wrote of the importance of students "flagging" technical terms and not only looking them up but also internalizing them and using them in context in other assignments (p. 3). This kind of repetition relates to the concept of tiered language.

The CCSS refer to Beck, McKeown, and Kucan (2002), who tier language according to commonality and applicability. Tier 1 words are everyday words learned early by most students. Tier 2 words are commonly found in texts and are more specific. An example provided in Appendix A of the CCSS document for ELA/Literacy is *saunter* rather than *walk*. These words are less common and applicable than Tier 1 words because of their specificity, but they are still "highly generalizable." Tier 3 words are "domain-specific" and are typically most difficult for students to comprehend without scaffolding such as the use of a glossary or explicit definition within the text. The authors of the CCSS caution that teachers must be watchful of their students to determine whether they have a clear understanding of the Tier 2 words since, unlike Tier 3 words, they may not be as accessible in a glossary. Regarding Tier 3 words, they write, "Vocabulary development for these words occurs most effectively through a coherent course of study in which subject matters are integrated and coordinated across the curriculum and domains become familiar to the student over several days or weeks" (NGA Center/CCSSO, 2010c, p. 33). According to Adams (2010–2011), "The challenge then, lies in organizing our reading regimens in every subject and every class such that each text bootstraps the language and knowledge that will be needed for the next" (p. 10). In other words, teachers across disciplines and grades should be teaching texts that build on each other's vocabulary and ideas.

In addition to vocabulary, according to the second "Craft and Structure" Anchor Standard, students must be aware of the effective use of language in terms of a bigger picture—the structure of texts. Heller and Greenleaf (2007) discussed the temptation to relegate weak readers in the upper grades to reading remediation classes, thus limiting those students' exposure to content-area texts. This puts the weak readers at a greater disadvantage. They state that such support classes must be just that—support rather than replacements—because all students need to be challenged with a variety of content-specific vocabulary and writing styles within the various content areas.

> If students do not have the opportunity to learn subject area concepts and vocabulary, their word knowledge and capacity to read a broader range of texts will be further diminished . . . teachers should assume that all students are capable of doing rigorous academic work—even if they struggle with fluency, vocabulary, reading comprehension, or decoding—and they should provide every student with meaningful and interesting opportunities to learn high-level skills by reading, writing, and talking about rich intellectual content. (p. 22)

Students who can assess the use of language and structure in the texts that they are reading can develop sophisticated reading habits that will allow them to better comprehend the information presented and to become more critical of their sources of information.

The final "Craft and Structure" Anchor Standard calls for students to assess how point of view or purpose shapes the style or content of a text. Elementary Science Integration Project (ESIP) (*Science/Inquiry Literature Circles*, 2011) suggests an approach that helps students meet this standard:

> Have students examine the various choices that authors make by having each group read a different book about the same science notable. Afterwards, have the groups share and compare what they learned about the person and the books that were read. (p. 2)

This approach is especially effective in social studies, where events told from different perspectives require students to analyze and evaluate the sources. History relies heavily on document analysis (primary, secondary, etc.), so teaching students how to select and evaluate historical documents develops their critical thinking skills.

INTEGRATION OF KNOWLEDGE AND IDEAS

The "Integration of Knowledge and Ideas" Anchor Standards create guidelines for students to apply their literacy skills by thinking at a higher level about varied texts.

> 7. *Integrate* and *evaluate* content presented in diverse formats and media, including visually and quantitatively, as well as in words.
>
> 8. *Delineate* and *evaluate* the argument and specific claims in a text, including the validity of the reasoning as well as the relevance and sufficiency of the evidence.
>
> 9. *Analyze* how two or more texts address similar themes or topics in order to build knowledge or to compare the approaches the authors take.

These Anchor Standards include verbs that align with the higher-order thinking skills in Bloom's Taxonomy. Words such as *integrate, delineate, evaluate,* and *analyze* denote advanced and sophisticated cognitive processing of information. College- and career-ready students must be able to break down information (analyze), solve problems by applying facts and knowledge in different ways (apply), integrate knowledge and ideas (synthesize), and assess the validity of and make judgments on ideas and works (evaluate).

If purposeful education is the preparation for college and career through the development of skills that students will use once they are in those settings, it is logical to practice the application of skills across disciplines. Sometimes application happens naturally. We have all enjoyed watching the lightbulb moment when a student says, "This is like what I am studying in _____." However, all too often in our schools, subjects are taught in their own wing or on their own floor (e.g., math classes are held on the third floor and English Language Arts [ELA] on the second floor). Unfortunately, this reflects our approach to educating our students. Yet the types of thinking used in math are not limited to math. The types of thinking used in any subject are not limited to that subject.

According to Nichols, Young, and Rickelman (2007), students and teachers use varied literacy strategies, depending on the subject. For instance, graphic organizers may be used in social studies, word walls in science, and the writing process in English. Students and teachers alike need the CCSS to help guide them toward better integration of these and other strategies across the subjects. After all, when students enter their careers, it is not likely that they will be asked to focus only on math for 40 minutes and then on ELA for 40 minutes. Rather, they will need to use a variety of thinking skills across a variety of disciplines. Keeping this in mind relates back to Dewey's (1916, 1938) concept of purposeful education.

Students can often recognize the *content*-based connections among their classes. The challenge is getting students to realize that the reading *skills* they use in one subject area can be transferred to work in other subject areas. We must be more cognizant of encouraging students to make connections in relation to the thinking skills they are using when they read for any of their courses. This is especially important as students are applying their skills to several mediums through which we gather information (e.g., screen images, video, quantitative data). If students can recognize the need to transfer their skills across subject areas, it follows that they can see how the same skills can be applied to the various mediums of expression they are encountering.

The second and third "Integration of Knowledge and Ideas" Anchor Standards call for students to be critical of the pieces that they read. They must consider the validity of their sources. Also, once they decide on multiple pieces as strong sources of information, they should be able to compare how two or more writers approach a similar topic or theme. This incorporates not only consideration of bias but also analysis of style.

According to the State Educational Technology Directors Association (SETDA) (2011), the meaning of the word *content* has shifted in the past few years. "Prior to digital technology, content meant a textbook and possibly a filmstrip or movie as the source of information for instruction. Now, technology can engage the 21st century learner and promote creative, collaborative, interactive, student-centered learning. With technology, teachers and students can access rigorous, high-quality digital content and resources" (p. 25). The CCSS note this shift by mentioning both print and digital sources in the first Anchor Standard for "Integration of Knowledge and Ideas." The acceptance of digital sources as educational content has created a drastic change in how students learn.

One important result to note when considering the Anchor Standards for "Integration of Knowledge and Ideas" is Project-Based Learning (PBL), a method whereby students use collaboration, communication, and critical-thinking skills to respond to a complex question or problem. SETDA (2011) notes,

Technology facilitates deeper learning and enhances PBL for students through participation in online, collaborative projects. Students have the opportunity to build group documents online and to participate in videoconferencing with peers or experts in other states or countries, which exposes students to different cultures and global perspectives. (p. 22)

This high-tech 21st-century skills-based approach to learning can be used in any content area and provides a genuine application of skills and content knowledge. This relates to all three major theorists that we discuss in this book. Bloom would be pleased with the higher-order thinking demands of PBL, Gardner with the applications for multiple intelligences, and Dewey with the real-life application of learning to solve a problem.

RANGE OF READING AND LEVEL OF TEXT COMPLEXITY

Not only do students need to develop more advanced thinking skills, they need to be able to apply those skills to more sophisticated texts. As we shared earlier, according to ACT (2010), only 31% of students are able to understand complex texts. Also, students struggle especially with the types of expository texts that are required in the content areas.

> What little expository reading students are asked to do is too often of the superficial variety that involves skimming and scanning for particular, discrete pieces of information; such reading is unlikely to prepare students for the cognitive demand of true understanding of complex text. (NGA Center/CCSSO, 2010c, p. 3)

The Range of Reading and Level of Text Complexity Anchor Standard reflects the need for improvement in this area:

> 10. Read and comprehend complex literary and informational texts independently and proficiently.

Students need to read a range of sophisticated texts and to practice a range of thinking—from making connections to evaluating the verity and quality of writing in various sources. In measuring the complexity of texts, the CCSS consider three factors:

1. Qualitative evaluation of the text: Levels of meaning, structure, language conventionality and clarity, and knowledge demands

2. Quantitative evaluation of the text: Readability measures and other scores of text complexity

3. Matching reader to text and task: Reader variables (such as motivation, knowledge, and experiences) and task variables (such as purpose and the complexity generated by the task assigned and the questions posed). (NGA Center/CCSSO, 2010c)

Appendix A of the CCSS Document for ELA includes an extensive explanation of the measures for the three factors listed above. To give you a general idea of their meaning, we include a few samples for each factor.

Within the *qualitative factor,* levels of meaning may range from explicit purpose to implicit. Structure may range from chronological to nonchronological (e.g., using flashback or thematic organization). Language may be literal or figurative, contemporary or archaic. Knowledge demands may include a perspective that is similar to the reader's or one that is very different, many allusions to other texts or very few, general vocabulary/content base or very specific content understanding (NGA Center/CCSSO, 2010c).

The *quantitative factor* for reading includes the measurement of word length, sentence length, and frequency of familiar versus unfamiliar vocabulary, syntactic complexity, and cohesiveness of text. If you are reading this and feeling overwhelmed, you are not alone. In a discussion of the Quantitative factor for "Range, Quality, and Complexity of Student Reading," the CCSS compared various tests. One that stood out as a strong measure was the nonprofit service Coh-Metrix. Though this seems to be a more efficient and reliable system than its competitors, it is still not flawless. The CCSS stated that the "greatest value of these factors may well be the promise they offer of more advanced and usable tools yet to come" (NGA Center/CCSSO, 2010c, p. 7).

Given the complexity of the quantitative factor, it is heartening to see the CCSS include a human factor of *matching reader to text and task* by considering the reader's cognitive capabilities, motivation, knowledge, and background knowledge (Rand Reading Study Group, as cited in NGA Center/CCSSO, 2010c).

The CCSS provide a frame for evaluating reading choices for students. For example, they provide examples of the analysis of text complexity in Appendix A of the CCSS for ELA/Literacy document. Specifically, they include a sample evaluation of *Narrative of the Life of Fredrick Douglass* (see http://www.core standards.org/assets/Appendix_A.pdf, p. 12).

The CCSS also include an extensive book list for ELA, social studies, science, and technical subjects for each grade level. The CCSS stress that these are "guideposts" or "exemplars," not dictated curriculum. Titles include Henry Petroski's "The Evolution of the Grocery Bag" (6–8), Euclid's "Elements" (9–10), and U.S. General Services Administration *Executive Order 13423: Strengthening Federal Environmental, Energy, and Transport Management* (11–12) (NGA Center/CCSSO, 2010d). To further assist teachers in making informed decisions regarding appropriate texts for their students, the CCSS list text exemplars in Appendix B of the CCSS for ELA/Literacy document (see http://www .corestandards.org/assets/Appendix_B.pdf).

The importance of evaluating "Range, Quality, and Complexity of Student Reading" is emphasized in the introduction to Appendix A of the CCSS for ELA/ Literacy document. The CCSS note that what distinguished the high-performing students from lower-performing students on the ACT preliminary test was not the ability to make inferences, determine the main ideas, or define vocabulary in context. Rather, it was the ability of high-performing students to work with complex texts that set them apart from their peers.

Pedagogy focused only on 'higher-order' or 'critical' thinking was insufficient to ensure that students were ready for college and careers:

what students could read, in terms of its complexity, was at least as important as what they could do with what they read. (NGA Center/ CCSSO, 2010c)

It is important for teachers to help students enhance their reading and analytical skills. However, as the findings above show, it is not enough to teach students how to comprehend "Key Ideas and Details," analyze "Craft and Structure," and apply "Integration of Knowledge and Ideas." Rather, we must also help them to develop these skills with an increased "Range of Reading and Level of Text Complexity."

A CLOSER LOOK

Let's look at the grade-specific standards for the first set of standards under "Key Ideas and Details" for History/Social Studies 6–8, 9–10, and 11–12 (see Table 2.2). Students progress from citing evidence to supporting their analysis of primary and secondary sources in Grades 6–8 to attending to textual details, such as the date and source. Finally, by Grades 11–12, students practice synthesis and evaluation by using knowledge of the parts of a text to understand the whole.

The same advanced thinking is required with regard to the second set of grade-specific standards for "Key Ideas and Details." In Grades 6–8, students need to be able to determine the central ideas of a text and provide a summary of the text that reflects newfound knowledge from the reading rather than prior knowledge. In Grades 9–10, students must "provide an accurate summary of how key events or ideas develop over the course of the text." Finally, in Grades 11–12, students engage in a higher level of thinking required in history and social studies, which consists of providing a clear summary that reflects an understanding of the relationships of key events or ideas in the text.

The third set of grade-specific standards for "Key Ideas and Details" requires students to move from simple identification in Grades 6–8 to analysis in Grades 9–10 and evaluation in Grades 11–12. Specifically, in the earlier grades, students identify the steps in a process as described in a text. In Grades 9–10, students analyze the course of events and determine cause-and-effect relationships among these events, what came before and what came after. Finally, in Grades 11–12, students must evaluate explanations of events and actions and determine the explanation that corroborates the textual evidence, "acknowledging where the text leaves matters uncertain." This scaffolded thinking that advances students to a higher cognitive level (from *delineate* in Grades 6–8, to *analyze* in Grades 9–10 and *evaluate* in Grades 11–12) is supported by students' ability to meet the "Craft and Structure" and "Integration of Knowledge and Ideas" standards.

Let's look at the grade-specific standards for the first set of standards under "Key Ideas and Details" for Science and Technical Subjects 6–8, 9–10, and 11–12 (see Table 2.3). Students advance from citing evidence in Grades

Table 2.2   Reading Standards for History/Social Studies 6–12

Grade 6–8 Students	*Grade 9–10 Students*	*Grade 11–12 Students*
Key Ideas and Details	**Key Ideas and Details**	**Key Ideas and Details**
1. Cite specific textual evidence to support analysis of primary and secondary sources.	1. Cite specific textual evidence to support analysis of primary and secondary sources, attending to such features as the date and origin of the information.	1. Cite specific textual evidence to support analysis of primary and secondary sources, connecting insights gained from specific details to an understanding of the text as a whole.
2. Determine the central ideas or information of a primary or secondary source; provide an accurate summary of the source distinct from prior knowledge or opinions.	2. Determine the central ideas or information of a primary or secondary source; provide an accurate summary of how key events or ideas develop over the course of the text.	2. Determine the central ideas or information of a primary or secondary source; provide an accurate summary that makes clear the relationships among the key details and ideas.
3. Identify key steps in a text's description of a process related to history/social studies (e.g., how a bill becomes law, how interest rates are raised or lowered).	3. Analyze in detail a series of events described in a text; determine whether earlier events caused later ones or simply preceded them.	3. Evaluate various explanations for actions or events and determine which explanation best accords with textual evidence, acknowledging where the text leaves matters uncertain.

6–8 to "attending to precise details of explanations or descriptions" in Grades 9–10. Finally, by the end of high school, they practice higher-order thinking in their attention to those specifics by considering "inconsistencies in the account."

The same advanced thinking is required with regard to the second set of grade-specific standards for "Key Ideas and Details." In Grades 6–8, students need to be able to determine the central idea of a text and provide a summary of the text that reflects newfound knowledge from the reading rather than prior knowledge. In Grades 9–10, the text becomes more sophisticated and students must "*trace* the text's explanation or depiction of a complex process, phenomenon, or concept." Finally, in Grades 11–12, deeper comprehension is reflected in students' ability to move from simply

Table 2.3	Reading Standards for Science and Technical Subjects 6–12	
Grade 6–8 Students	*Grade 9–10 Students*	*Grade 11–12 Students*
Key Ideas and Details	**Key Ideas and Details**	**Key Ideas and Details**
1. Cite textual evidence to support analysis of science and technical texts.	1. Cite textual evidence to support analysis of science and technical texts, attending to the precise details of explanations or descriptions.	1. Cite textual evidence to support analysis of science and technical texts, attending to important distinctions the author makes and to any gaps or inconsistencies in the account.
2. Determine the central ideas or conclusions of a text; provide an accurate summary of the text distinct from prior knowledge or opinions.	2. Determine the central ideas or conclusions of a text; trace the text's explanation or depiction of a complex process, phenomenon, or concept; provide an accurate summary of the text.	2. Determine the central ideas or conclusions of a text; summarize complex concepts, processes, or information presented in a text by paraphrasing them in simpler but still accurate terms.
3. Follow precisely a multistep procedure when carrying out experiments, taking measurements, or performing technical tasks.	3. Follow precisely a complex multistep procedure when carrying out experiments, taking measurements, or performing technical tasks, attending to special cases or exceptions defined in the text.	3. Follow precisely a complex multistep procedure when carrying out experiments, taking measurements, or performing technical tasks; analyze the specific results based on explanations in the text.

tracing sophisticated information to being able to *paraphrase* the complex processes presented in the text.

The third set of grade-specific standards for "Key Ideas and Details" connects student action with reading. In Grades 6–8, students must "follow precisely a multistep procedure." This continues in Grades 9–10; however, the simplicity of following a set of steps is replaced with a call for students to understand and be aware of "special cases or exceptions defined in the text." Students' choices and actions are determined by their understanding of the text. Finally, in Grades 11–12, students must reflect on their actions when they "analyze the specific results based on explanations in the text." This type of higher-order thinking (application and analysis) is supported by students' ability to meet the "Craft and Structure" and "Integration of Knowledge and Ideas" standards.

CONCLUSION

As you read this chapter and take in the standards, we hope that you are thinking to yourselves, "I do this already!" If so, then the CCSS should serve as reinforcement of the good decisions that you are making regarding your instruction. Perhaps you have thought to yourself, "I would like to help my students be more able to_____." If so, then the standards can help make you more aware of a need for enhanced instruction. In the next chapter, we present reading lessons that target the Reading Standards within the CCSS for Literacy. We hope that they will serve as models for your own lesson planning.

Reading Lessons in History/Social Studies **3**

In this chapter, we present three history/social studies lessons that we believe are particularly effective for addressing the Common Core State Standards (CCSS) for Reading. These lessons involve many reading and writing skills and thus address the majority of the CCSS. However, we have designated each lesson according to the CCSS Reading strands that it addresses most fully:

- Key Ideas and Details: Grades 6–8 lesson, "Nationalism: The Good, the Bad, the Ugly"
- Craft and Structure: Grades 9–10 lesson, "Social Causes of New Imperialism"
- Integration of Knowledge and Ideas: Grades 11–12 lesson, "Vietnam: The Human Face of an Inhumane Time"

Within the first lesson, students examine various forms of media that promote nationalism from both World War II and post-9/11. They compare two sources and develop an argument essay regarding which is best at promoting nationalism.

Students engaged in the lesson on New Imperialism use Rudyard Kipling's (1899) poem "White Man's Burden" as a lens through which to view this time in history. The satirical voice in this poem affords students some emotional connection to the victims of Imperialism. Based on their analysis of the poem, students create their own poems to represent their understanding of the time period.

Similarly, in the third lesson, on Vietnam, students analyze several poems, songs, and excerpts from longer texts and integrate their understanding of multiple perspectives into a final writing piece, a conversation between two characters from two different works.

As you read through these lessons—and as you develop your own lessons—we encourage you to focus on how you can best guide your students to meet the CCSS for Reading that you examined in Chapter 2.

READING ANCHOR STANDARDS REFLECTIVE QUESTIONS

How does the lesson require students to do one or more of the following?

1. Determine what the text says explicitly and make logical inferences from it

2. Cite specific textual evidence when writing or speaking to support conclusions drawn from the text

3. Determine the main ideas and details of a text

4. Analyze the development of ideas in a text

5. Interpret words or phrases in a text and analyze how they shape meaning

6. Analyze the structure of a text, and analyze how sentences, paragraphs, and larger portions of the text shape meaning

7. Assess how point of view of a text shapes the meaning and style

8. Integrate and evaluate the content of texts presented in diverse media and formats

9. Evaluate the argument and claims in a text

10. Analyze how two or more texts address similar themes or topics

LESSON DESIGN REFLECTIVE QUESTIONS

1. How does the lesson require close and multiple readings of grade-level complex text?

2. How does my questioning require students to use the text as support for their interpretations/arguments?

3. How does the lesson incorporate varied thinking skills (e.g., read, summarize, analyze, interpret)? (Bloom)

4. How does the lesson include the three components of Backward Design: (a) desired results, (b) acceptable evidence, and (c) learning experiences?

5. How do I differentiate instruction, materials, and expectations for this particular lesson so that all students can be successful?

6. How does the lesson provide opportunities for technology/media use?

7. How does the lesson include research-based instructional strategies to promote effective teaching?

8. How does the lesson present opportunities for interdisciplinary connections?

9. How does the lesson provide opportunities for students with varied Multiple Intelligences to be successful? (Gardner)

10. How do I present the lesson in a way that encourages students to see the value of what they are learning (e.g., service learning, college- and career-readiness skills)? (Dewey)

Nationalism: The Good, the Bad, the Ugly
History/Social Studies—U.S. History
(Grades 6–8; Key Ideas and Details)
Nicole Moriarty—Mineola High School, Garden City Park, NY

LESSON PLAN TEMPLATE

TOPIC:

Nationalism: The Good, the Bad, the Ugly (Grades 6–8)

TIMING:

7 class periods

CCSS STRAND:

Reading

BACKWARD DESIGN COMPONENTS:

DESIRED RESULTS/CCSS ADDRESSED:

Enduring Understandings

- Through a close examination of literary and informational texts in various formats, students will be able to develop an understanding of the use of propaganda throughout history [R.1, R.2, R.3, R.4, R.5, R.6, R.7, R.8, R.9].

Knowledge and Skills

- Students will be able to analyze the figurative meaning of several texts and compare the implications of those texts on society [R.1, R.2, R.3, R.4, R.5, R.6, R.8, R.9, R.10].

- Students will be able to develop an argument essay in which they analyze and compare the effectiveness of prominent speakers in history [W.1, W.4, W.5, W.9].

ACCEPTABLE EVIDENCE:

- Effective classroom discussion of *Hansel and Gretel*, World War II propaganda posters, FDR's "A Date Which Will Live in Infamy" speech, Bush's 9/11 speech, and U2's song—"Walk On"

- Completed notes for *Hansel and Gretel* Analysis handout, including details that provide evidence of the fairy tale as a vehicle for encouraging nationalism

- Accurate evidence on WWII Propaganda Jigsaw Notes handout to support a group conversation regarding propaganda and nationalism in the United States

- Annotations on presidential speeches noting key details, the meaning of the details, and implications for the American public

- Argument essay regarding which is the better presidential speech, including valid reasoning and evidence in the form of textual and historical references

- Annotated U2 lyrics indicating how the song, "Walk On," might have taken on greater meaning after 9/11

- Logical rationale for song choice on Historical CD Song Choice handout through which students consider how other songs might take on greater meaning in relation to a historical event

LEARNING EXPERIENCES AND INSTRUCTION:

- Day 1—Use KWL (what students know, what students want to know, what students learned) to consider forms of nationalism in the United States, and read *Hansel and Gretel* to consider forms of nationalism abroad.

- Day 2—Deconstruct *Hansel and Gretel*.

- Day 3—Jigsaw activity—examine examples of Nationalism through propaganda in the United States during World War II.

- Day 4—Analysis of FDR's "A Date Which Will Live in Infamy" speech.

- Day 5—Analysis of Bush's 9/11 speech. Begin drafting argument essay regarding which speech is better.

- Day 6—Peer editing and discussion of the popularity of "Walk On" by U2 after 9/11. Begin compiling a CD of songs that would fit a time period in U.S. history.

- Day 7—Share songs.

STRATEGIES:

- Modeling

- Discussion

- Cooperative learning

MATERIALS NEEDED:

- *Hansel and Gretel* (1857) (http://www .pitt.edu/~dash/grimm015a.html)

- Printed copies of War Propaganda Posters:

  o http://www.crestock.com/uploads /blog/2008/propagandaposters /us_propaganda-31.jpg

  o http://faculty.polytechnic.org /gfeldmeth/Ww2_poster_oct0404.jpg

  o http://www.ww2shots.com /gallery/d/2765–1/Anti_Japanese _Propaganda4-ww2shots.jpg

  o http://sas.guidespot.com/bundles /guides_0d/assets/widget _dawLYXRZve2itbGymraEeZ.jpg

- Audio of FDR's "A Date Which Will Live in Infamy" speech(http://historymatters .gmu.edu/d/5166/)

- Video of Bush's 9/11 speech (http:// www.youtube.com /watch?v=YMiqEUBux3o)

- "Walk On" lyrics (http://www.elyrics.net /read/u/u2-lyrics/walk-on-lyrics.html)

- Paper and pens

- Handouts (reproducible forms for each handout appear at the end of this section)

SUPPLEMENTAL RESOURCES:

- World War II background (http:// americanhistory.about.com/od /worldwarii/a/wwiioverview.htm)

- Brothers Grimm National Geographic link (http://www.nationalgeographic .com/grimm/index2.html)

TECHNOLOGY/MEDIA OPPORTUNITIES:

- Use of audio or video of *Hansel and Gretel,* FDR's speech, and Bush's speech.

- Lyrics.com for song lyrics.

- Youtube.com to project song lyrics while sharing.

SERVICE LEARNING LINKS:

- Students create a CD with songs for our troops and send them with care packages.

- Students evaluate the ways that advertising manipulates them in similar ways to the propaganda that they examined. Students rate companies based on their advertising campaigns and encourage their peers to give their business to those companies that use positive advertising methods.

VARIATIONS:

- Students evaluate other presidential speeches during difficult times in U.S. history.

- Students design their own posters related to current events. These posters can contain several elements of nationalism.

- Students create a Photo Story with pictures of the time period/historical figure that they have connected with their song. This serves as a visual support of their rationale for the connection.

NATIONALISM: THE GOOD, THE BAD, THE UGLY

History/Social Studies—U.S. History

(Grades 6–8; Key Ideas and Details)

*Nicole Moriarty—Mineola High School,
Garden City Park, NY*

Although the concept of nationalism and its many examples may be highly interesting to historians, it can often be presented to high school students in a rather dull, sequential manner that focuses on dates and facts. And as a result, all too often, students have forgotten the information by the end of the school year. Nationalism presented in this lockstep fashion does not assist learners in making the much-needed connections among events across time periods and regions or enable them to transfer the information learned from one unit of study on nationalism to other seemingly unrelated units of study. Unfortunately, students who lack these skills are at a disadvantage in the study of U.S. and world history. Thus, if we look at nationalism in its entirety, introducing the students to an array of nationalistic events across time and space and providing them with myriad activities stemming from reading for information, the learning experience becomes more profound, equipping the learners with the coveted skills required to think like an investigator and to write like a journalist.

This *Hansel and Gretel* lesson has been adapted to fit an eighth-grade U.S. history course; it would work well in earlier grades also. Given the limited amount of time allocated for the study of World War II, some teachers may need to select activities from those described below instead of covering all of them. Another approach would be to complete the entire lesson by teaming with an English teacher to cover *Hansel and Gretel* and the presidential speeches. Depending on the reading level of your students, you might also choose to present excerpts rather than the full-length transcripts.

Materials Needed

- *Hansel and Gretel* (1857) (http://www.pitt.edu/~dash/grimm015a.html)
- Printed copies of War Propaganda Posters:

  o http://www.crestock.com/uploads/blog/2008/propagandaposters/us_propaganda-31.jpg
  o http://faculty.polytechnic.org/gfeldmeth/Ww2_poster_oct0404.jpg
  o http://www.ww2shots.com/gallery/d/2765-1/Anti_Japanese_Propaganda4-ww2shots.jpg
  o http://sas.guidespot.com/bundles/guides_0d/assets/widget_daw LYXRZve2itbGymraEeZ.jpg

- Audio of FDR's "A Date Which Will Live in Infamy" speech (http://history matters.gmu.edu/d/5166/)
- Video of Bush's 9/11 speech (http://www.youtube.com/watch?v=YMiqEUBux3o

- "Walk On" lyrics (http://www.elyrics.net/read/u/u2-lyrics/walk-on -lyrics.html)
- Paper and pens
- Handouts (reproducible forms for each handout appear at the end of this section)

Timing

7 class periods

- Day 1—Use KWL (what students know, want to know, want to learn) to consider forms of nationalism in the United States and read *Hansel and Gretel* to consider forms of nationalism abroad.
- Day 2—Deconstruct *Hansel and Gretel.*
- Day 3—Complete jigsaw activity—examining examples of nationalism through propaganda in the United States during World War II.
- Day 4—Analyze FDR's "A Date Which Will Live in Infamy" Speech.
- Day 5—Analyze Bush's 9–11 Speech. Begin drafting argument essay regarding which speech is better.
- Day 6—Work on peer editing and discussion of the popularity of "Walk On" by U2 after 9/11. Begin compiling a CD of songs that would fit a time period in U.S. history.
- Day 7—Share songs.

Day 1

On the first day of the unit, students quickly brainstorm some of the symbols in the United States that reflect love for the country (e.g., the American flag, the eagle, images of the president) as well as symbols that invoke loyalty to the country (e.g. a soldier in uniform, a person with hand over heart reciting the Pledge of Allegiance). We record their answers in the K section of a KWL chart (**Handout 1**). Students then list some of the mediums that portray these symbols to the general public (e.g., flag pins, money, Mount Rushmore); we also record those answers in the KWL chart. Next, we engage in a class discussion about how these symbols can help unify a country and how the symbols can also be used in a negative manner to destroy other countries, ethnicities, or outsiders (e.g., burning of another country's flag). Based on this introductory activity, students formulate questions that they would like to explore throughout the unit, and we write these in the W section of the KWL chart.

 THEORY LINK (Dewey): Purposeful learning—the unit will answer their questions.

I introduce (or reintroduce) the students to *Hansel and Gretel,* a story that most know. For their analysis, I tell the students that the story was not just a beloved tale told to children; it was used as a tool for German unification. In 1812, motivated by a sense of nationalism, the Grimms published a collection of folktales to preserve aspects of traditional culture in an attempt to foster pride in Germanic past, increase loyalty to the state, and vilify outsiders to the German race. The Grimms preserved German culture and introduced readers to cultural and social ideologies through characterizations and symbolism.

CULTURAL/LINGUISTIC HIGHLIGHT: Students may share stories that highlight aspects of their own cultures.

CULTURAL/LINGUISTIC HIGHLIGHT: Listening while reading provides additional support for comprehension and language development.

THEORY LINK (Gardner): Appeals to Interpersonal Intelligence.

For the remainder of the class period, the students read the story of *Hansel and Gretel* silently as I read it aloud to them.

To do this, I move the students to the floor and we have circle time to remind them of the innocent and trusting perspective they likely held when they were first read this story as young children. I read from the text posted on http://www.pitt.edu/~dash /grimm015a.html because this site provides a side-by-side representation of the 1812 and the 1857 texts. For this reading, I instruct the students to pay careful attention to the characters and the setting. After I read the story this second time, the students break into small groups, where they quickly discuss the key ideas and details associated with characterization and setting.

After 5 to 10 minutes, we come back together as a class and develop class consensus on how these story elements are portrayed [R.1, R.2, R.3]. For example, in terms of characterization, students note the contrast between the father's kindness and mother's ruthlessness in their treatment of the children. In terms of setting, they also note that the woods are dark and the need for moonlight or sunlight to help Hansel and Gretel see.

Day 2

The next step in this process is to have students consider how the Grimms conveyed various nationalistic themes throughout the story of *Hansel and Gretel.* To foster student thinking and discussion, learners work together in small groups to decipher the embedded nationalistic symbols that encouraged German nationalism and the development of the Volk, Hitler's concept of the natural unit of mankind; promoted anti-Semitism; and advanced German cultural priorities, such as patriarchal societies, loyalty to the state, the idea that the individual is nothing and the state is everything, racial purity, good triumphing evil, and the evil outsider (**Handout 2**). The purpose of the activity is to encourage students to analyze how the symbols in the story might have had an influence on German society [R.4, R.5, R.6].

THEORY LINK (Bloom): Students move from basic comprehension to analysis and evaluation.

DIFFERENTIATION TIP: Struggling learners may use parts of the comparison chart rather than all of it. Advanced students may find a third version of the story for comparison.

Upon completion of the small-group analysis, whole-group discussion ensues. To extend student knowledge on the change of nationalism in Germany over time, I ask students to compare the 1857 edition of *Hansel and Gretel* with the original 1812 edition (see http://www.pitt.edu/~dash/grimm015a.html) [R.9].

We discuss the ways that the changes might have increased feelings of nationalism and fueled citizens' allegiance to the Nazi cause. I always enjoy seeing my students' reactions to this lesson. When I tell them that *Hansel and Gretel* was required reading in German schools, they express outrage at the "brainwashing" of the German children. This outrage provides a pivotal point at which I require students to reflect on the way nationalism has played a part in our own country's history.

Day 3

On the third day of this unit, students engage in a jigsaw activity through which they examine evidence of nationalism in the United States during World War II. Students form four different content-based groups. Each group must examine a different U.S. propaganda poster printed from the sites listed below. All members of each group receive a copy of the group's poster. The groups consider the details in their poster, the meaning of the details, and the implications of that meaning for Americans during World War II (**Handout 3**).

 THEORY LINK (Gardner): Appeals to Visual-Spatial Intelligence.

The first poster is for war bonds. It features Uncle Sam with a bundle over his shoulder wrapped in an American Flag (see http://www .crestock.com/uploads/blog/2008/propagandaposters/us_propaganda-31 .jpg). The second poster presents a comical picture of Hitler in his underwear (see http://faculty.polytechnic.org/gfeldmeth/Ww2_poster_oct0404.jpg). The third poster is a bit more aggressive, calling for people to buy war bonds in order to "blast 'em Japanazis" (see http://www.ww2shots.com /gallery/d/2765–1/Anti_Japanese_Propaganda4-ww2shots.jpg). It still maintains some humor since it features Popeye. The last poster is the most aggressive and demeaning to our enemies. It features Germans and Japanese "monsters" (see http://sas.guidespot.com/bundles/guides_0d/assets/widget _dawLYXRZve2itbGymraEeZ.jpg).

Each group analyzes a different poster. Then I reorganize the groups so that each new group contains four students—one who worked on each poster. Students bring a copy of the poster they analyzed, and the new groups compare the four posters, pointing out the pertinent details directly [R.4, R.6, R.7, R.9].

Day 4

Following the examination of the war posters, students delve into the more complex text of FDR's "A Date Which Will Live in Infamy" speech (**Handout 4**) [R.1, R.2, R.3, R.4, R.5, R.6, R.8, R.10]. They read along as I play the audio (http://historymatters.gmu.edu/d/5166/). I remind students that this experience of listening to the president's voice is much like that of the people during the time period of World War II listening to FDR over the radio. Just as they did with the posters the day before, students annotate the text, noting key details, the meaning of the details, and the implication of that meaning for the American people. This time, students annotate directly on the page, thus progressing toward what they would be expected to do in a high school or college setting.

CULTURAL/LINGUISTIC HIGHLIGHT: Listening while reading provides additional support for comprehension and language development.

THEORY LINK (Gardner): Appeals to Verbal-Linguistic Intelligence.

DIFFERENTIATION TIP: You may read the speech aloud a second time and use the think-aloud strategy to model and guide students in the analysis of the text.

TECH CONNECTION: Have students listen and read first. Then have them watch the speech. Discuss the effect of seeing the president give the speech rather than simply listening as they did with FDR.

CULTURAL/LINGUISTIC HIGHLIGHT: The graphic organizer helps highlight key information and scaffold learning.

THEORY LINK (Gardner): Appeals to Interpersonal and Verbal-Linguistic Intelligences.

To confirm understanding, I ask students to summarize the main ideas of the speech before we conduct a full-class discussion based on the deeper analysis represented in their notes.

Day 5

To help students see the relevancy of studying this speech, I compare FDR's words after the attack on Pearl Harbor with President George Bush's words after the 9/11 attacks (**Handout 5**) [R.1, R.2, R.3, R.4, R.5, R.6, R.8, R.9, R.10]. This time, students can watch Bush's speech (http://www.youtube.com /watch?v=YMiqEUBux3o).

Again, I ask students to summarize the main ideas of the speech and annotate this text, noting the meaning of the details and the implication of that meaning for the American people. Based on their notes on both FDR's and Bush's speeches, students use textual references to develop an argument essay on which speech is better at invoking nationalistic feelings and why [W.1, W.4, W.9]. I help students reflect on all of the information they have acquired regarding nationalism by completing the L section of the KWL organizer. I provide further support in the form of an essay organizer for the planning stage of the writing process (**Handout 6**).

Students begin planning in class, and they draft for homework.

Day 6

For the first 10 minutes, students pair and share their drafts.

Students underline clear examples of supporting evidence and place questions in the margins regarding any support that is not clear. They have two days to make the necessary revisions [W.4, W.5]. During the second half of class, we take this unit full circle by considering how a song that was popular in the United States, "Walk On" by U2, took on greater meaning after the 9/11 attacks. This is comparable to the way that the story of *Hansel and Gretel* took on new meaning during World War II [R.4, R.5, R.6, R.9]. The difference is that in the case of "Walk On," the meaning is one of survival, whereas the story of *Hansel and Gretel* took on a dark and sinister meaning. Students examine the lyrics of "Walk On," and we discuss which lines might have had a particularly important impact on listeners after the attacks (see http://www.elyrics.net/read/u/u2-lyrics/walk -on-lyrics.html).

As a culminating activity, students work together to create a historical CD. In pairs, they consider the following question: If you could play a song for someone in any time period, regardless of whether that song was actually written at the time, what song would it be and why?

THEORY LINK (Gardner): Appeals to Interpersonal, Musical-Rhythmic, and Verbal-Linguistic Intelligences.

The students answer this question in detail on **Handout 7** [R.1, R.2, R.3, R.4, R.5, R.6].

Day 7

Students share their songs. This is a great day because students often comment that they have learned something new about a favorite song by listening to it with a new perspective. This entire unit helps students recognize just how important perspective is!

HANDOUT 1

KWL CHART

K	W	L
What I Know	What I Want to Know	What I Learned

HANDOUT 2

HANSEL AND GRETEL ANALYSIS

Directions: As you read the story, note any examples of the following.

German nationalism:

The development of the Volk:

Anti-Semitism:

Patriarchal society:

Loyalty to the State:

Racial purity:

Good triumphing over evil:

Evil outsider:

HANDOUT 3

WWII PROPAGANDA

Jigsaw Notes

Posters printed out, one for each member of the assigned group:

1. Poster for war bonds: It features Uncle Sam with a bundle over his shoulder wrapped in an American Flag (http://www.crestock.com/uploads/blog/2008/propagandaposters/us_propaganda-31.jpg)

2. Poster presenting a comical picture of Hitler in his underwear (http://faculty.polytechnic.org/gfeldmeth/Ww2_poster_oct0404.jpg)

3. Poster featuring Popeye and calling for people to buy war bonds in order to "blast 'em Japanazis" (http://www.ww2shots.com/gallery/d/2765–1/Anti_Japanese_Propaganda4-ww2shots.jpg)

4. Poster featuring Germans and Japanese "monsters" (http://sas.guidespot.com/bundles/guides_0d/assets/widget_dawLYXRZve2itbGymraEeZ.jpg)

Poster Details	Meaning of Details	Implications of Details

HANDOUT 4

"A DATE WHICH WILL LIVE IN INFAMY": FDR ASKS FOR A DECLARATION OF WAR

Yesterday, December 7, 1941—a date which will live in infamy—the United States of America was suddenly and deliberately attacked by naval and air forces of the Empire of Japan.

The United States was at peace with that nation, and, at the solicitation of Japan, was still in conversation with its government and its emperor looking toward the maintenance of peace in the Pacific. Indeed, one hour after Japanese air squadrons had commenced bombing in the American island of Oahu, the Japanese ambassador to the United States and his colleague delivered to our secretary of state a formal reply to a recent American message. While this reply stated that it seemed useless to continue the existing diplomatic negotiations, it contained no threat or hint of war or armed attack.

It will be recorded that the distance of Hawaii from Japan makes it obvious that the attack was deliberately planned many days or even weeks ago. During the intervening time the Japanese government has deliberately sought to deceive the United States by false statements and expressions of hope for continued peace.

The attack yesterday on the Hawaiian Islands has caused severe damage to American naval and military forces. I regret to tell you that very many American lives have been lost. In addition, American ships have been reported torpedoed on the high seas between San Francisco and Honolulu.

Yesterday the Japanese government also launched an attack against Malaya.

Last night Japanese forces attacked Hong Kong.

Last night Japanese forces attacked Guam.

Last night Japanese forces attacked the Philippine Islands.

Last night Japanese forces attacked Wake Island.

And this morning the Japanese attacked Midway Island.

Japan has, therefore, undertaken a surprise offensive extending throughout the Pacific area. The facts of yesterday and today speak for themselves. The people of the United States have already formed their opinions and well understand the implications to the very life and safety of our nation.

As commander in chief of the Army and Navy I have directed that all measures be taken for our defense. But always will our whole nation remember the character of the onslaught against us . . .

Source: http://historymatters.gmu.edu/d/5166/ Franklin D. Roosevelt Library, Hyde Park, NY.

HANDOUT 5

9/11 SPEECH BY PRESIDENT GEORGE W. BUSH

Good evening. Today, our fellow citizens, our way of life, our very freedom came under attack in a series of deliberate and deadly terrorist acts. The victims were in airplanes, or in their offices; secretaries, businessmen and women, military and federal workers; moms and dads, friends and neighbors. Thousands of lives were suddenly ended by evil, despicable acts of terror.

The pictures of airplanes flying into buildings, fires burning, huge structures collapsing, have filled us with disbelief, terrible sadness, and a quiet, unyielding anger. These acts of mass murder were intended to frighten our nation into chaos and retreat. But they have failed; our country is strong.

A great people has been moved to defend a great nation. Terrorist attacks can shake the foundations of our biggest buildings, but they cannot touch the foundation of America. These acts shattered steel, but they cannot dent the steel of American resolve.

America was targeted for attack because we're the brightest beacon for freedom and opportunity in the world. And no one will keep that light from shining.

Today, our nation saw evil, the very worst of human nature. And we responded with the best of America—with the daring of our rescue workers, with the caring for strangers and neighbors who came to give blood and help in any way they could.

Immediately following the first attack, I implemented our government's emergency response plans. Our military is powerful, and it's prepared. Our emergency teams are working in New York City and Washington, D.C. to help with local rescue efforts.

Our first priority is to get help to those who have been injured, and to take every precaution to protect our citizens at home and around the world from further attacks.

The functions of our government continue without interruption. Federal agencies in Washington, which had to be evacuated today are reopening for essential personnel tonight, and will be open for business tomorrow. Our financial institutions remain strong, and the American economy will be open for business, as well.

The search is underway for those who are behind these evil acts. I've directed the full resources of our intelligence and law enforcement communities to find those responsible and to bring them to justice. We will make no distinction between the terrorists who committed these acts and those who harbor them.

I appreciate so very much the members of Congress who have joined me in strongly condemning these attacks. And on behalf of the American people, I thank the many world leaders who have called to offer their condolences and assistance.

America and our friends and allies join with all those who want peace and security in the world, and we stand together to win the war against terrorism. Tonight, I ask for your prayers for all those who grieve, for the children whose worlds have been shattered, for all whose sense of safety and security has been threatened. And I pray they will be comforted by a power greater than any of us, spoken through the ages in Psalm 23: "Even though I walk through the valley of the shadow of death, I fear no evil, for You are with me."

This is a day when all Americans from every walk of life unite in our resolve for justice and peace. America has stood down enemies before, and we will do so this time. None of us will ever forget this day. Yet, we go forward to defend freedom and all that is good and just in our world.

Source: http://www.famous-speeches-and-speech-topics.info/presidential-speeches/george-w-bush-speech-9–11-address-to-the-nation.htm

HANDOUT 6

ARGUMENT ORGANIZER FOR BEST SPEECH

Directions: Tell which speech was better at invoking nationalistic feelings (FDR's or Bush's). Be sure to follow the format outlined below and to include at least two direct quotes from the speech.

Paragraph 1: Introduction (10 Points)

Tell the social and historical context of the speeches you are comparing.

Clearly state which speech you believe is better.

Paragraph 2: Supporting Evidence (40 Points)

How does the speech appeal to nationalism?

    —Reference to traditional culture

    —Fostering of pride

    —Vilifying outsiders

How does the speech appeal to emotion?

How does the speech appeal to logic?

Paragraph 3: Counterargument (20 Points)

Concede opposite viewpoint:

—Some might say the other speech is better because . . .

Refute opposite viewpoint:

However, I believe _____ speech is better because . . .

(Be specific about what you conceded above)

Paragraph 4: Conclusion (10 Points)

Tell why it is important for students like you to read this speech today.

Conventions (20 Points)

—Grammar

—Spelling

—Transitions

—Topic sentences

HANDOUT 7

HISTORICAL CD SONG CHOICE

Directions: If you could play a song for someone in any time period, regardless of whether that song was actually written at the time, what song would it be and why? Choose any time period that we have covered this year. Name a song that would be fitting to play for a figure living during that time period. The person could be a famous figure or an average citizen. You choose. Be sure to provide a clear explanation as to why this song fits this person and this time period.

Describe the historical time period:

Describe the person for whom you would play this song:

Cite two lines from the lyrics that make this song particularly appropriate for this person:

1. _____

    Explain why this is appropriate for your person:

2. _____

    Explain why this is appropriate for your person:

Social Causes of New Imperialism
History/Social Studies—World History
(Grades 9–10; Craft and Structure)
Jena Malinowski—Molloy College, Rockville Centre, NY

LESSON PLAN TEMPLATE

TOPIC:

Social Causes of New Imperialism (Grades 9–10)

CCSS STRAND:

Reading

TIMING:

5 class periods

BACKWARD DESIGN COMPONENTS:

DESIRED RESULTS/CCSS ADDRESSED:

Enduring Understandings

- Through the close examination of poetry from a historical period, students will understand social and cultural beliefs that lead to and create support for social power structures [R.1, R.2, R.4, R. 6, R.7, R.8].

Knowledge and Skills

- Students will be able to analyze poetry by examining the structure of the text, considering the effect of specific words or phrases on the overall meaning, and assessing how point of view influences the style and meaning [R.4, R.5, R.6].

- Students will be able to engage in the writing process to develop a poem with a message that makes a statement about society [R.4, W.4, W.5, W.6].

- Students will be able to write a clear and coherent argument about how poetry can inform us about history [W.1, W.4].

ACCEPTABLE EVIDENCE:

- Stop and Jot writing segments about "White Man's Burden"—mood, language, and cultural/historical context

- Student-created poem highlighting and contrasting the ideas of Kipling's "White Man's Burden" and New Imperialism

- Paragraph answering the lesson's aim: "What do you think the belief in Social Darwinism and the 'White Man's Burden' poem by Rudyard Kipling tell you about New Imperialism from the 1870s through 1914?"

LEARNING EXPERIENCES AND INSTRUCTION:

- Day 1—Discuss and take notes about the social causes of New Imperialism. Read, reflect, and analyze the poem, "White Man's Burden" by Rudyard Kipling.

- Day 2—Create student poems.

- Day 3—Peer-edit poems.

- Day 4—Write paragraphs answering the lesson's aim about New Imperialism and Social Darwinism; edit poems.

- Day 5—Share the poems with the class.

STRATEGIES:

- Discussion

- Modeling

- Questioning

- Cooperative Learning

- Writing Process

MATERIALS NEEDED:

- Copy of "White Man's Burden" by Rudyard Kipling (http://www.fordham .edu/halsall/mod/kipling.asp)

- Computer/projector/SMART Board or projector screen

- PowerPoint

- Whiteboard and markers or blackboard and chalk

- Paper and pens

- Handouts (reproducible forms for each handout appear at the end of this section)

SUPPLEMENTAL RESOURCES:

- Beck, R., Black, L., Krieger, L., Naylor, P., & Shabaka, D. (2003). *World history: patterns of interaction*. New York, NY: McDougal.

- Dictionary.com, LLC. (2012). Thesaurus .com. Retrieved from http://thesaurus .com/

- *Brief review for New York global history and geography*. (2004). New York, NY: Prentice Hall.

TECHNOLOGY OPPORTUNITIES:

- Students can enhance their poems and vocabulary by using Thesaurus.com.

- The students will look up visuals on the Internet to accompany their poems.

- Students with disabilities that need assistive technology can use the computer to take notes and write their poems and paragraphs.

- A projector and SMART Board or Whiteboard are used to display visuals and cartoons about New Imperialism and the White man's burden.

SERVICE LEARNING LINKS:

- Students share their poems as part of the school's or the town's antibullying campaign. This is a good match because the poems address the need for tolerance and understanding between cultures to prevent another age of imperialism and injustice from occurring again.

- Students compose a satirical piece based on a current issue and submit it for publication online or in a local paper.

VARIATIONS:

- Apply this lesson to other time periods to compare and contrast cultural norms and the development of social justice (e.g., slavery, Civil Rights Movement, the Holocaust, the women's suffrage movement, etc.).

- To make the assignment more challenging, require students to take on the beliefs of various historic cultures and write a poem, diary entry, or essay justifying these beliefs and their effects on history.

- Have students participate in a mini-debate using historical analysis and cultural influences of today to decide if belief in the White man's burden can be justified.

- Encourage students to analyze further by asking students to decide if Kipling wrote the poem because he truly believed in the White man's burden or if he wrote the poem to highlight the injustices of New Imperialism.

SOCIAL CAUSES OF NEW IMPERIALISM

History/Social Studies—World History

(Grades 9–10; Craft and Structure)

Jena Malinowski—Molloy College, Rockville Centre, NY

This lesson helps students understand and analyze historic events while also analyzing their own society's understandings of social justice. This application to their own lives helps students connect the material to already developed schemata. It relates to students' lives because it has undertones that connect to the central ideas of antibullying campaigns and multiculturalism (e.g., tolerance, understanding, and respect).

Through this lesson, students form an understanding of the social and cultural beliefs that were tied to New Imperialism from 1870 to 1914. Similar to the first wave of Imperialism, which was driven by the "Three G's" (gold, God, and glory), New Imperialism was also driven by economics, global power, and beliefs; however, it was much more devastating to the countries that were occupied, because of Europe's intense militaristic drive, racist policies, and unbounded exploitation of natural resources. Students need to know these differences between the two waves of Imperialism because the second wave set the stage for the global politics of the 20th century (particularly during WWII, the Cold War, and post-Cold War) regarding developing nations. Through Rudyard Kipling's poem "White Man's Burden" (1899), students examine the social causes, influences, and justifications of New Imperialism and contrast these beliefs and ideals with cultural beliefs of today.

Materials Needed

- Copy of "White Man's Burden" by Rudyard Kipling (http://www.fordham.edu/halsall/mod/kipling.asp)
- Computer/projector/SMART Board or projector screen
- PowerPoint
- Whiteboard and markers or blackboard and chalk
- Paper and pens
- Handouts (reproducible forms for each handout appear at the end of this section)

Timing

5 class periods

- Day 1—Discuss and take notes about the social causes of New Imperialism. Read, reflect, and analyze the poem "White Man's Burden" by Rudyard Kipling.
- Day 2—Create student poems.
- Day 3—Peer-edit poems.

- Day 4—Write paragraphs answering the lesson's aim about New Imperialism and Social Darwinism; edit poems.
- Day 5—Share the poems with the class.

Day 1

When the class starts, students complete a brief two- to three-minute Do Now activity. I write the question, "What do you think is meant by the phrase 'White man's burden'?" on the board. I want students to respond in writing to this question. I want them to think creatively about this, and as we discuss the students' ideas as a class, I pose questions to them regarding the connotation of the word burden and the phrase White man, and of exchange words such as moral obligation and duty for burden. I also ask how each phrase makes the students feel.

CULTURAL/LINGUISTIC HIGHLIGHT: Vocabulary sheets and sentence starters provide linguistic support.

Once students complete the Do Now activity and review, I hand out the work packet that contains the materials for the lesson (Handouts 1–7) and supports for English Language Learners (ELLs) and students with disabilities (SWD), such as a vocabulary sheet and sentence starters (**Handout 6**).

The next part of the lesson is the note-taking session. This takes just a few minutes because the purpose of the lesson is not a focus on the material but rather the analysis of Kipling's poem and students' creation of their own poem. I review the notes that students took the day before called, "Yesterday's Notes" (see **Handout 1**) and provide direct instruction on the day's lesson for which students take notes. (A student sample of "Today's Notes" is provided in Handout 1 for your reference.) This direct instruction is in the form of a PowerPoint presentation that includes a visual representation of the social motives through political cartoons, photographs, and sometimes even medical diagrams. These visuals deepen the lesson discussion because they help students make connections to the notes and also demonstrate the intense power of racist social beliefs and how imbedded in the culture they really were.

THEORY LINK (Gardner): Appeals to Visual-Spatial Intelligence.

The notes are on additional background material regarding the social causes of and influences on New Imperialism. This information better enables students to analyze Kipling's poem. The students use a graphic organizer that groups the causes of New Imperialism into economic, political/military, social, and science and technology categories; the social causes are further categorized into nationalism, Social Darwinism, and White man's burden (**Handout 1**).

CULTURAL/LINGUISTIC HIGHLIGHT: Visual representations deepen students' comprehension of content and language.

Once the graphic organizer is completed, I read aloud the entire poem, "White Man's Burden" by Rudyard Kipling. I reread the entire poem and then read the first stanza a third time. I want students to do a close reading and focused analysis of only the

CULTURAL/LINGUISTIC HIGHLIGHT: Graphic organizers help highlight key information and scaffold learning.

first stanza so that they can create their own stanzas modeled after Kipling's. I read the poem emphatically to highlight the negative terms used in the poem and to give students the sense of what the poem is about. After hearing the first stanza, the students do a Stop and Jot—they stop and use **Handout 2** to jot down their reaction. I ask them specifically to consider how the poem makes them feel, how the people of Africa and Asia would have felt after hearing the poem, why Kipling uses such harsh language, and what the poem demonstrates about European beliefs about other cultures.

TECH CONNECTION: Students could listen to the teacher's pre-recorded reading of the poem.

After students have quickly jotted some ideas down, the students share their thoughts with their neighbors and begin to analyze the meaning and purpose of the poem. Some questions that students may discuss during this think-pair-share time include the following:

- How do you and your partners feel about the poem? Why?
- How are people from non-European lands described?
- What does this language show you about the beliefs of the European Imperialists?
- Were the European nations really better than nations in Africa and Asia?
- Why did the Europeans have such mistaken beliefs about the Africans and Asians?

TECH CONNECTION: These questions may be projected on the board to aid students' conversations.

CULTURAL/LINGUISTIC HIGHLIGHT: An exchange about racist beliefs and actions—how and why they evolved—can lead to cross-cultural understanding.

After about a minute, the class comes back together and I guide a classroom analysis of the poem using the students' own jotted responses and other ideas generated during their think-pair-share time, thereby making sure all the students understand the meaning and purpose of the poem [R.1, R.2, R.4, R.5, R.6, R.7, R.8]. It is interesting to point out to students that the analysis of the poem presents many of the same challenges as the analysis of political cartoons because both involve satire. This is a concept that requires guided understanding for most students.

Day 2

THEORY LINK (Bloom): Students interpret and analyze the poem.

Once I feel that the students fully understand the meaning and purpose of the poem, I then guide them in the creation of their own poems. The poems should include acknowledgment of European racist beliefs of the time, present the need for tolerance and understanding to prevent such events from happening again, and be written from a perspective other than that of European imperialists, such as an African, Chinese, or Filipino.

I read an example poem to students (**Handout 2**), and as a class we verbally contrast the example poem to Kipling's to ensure understanding of what is required for the poem-writing assignment. I provide various poetic structures (**Handout 2**), but I do not limit students to these options. To guide the students, I also provide the rubric by which they will be assessed (**Handout 7**).

Day 3

Students engage in peer-editing using a worksheet (**Handout 3**). Once their peers have had a chance to respond to their poems, students submit them to me for feedback.

CULTURAL/LINGUISTIC HIGHLIGHT: When students are allowed to express their creativity through their own self-created poems that require them to take a different cultural and historic perspective, they gain a global perspective.

Day 4

I hand back the poems with my feedback so students can revise their poems incorporating their peers' and teacher's suggestions. They retype them and add visuals [R.4, W.4, W.5, W.6]. We continue our unit on New Imperialism. Students write a paragraph answering the aim regarding Social Darwinism and European Imperialism (**Handout 4**). I provide a scaffolded paragraph to support ELLs (**Handout 5**), and I include a list of defined vocabulary words (**Handout 6**) to support ELLs and struggling learners. As noted, I include a rubric to guide students as they work (**Handout 7**).

Day 5

Students share and display their typed poems to remind each other that lessons learned from history are still relevant to their lives.

As a class, we discuss how they must still work to understand and respect all people. This makes for a good learning environment and a truly culturally sensitive classroom. We also display students' poems throughout the school to help promote a tolerant and respectful learning environment and assist with antibullying campaigns.

THEORY LINK (Gardner): Appeals to Interpersonal Intelligence.

THEORY LINK (Dewey): Developing citizenry—students are enhancing their understanding of diversity.

HANDOUT 1

Yesterday's Notes

Motives of New Imperialism

Economic	Political and Military	Social (Today's lesson)	Science and Invention
- Need for natural resources - Need for new markets - Place for growing population to settle - Place to invest profits	- Bases for trade and navy ships - Power and security of global empire - Spirit of nationalism	- Nationalism - Social Darwinism - "White Man's Burden" - Wish to spread Christianity - Wish to share Western Civilization - Belief that Western ways are best	- New weapons - New medicines - Improved ships

Today's Notes

Social Causes of New Imperialism

Nationalism	Social Darwinism	White Man's Burden
- Idea of national superiority - Idea of "we have a right to take over your country because we are better"	- Non-Europeans considered to be on lower scale of cultural and physical development because they did not have Europe's technology - Europeans thought they were "fittest" so they had right to imperialize other ethnic groups - racist idea	- Poem written by Rudyard Kipling - Belief that it was White man's moral duty to civilize and/or make more human the savage nations of Africa and Asia - very racist belief

HANDOUT 2

STOP AND JOT

Excerpt from: "White Man's Burden"- Rudyard Kipling

Stanza 1

Take up the White Man's burden—
Send forth the best ye breed—
Go, bind your sons to exile
To serve your captives' need;
To wait, in heavy harness,
On fluttered folk and wild—
Your new-caught sullen peoples,
Half devil and half child.

My Reaction to the Poem:

_____

_____

_____

_____

_____

_____

_____

_____

Full poem found at http://www.fordham.edu/halsall/mod/kipling.asp

Example poem:

"The World's Burden"

Take up the new World's Burden

It's time for our views to broaden

We all need to learn some tolerance

To help the world bridge the distance.

The Colonizers believed they were the best of all Creation

That is why their policies hurt many other nations

Now Understanding will help us too.

To create love for others that's true.

This is the new World's Burden

Let's work together to make it happen.

Examples of Poem Patterns:

Rhyme A	Rhyme A
Rhyme A	Rhyme B
Rhyme B	Rhyme A
Rhyme B	Rhyme B
Rhyme C	Rhyme C
Rhyme C	Rhyme D
Rhyme D	Rhyme C
Rhyme D	Rhyme D

Acrostic Poem Starters:

T_____	I_____
O_____	M_____
L_____	P_____
E_____	E_____
R_____	R_____
A_____	I_____
N_____	A_____
C_____	L_____
E_____	I_____
	S_____
	M_____

Rhyming Poem Starter:

Take up the _____
It's time for _____
We all need _____
To _____
The Colonizers believed _____
That is why their policies _____
Now Understanding will _____
To _____
This is the _____
Let us _____

HANDOUT 3

PEER-EDITING WORKSHEET

My name:

Partner's name:

Assignment:

1. Does the poem address the need for tolerance and understanding?

   Yes ___ No___

   If yes, explain:

2. Does the poem address European racist beliefs justifying Imperialism?

   Yes ___ No ___

   If yes, explain:

3. Does the poem have comprehensible spelling and grammar?

   Yes ___ No ___

   If yes, explain.

4. Does the poem have correct poetic structure and rhythm, and is it at least eight lines?

   Yes___ No ___

   If yes, explain the poem structure and rhythm.

5. Is the poem written from a perspective other than that of European Imperialists?

   Yes ___ No ___

   If yes, explain.

HANDOUT 4

SOCIAL CAUSES OF NEW IMPERIALISM

Directions: Write a paragraph answering the questions below.

What are Social Darwinism and the "White Man's Burden"? How did the beliefs in Social Darwinism and "White Man's Burden" affect the policies of the European imperialists during New Imperialism? Do you think the colonists treated the people of Africa and Asia fairly and created policies that benefited (helped) the people? How do you think the people of Africa and Asia felt about being colonized?

_____

_____

_____

_____

_____

_____

_____

_____

_____

_____

_____

_____

_____

_____

_____

_____

_____

HANDOUT 5

SOCIAL CAUSES OF NEW IMPERIALISM (FOR ELLS)

Directions: Write a paragraph answering the questions below.

What are Social Darwinism and the "White Man's Burden"? How did the beliefs in Social Darwinism and "White Man's Burden" affect the behavior and policies of the European Imperialists during New Imperialism? Did you think the colonists treated the people of Africa and Asia fairly and created policies that benefited (helped) the people? How do you think the people of Africa and Asia felt about being colonized?

Social Darwinism is _____

The "White Man's Burden" is _____

These racist beliefs of the European colonists caused the policies of the colonizing nations to be

_____ because _____

_____

_____

The colonists did/did not (circle one) treat the people of Africa and Asia_____

because they did not have _____and _____for the other _____

_____

_____

I think the people of Asia and Africa felt _____ about being colonized because _____

_____

_____

HANDOUT 6

NEW IMPERIALISM VOCABULARY LIST

Burden—duty, responsibility

Civilized—cultured, educated, sophisticated

Imperialism—the takeover of a country or territory by a stronger nation

Nationalism—feeling of pride and devotion to one country

Respect—consideration or thoughtfulness

Racism—belief that one race is superior to others

Savage—unrestrained, violent, or vicious

Social—relating to society and people

Social Darwinism—the application of Charles Darwin's ideas about evolution and "survival of the fittest" to human societies, particularly as justification for imperialist expansion

Tolerance—acceptance, open-mindedness

Uncivilized—socially or culturally undeveloped

Understanding—considerate, acknowledgment of another culture

White Man's Burden—European and American duty to take over "inferior" countries to make them "civilized"

Translation of "White Man's Burden" to American English

Take a job doing the White Man's burden

Send your strongest men

Send your sons far away to uncivilized lands

To make the people we are conquering civilized

To do very hard work serving and making better

The easily tempted, wild and savage people

The people you have just captured by force

The people who are so uncivilized they act like the devil and behave like children

HANDOUT 7

RUBRICS

Poem Checklist

_____ Addresses need for tolerance and understanding (3 points)

_____ Addresses European racist beliefs justifying Imperialism (3 points)

_____ Has comprehensible spelling and grammar (1 point)

_____ Has correct poem structure and rhythm and is at least 8 lines (1 point)

_____ Poem is written from a perspective other than that of European imperialists (2 points)

Paragraph—Social Causes of New Imperialism Checklist

_____ Answers all questions (1 point)

_____ Has comprehensible spelling and grammar (1 point)

_____ Uses full sentences (1 point)

_____ Addresses European beliefs of superiority appropriately (3 points)

_____ Supports predictions with evidence from class or appropriate prior knowledge (4 points)

Vietnam: The Human Face of an Inhumane Time
History/Social Studies—U.S. History
(Grades 11–12; Integration of Knowledge and Ideas)
Eileen Burke and Vincent Russo—Mineola High School, Garden City Park, NY

LESSON PLAN TEMPLATE

TOPIC:

Vietnam: The Human Face of an Inhumane Time (Grades 11–12)

TIMING:

7 class periods

CCSS STRAND:

Reading

BACKWARD DESIGN COMPONENTS:

DESIRED RESULTS/CCSS ADDRESSED:

Enduring Understandings

- Through a close examination of literary and informational texts in various formats, students will understand a historical time period and appreciate the varied points of view regarding the cost of war and the lasting effects of war on the human psyche [R.1, R.4, R.5, R.6, R.7, R.8, R.9, R.10].

Knowledge and Skills

- Students will be able to analyze, synthesize, and evaluate multiple sources of information presented in diverse formats and media in order to develop an understanding of varied points of view regarding a period in history [R.1, R.4, R.5, R.6, R.7, R.8, R.9, R.10].

- Students will be able to reflect on their analysis of writers' narrative techniques in order to write (a) their own personal narratives of things they literally and metaphorically carry and, later, (b) narrative works in which they represent the voices of people affected by war [R.4, R.5, R.6, R.7, R.8, R.9, W.2, W.7, W.8, W.9].

ACCEPTABLE EVIDENCE:

- Answers to guiding questions for *The Things They Carried*

- Writing Organizer for items students literally and metaphorically carry with them, like the soldiers in *The Things They Carried*

- Discussion Chart for song lyrics and poetry on which students note and provide evidence for their understanding and analysis of information presented, attitude of speaker, and intent of writer

- Conversation Between Two Characters in two different works studied during the unit that includes historical information and captures the style of each character

LEARNING EXPERIENCES AND INSTRUCTION:

Timing:

7 class periods (lessons do not have to be conducted on consecutive days)

- Day 1—Review Vietnam History packet. Introduce *The Things They Carried*.

- Day 2—Discuss and analyze *The Things They Carried*, view Time Magazine Photo Story, "The Things They Carry." Compose own "The Things I Carry."

- Day 3—Discussion Chart: Analyze songs of the Vietnam War and home front protest era.

- Day 4—View *Dateline*: "A Few Good Men."

- Day 5—Examine the human cost: excerpt from nonfiction—*Born on the*

Fourth of July; accounts from combat nurses from *A Piece of My Heart: The Stories of 26 American Women Who Served in Vietnam*.

- Day 6—Analyze other voices through poetry: Vietnamese writers; synthesize diverse sources by composing a conversation between two characters.

- Day 7—Small-group sharing of completed writing assignment.

STRATEGIES:

- Guidance and Monitoring

- Modeling

- Discussion

- Cooperative Learning

MATERIALS NEEDED:

- YouTube videos of songs

  o "Ballad of the Green Beret" by Staff Sergeant Barry Sadler and Robin Moore (http://www.lyricsmode.com /lyrics/b/barry_sadler/ballad_of_the _green_beret.html)

  o "Eve of Destruction" by Barry McGuire (http://www.lyricsmode. com/lyrics/b/barry_mcguire/eve_of _destruction.html)

  o "The Fish Cheer & I-Feel-Like-I'm-Fixin'-to-Die Rag" by Country Joe and the Fish (http://www.well .com/~cjfish/game.htm)

  o "Goodnight Saigon" by Billy Joel (http://www.lyricsmode.com/lyrics/b /billy_joel/goodnight_saigon.html)

  o Video of *Dateline*: "A Few Good Men" (available from http://www .nbcuniversalarchives.com/nbcuni /clip/5112995113_s05.do)

- O'Brien, T. (1990).The things they carried. In *The things they carried*. New York, NY: Houghton Mifflin Harcourt.

- "The things they carry," Photo Story (http://www.time.com/time /photoessays/2006/talismans _multimedia_new/)

- Walker, K. (1985). *A piece of my heart*. New York: Random House.

- Excerpt from Kovic, R. (1976). *Born on the fourth of July*. New York, NY: Akashic.

- Poems by Duc Thanhat (http://www3 .crk.umn.edu/newsarchive/umcnews /stories/story1609.html)

- Poems from Palmer, L. (1987). *Shrapnel in the heart*. New York, NY: Random House.

- Excerpt from Hayslip, L. L. (1989). *When heaven and earth changed places*. New York, NY: Penguin.

- Paper and pens

- Handouts (reproducible forms for each handout appear at the end of this section)

SUPPLEMENTAL RESOURCES:

- *The Americans*. (2003). New York, NY: McDougal Littell

- Movie clips from Oliver Stone's *Platoon* (1986), Oliver Stone's *Born on the Fourth of July* (1989), or Robert Zemeckis's *Forrest Gump* (1994)

TECHNOLOGY/MEDIA OPPORTUNITIES:

- Youtube.com

- Students can use Photo Story or iMovie for an optional music assignment.

SERVICE LEARNING LINKS:

- Students write letters or cards of encouragement to Vietnam-era veterans at a local VA hospital and collect "comfort" supplies such as crossword puzzles, razors, socks, and so forth as a sign of gratitude and support for their actions during the war.

VARIATIONS:

- Interview someone from the Vietnam era.

- Adapt this lesson to study multiple perspectives of a war other than Vietnam.

VIETNAM: THE HUMAN FACE OF AN INHUMANE TIME

History/Social Studies—U.S. History

(Grades 11–12; Integration of Knowledge and Ideas)

Eileen Burke and Vincent Russo—Mineola High School, Garden City Park, NY

Adolescents live in the moment, so the term recent history has quite a different meaning to them. Already "Y2K Worries" are as quaint and distant as the concern over Model Ts and horse-drawn carriages sharing the same roads. For today's teens, the Vietnam War—a cultural, political, and social watershed of the second half of the 20th century—is as remote as WWI or the Civil War. Putting a "human face" on the conflict helps the students connect and care more deeply and, in doing so, understand the historical significance of the Vietnam era.

This unit is designed to complement the background and factual information presented in an 11th-grade class. Prior to this lesson, students will have studied the following types of background information already: Cold War tensions/Domino theory of foreign policy, specific causes and key events of the Vietnam Conflict, and so on. They will also be familiar with the geography, key military battles, and important people connected to the conflict. All this information will be referred to and reinforced using the materials chosen for this unit.

Materials Needed

- YouTube videos of songs
- "Ballad of the Green Beret" by Staff Sergeant Barry Sadler and Robin Moore   (http://www.lyricsmode.com/lyrics/b/barry_sadler/ballad_of_the_green_beret.html)
- "Eve of Destruction" by Barry McGuire (http://www.lyricsmode.com/lyrics/b/barry_mcguire/eve_of_destruction.html)
- "The Fish Cheer & I-Feel-Like-I'm-Fixin'-to-Die Rag" by Country Joe and the Fish (http://www.well.com/~cjfish/game.htm)
- "Goodnight Saigon" by Billy Joel (http://www.lyricsmode.com/lyrics/b/billy_joel/goodnight_saigon.html)
- Video of Dateline: "A Few Good Men" (available from http://www.nbcuniversalarchives.com/nbcuni/clip/5112995113_s05.do)
- O'Brien, T. (1990).The things they carried. In *The things they carried*. New York, NY: Houghton Mifflin Harcourt.
- The things they carried, Photo Story (http://www.time.com/time/photoessays/2006/talismans_multimedia_new/)
- Walker, K. (1985). *A piece of my heart*. New York: Random House.
- Excerpt from Kovic, R. (1976). *Born on the fourth of July*. New York, NY: Akashic.

- Poems by Duc Thanhat (http://www3.crk.umn.edu/newsarchive/umcnews/stories/story1609.html)
- Poems from Palmer, L. (1987). *Shrapnel in the heart.* New York, NY: Random House.
- Excerpt from Hayslip, L. L. (1989). *When heaven and earth changed places.* New York, NY: Penguin.
- Paper and pens
- Handouts (reproducible forms for each handout appear at the end of this section)

Timing

5–7 class days (lessons do not have to be conducted on consecutive days)

- Day 1—Review students' knowledge of Vietnam War. Introduce *The Things They Carried.*
- Day 2—Discuss and analyze *The Things They Carried*; view *Time Magazine* Photo Story, "The Things They Carry." Compose own "The Things I Carry."
- Day 3—Discussion Chart—Analyze songs of the Vietnam War and home front protest era.
- Day 4—View *Dateline*: "A Few Good Men."
- Day 5—Examine the human cost: excerpt from nonfiction—*Born on the Fourth of July*; accounts from combat nurses from *A Piece of My Heart: The Stories of 26 American Women Who Served in Vietnam.*
- Day 6—Analyze other voices: Vietnamese writers; synthesize diverse sources—compose writing assignment, Conversation Between Two Characters.
- Day 7—Small-group sharing of completed writing assignment.

Day 1

On the first day, we ask students to read an excerpt from *The Things They Carried*, a novel about Vietnam written by Tim O'Brien, who served in the infantry in Vietnam [R.4, R.5, R.6, R.10]. Then students answer guiding questions (**Handout 1**).

Day 2

Students discuss the chapter, connecting fictional description to factual information. We ask them to pay particular attention to O'Brien's style, which combines factual historical information and technical vocabulary yet conveys the emotions of young soldiers stationed in a combat zone [R.4, R.5, R.6].

THEORY LINK (Bloom): Students interpret and analyze the chapter.

Students then watch a Photo Story from Time magazine, "The Things They Carry," which profiles the items carried by soldiers currently stationed in Iraq and Afghanistan. This Photo Story can be found at http://www.time.com/time/photoessays/2006/talismans_multimedia_new/.

Finally, students compose their own "The Things I Carry" (in a backpack, a purse, or pockets), attempting to imitate O'Brien's style. When the assignment is complete, Eileen asks students to share something that they "carry"

 CULTURAL/LINGUISTIC HIGHLIGHT: Visual representations deepen students' comprehension of content and language.

 THEORY LINK (Gardner): Appeals to Verbal-Linguistic, Interpersonal, and Intrapersonal Intelligences.

 CULTURAL/LINGUISTIC HIGHLIGHT: Any opportunity provided to students to share their cultural experiences and backgrounds can lead to cross-cultural understanding and respect.

 THEORY LINK (Gardner): Appeals to Verbal-Linguistic and Musical Intelligences.

 CULTURAL/LINGUISTIC HIGHLIGHT: Music and music videos provide linguistic support.

 DIFFERENTIATION TIP: The number and selection of songs may be adapted to fit timing and students' needs.

 TECH CONNECTION: Students can create their own Photo Story or iMovie "illustrating" the song lyrics with appropriate photos from the time period.

with the class. Some students feel comfortable sharing the entire assignment; most share one or two sentences (**Handout 2**) [R.4, R.5, R.6, R.7, W.2, W.7].

This is such a wonderful glimpse into the inner life of our students. One of our favorite closing lines from a student's essay is "Along with his not-so-good graded papers, Christopher carries his unsuccessful determination to attract girls, annoyance at school, and knowledge of Greek mythology and comic book superheroes." One time, a teacher's aide who was working with a student with special needs also completed this assignment. Her piece began: "I carry my need to be needed in my bag." The students applauded when she read it aloud!

Day 3

Day 3 involves analyzing music. This is one of the most enjoyable parts of the unit for students. Vincent selects songs and distributes copies of the lyrics for students to look at while they listen and watch videos of the music (**Handout 3**).

First, we listen to the "Ballad of the Green Beret," a song from 1965 written and performed by Sgt. Barry Sadler. It offers a wonderful glimpse into the early attitudes toward the war, as it is very patriotic and respectful. We follow this with two songs with very different feelings from Sadler's: "Eve of Destruction" by Barry McGuire and, if appropriate for the class, the more controversial songs, Country Joe and the Fish's "The Fish Cheer & I-Feel-Like-I'm-Fixin'-to-Die Rag" which brings out the growing dissatisfaction with the war. Finally, students listen to Billy Joel's "Goodnight Saigon," a song written in the 1980s that combines respect for the sacrifice of the young soldiers and evidence of the disillusionment felt by many Americans of the time.

In small groups, students then compare and contrast the information, attitudes, and intent evident in each song. We ask students to connect factual information from their notes and previous discussion to the songs on a Discussion Chart (**Handout 4**) [R.1, R.7, R.8, R.9].

Day 4

Students view the episode from *Dateline:* "A Few Good Men" (available from http://www.nbc universalarchives.com/nbcuni/clip/5112995113 _s05.do). This excellent episode focuses on one military engagement, the Battle for 881 at Khe San.
It combines archival news footage and recent interviews with Vietnam veterans, and it serves as an excellent mini-lesson on the war and its aftermath. It leads well into the discussion on Day 5.

CULTURAL/LINGUISTIC HIGHLIGHT: Visual representations deepen students' comprehension of content and language.

Day 5

On this day, students read, discuss, and reflect on several nonfiction excerpts that focus on the terrible human cost of war. Students begin with an excerpt from Ron Kovic's *Born on the Fourth of July*, which describes the spinal injury the author suffered in Vietnam and the time he spent in a VA hospital when he first returned to the United States. It is depressing, powerful, and enlightening. Students also read excerpts from *A Piece of My Heart: The Stories of 26 American Women Who Served in Vietnam*. Finally, students read and discuss a poem called "Hello David," (retrieved from http://www.stg.brown.edu /projects/WritingVietnam/readings/lp_read_Dusty.html), which is written from the point of view of a nurse. Although the poem is fiction, it is very realistic and touching. They also read a response to this poem, "Hello Dusty," written by a soldier who was wounded in Vietnam (**Handout 5**). Students work to connect these readings to each other and to the topic of the human cost of the war [R.7, R.9, R.10].

This is a good point in the unit to introduce a service learning project for veterans at a local VA hospital. The project can involve letters of encouragement, gratitude, and so forth and may be combined with a collection of items such as toiletries, socks, and DVDs, which are often requested by long-term residents of the hospitals.

THEORY LINK (Dewey): Developing citizenry—students' understanding of this issue prompts them to help others.

Day 6

During this class, students look at the conflict from the "enemy's" viewpoint. They examine two readings, a poem by Duc Thanh and an excerpt from *When Heaven and Earth Changed Places* by Le Ly Hayslip. Both of these Vietnamese writers were living in Vietnam during "The American War" as it is called there. We ask students to analyze how the change in perspective alters their understanding of the situation. They then compare and contrast these views of the Vietnamese civilians with previous knowledge and readings [R.7, R.8, R.9, R.10].

CULTURAL/LINGUISTIC HIGHLIGHT: Using texts written by diverse authors can lead to cultural understanding and respect.

As a cumulative assessment, we require the students to write a conversation between two people, either fictional or real, from the readings, songs,

THEORY LINK (Bloom): Students apply their analysis and evaluation of the poems by synthesizing two characters into a new writing piece.

poems, and excerpts in this unit (**Handout 6**). We supply a rubric so they understand how this conversation will be assessed (**Handout 7**).

Students must choose the characters and create an appropriate setting. For example, a student may have a soldier from "The Ballad of the Green Beret" confront a protester from one of the antiwar songs. Other pairings might include a U.S. soldier from The Things They Carried, who meets and has a conversation with one of the Vietnamese writers, or a nurse who talks to any of the young soldiers, those who were injured, or those who escaped injury [R.7, R.8, R.9, W.8, W.9].

Day 7

We ask students to select a partner and present the conversations that they wrote individually. Working in pairs, students then share their dialogues with either the full class or in small groups.

This unit is always one of the most successful that we teach. When students are able to put a "human face" on the Vietnam Conflict—whether it is the face of a nurse, a young soldier close to their own age, an antiwar protestor on the home front, or even a Vietnamese civilian—it increases their interest level and gives them a reason to remember the facts about the war. Students seem truly to connect with the time period and understand more fully the lasting influence this conflict had on the American psyche.

CULTURAL/LINGUISTIC HIGHLIGHT: Pair and group work opportunities develop ELL students' language skills and promote cross-cultural understanding.

HANDOUT 1

THE THINGS THEY CARRIED

Chapter 1

Reading Questions for *The Things They Carried* (Chapter 1)

Directions: Please answer in full sentences and include lots of details!

1. Who are the "they" in this excerpt? What is the effect of this being told in the third person?

2. Categorize or group three types of "things" the soldiers carried and list some of the "items" in each group.

3. What happens to Lt. Jimmy Cross by the end of the story? Explain.

4. Read the epigraph (just before the first chapter) and explain what it means to you. Try to relate it to something else we read this year.

HANDOUT 2

THE THINGS I CARRY

Writing Organizer

Directions: Think about what you carry and the way you would write about these things, if you were Tim O'Brien.

1. Choose a carrier: your backpack, purse, pockets, etc.

2. List everything that you have with you on a regular basis (choose either a school day, a weekend, etc.).

3. Describe all the things on your list, and be sure to include both physical "real" items as well as emotional things.

4. Organize your writing by using some of the traits of O'Brien's writing.

   (Consider how O'Brien includes personal facts, historical information, sophisticated vocabulary, and appeal to emotion.) Outline your plan below.

HANDOUT 3

SONG LYRICS

- "Ballad of the Green Beret" by Staff Sergeant Barry Sadler and Robin Moore

  (http://www.lyricsmode.com/lyrics/b/barry_sadler/ballad_of_the_green_beret.html)

- "Eve of Destruction" by Barry McGuire

  (http://www.lyricsmode.com/lyrics/b/barry_mcguire/eve_of_destruction.html)

- "The Fish Cheer & I-Feel-Like-I'm-Fixin'-to-Die Rag" by Country Joe and the Fish

  (http://www.well.com/~cjfish/game.htm)

- "Goodnight Saigon" by Billy Joel

  (http://www.lyricsmode.com/lyrics/b/billy_joel/goodnight_saigon.html)

HANDOUT 4

DISCUSSION CHART

SONG	Information Presented	Attitude of Speaker	Intent of Writer
"Ballad of the Green Beret"	Your thoughts: Textual evidence:	Your thoughts: Textual evidence:	Your thoughts: Textual evidence:
"Eve of Destruction"	Your thoughts: Textual evidence:	Your thoughts: Textual evidence:	Your thoughts: Textual evidence:
"The Fish Cheer & I-Feel-Like-I'm-Fixin'-to-Die Rag"	Your thoughts: Textual evidence:	Your thoughts: Textual evidence:	Your thoughts: Textual evidence:
"Goodnight Saigon"	Your thoughts: Textual evidence:	Your thoughts: Textual evidence:	Your thoughts: Textual evidence:

HANDOUT 5

TWO VOICES

1. Hello David by "Dusty"

Dusty. (1987). Hello, David. *Shrapnel in the heart*. New York, NY: Random House. Retrieved from http://www.stg.brown.edu/projects/WritingVietnam/readings/lp_read_Dusty.html

2. Hello Dusty

"Hello, Dusty," I am Specialist Miller,

But my Mama calls me "Donnie."

I am scared, but I can see you care.

I can feel your hand smoothing my hair.

But I can't see that hand.

I can see your other hand on my arm,

But I can't feel it?

May I watch your face, your eyes, your smile.

Will you tell them I need to feel your hand?

I remember "Doc" said, after the battle,

"Man you got five too many holes in ya!"

I think I remember a chopper

and then your face.

Is it getting colder in here?

Did "Doc" count right?

What were they saying about my Lung?

I don't like the taste of blood!

What are you putting in my IV?

I am talking, but I can't hear me?

I am getting colder,

and more scared!

The table is moving?

Sorry I messed up your uniform.

Did I tell you that I Love You?

I wanted to.

May I have just one more smile Please?

A smile to last me a life time,

Thank You "Dusty"

I Love You!

This is dedicated to all the "Dustys" that cared for all the wounded in all the Battles of all the wars. But mainly to the one "Dusty" who helped me throughout the hardest hours of my life. I was wounded rather severely in Vietnam on September 11th 1968 at around 2:30 AM. I was told that I bled out twice before I arrived at the Hospital in An-Loc that following morning at around 9:30 AM. That is where, when, and why I met "My Dusty." Yes her smile has lasted me "a Life Time" And yes I still love her.

—Donald (Blind Dog) Miller 168th Combat Engineers "C" Company 1967–68
Phoenix, AZ USA—Wednesday, December 09, 1998 at 18:51:14 (CST)

HANDOUT 6

CONVERSATION BETWEEN TWO CHARACTERS

In this unit, we have read fiction and nonfiction, stories, and poems. The literature was from the perspective of an American soldier, a nurse, an antiwar protester, a Vietnamese soldier, and a Vietnamese civilian. All experienced the Vietnam War but in very different ways. Imagine how interesting it would be to eavesdrop on a conversation between two of these people!

Your assignment:

1. Choose two characters (persons), each one from different works studied in this unit.

2. Create and describe a believable situation in which your two characters have a conversation (for example, waiting for a delayed train or plane, at a museum or monument for the war).

3. Set the scene; in other words, explain how they meet.

4. Using the script format* shown in class, write the dialogue (conversation) between your characters. Included in your conversation should be specific references to the works we read in class; for example, refer to an event that was described, use a quotation from something a character actually said, and so on. Think about whether your characters would argue because they are so different or have a great deal in common; your dialogue should reflect this.

5. You should also include facts and historical information from the fact packet and content discussed in class.

6. Try to capture the style of speaking appropriate for your character. (A soldier would use different vocabulary from a civilian; a combat nurse would speak differently from someone who was never in Vietnam, etc.).

7. Each character should have a minimum of 10 lines.

Remember: Your goal is to create a conversation that sounds realistic and reflects important information that you learned from this unit.

*Script Format Reminder

- Use italics for description of setting or emotions of characters.

Example:

At midnight, the hospital is dim and sad. Light squeezes through a door as a nurse walks in.

- Use BOLD CAPITALS followed by a colon to indicate the speaker.
- Use plain text for the dialogue.

Example:

DUSTY: I am going to take care of you.

HANDOUT 7

GRADING RUBRIC

Vietnam Unit Culminating Writing Assignment

"Voices from Vietnam"

	Points Earned
Evidence of information learned from this unit: 4 to 5 specific facts or details from literature studied. Details and facts are accurate and appropriate for each character Comment:	/15
Evidence of information learned from this unit: 4 to 5 specific facts from historical fact packet. Details and facts are accurate and appropriate for each character Comment:	/15
Setting is appropriate and realistic Comment:	/10
Language of each "character" reflects an understanding of the background and Vietnam experience of this person Comment:	/10
Minimum of 10 lines of dialogue for each character Comment:	/20
Shows evidence of effort to be creative Comment:	/20
Correct dialogue format used Comment:	/10
Total/grade earned	

Reading Lessons in Science and Technical Subjects 4

In this chapter, we present three science and technical subject lessons that we believe are particularly effective for addressing the CCSS for Reading. These lessons involve many reading and writing skills and thus address the majority of the CCSS. However, we have designated each lesson according to the CCSS Reading strands that it addresses most fully:

- Key Ideas and Details: Grades 11–12, "Bonus Science Articles"
- Craft and Structure: Grades 9–10, "Vocabulary Videos"
- Integration of Knowledge and Ideas: Grades 6–8, "Continental Drift"

In the first lesson, students read and answer text-based questions on timely science articles. They must develop a strong understanding of the development of ideas within the articles in order to be successful.

The second lesson calls for students to interpret vocabulary words and assess how the words can be used in a variety of contexts by producing a video that exemplifies the meaning of a vocabulary word in three different ways.

For the third lesson, students conduct research and compare findings from a variety of sources on continental drift and magnetic reversal. They must analyze the argument presented in their sources and integrate their findings to make a claim regarding their research topic.

As you read these lessons and as you develop your own, we encourage you to focus on how you can best guide your students to meet the CCSS for Reading that you examined in Chapter 2.

READING ANCHOR STANDARDS REFLECTIVE QUESTIONS

How does the lesson require students to do one or more of the following?

1. Determine what the text says explicitly and make logical inferences from it

2. Cite specific textual evidence when writing or speaking to support conclusions drawn from the text

3. Determine the main ideas and details of a text

4. Analyze the development of ideas in a text

5. Interpret words or phrases in a text, and analyze how they shape meaning

6. Analyze the structure of a text and analyze how sentences, paragraphs, and larger portions of the text shape meaning

7. Assess how point of view of a text shapes the meaning and style of a text

8. Integrate and evaluate the content of texts presented in diverse media and formats

9. Evaluate the argument and claims in a text

10. Analyze how two or more texts address similar themes or topics

LESSON DESIGN REFLECTIVE QUESTIONS

1. How does the lesson require close and multiple readings of grade-level complex text?

2. How does my questioning require students to use the text as support for their interpretations/arguments?

3. How does the lesson incorporate varied thinking skills (e.g., read, summarize, analyze, interpret)? (Bloom)

4. How does the lesson include the three components of Backward Design: (a) desired results, (b) acceptable evidence, and (c) learning experiences?

5. How do I differentiate instruction, materials, and expectations for this particular lesson so that all students can be successful?

6. How does the lesson provide opportunities for technology/media use?

7. How does the lesson include research-based instructional strategies to promote effective teaching?

8. How does the lesson present opportunities for interdisciplinary connections?

9. How does the lesson provide opportunities for students with varied Multiple Intelligences to be successful? (Gardner)

10. How do I present the lesson in a way that encourages students to see the value of what they are learning (e.g., service learning, college- and career-readiness skills)? (Dewey)

Bonus Science Articles
Science—Biology
(Grades 11–12; Key Ideas and Details)
Sue Kennedy—Mineola High School, Garden City Park, NY

LESSON PLAN TEMPLATE

TOPIC:

Bonus Science Articles (Grades 11–12)

CCSS STRAND:

Reading

TIMING:

5 class periods

BACKWARD DESIGN COMPONENTS:

DESIRED RESULTS/CCSS ADDRESSED:

Enduring Understandings

- After reading several current science articles, students will demonstrate an understanding of key ideas and details related to scientific developments in today's society [R.1, R.2].

Knowledge and Skills

- Students will be able to access articles from the Internet (if needed) and to interpret information represented in the articles in the form of words, in the form of visuals, and quantitatively [R.7].

- Students will be able to analyze and evaluate the information and opinions presented in articles and interpret them based on their scientific knowledge through other texts [R.6, R.8, R.9].

ACCEPTABLE EVIDENCE:

- Completed reading quizzes to assess understanding of the key ideas and details of the articles.

- Effective classroom discussion in which students use textual evidence and scientific knowledge to support their arguments regarding the articles.

LEARNING EXPERIENCES AND INSTRUCTION:

- Day 1—Introduce the Bonus Reading option and distribute articles.

- Days 2–5—Take daily 5-minute quizzes on each article.

STRATEGIES:

- Modeling

- Discussion

- Cooperative Learning

MATERIALS NEEDED:

- Copies of articles and/or computer access to articles:

  o Carpenter, B. (2004, August 8). Feeling the sting. Retrieved from http://www.usnews.com/usnews /culture/articles/040816/16jelly.htm

  o Lobster's life: A New England bestseller unveils the mysteries of America's favorite crustacean. (2004, August 8). Retrieved from http:// www.usnews.com/usnews/culture /articles/040816/16lobster.htm

  o Querna, E. (2004, August 8). Fixing fish farms: Aquaculture has a bad rep, but innovators are finding healthy ways to return it to U.S. waters. Retrieved from http://www.usnews .com/usnews/culture /articles/040816/16aquaculture.htm

  o Harmon, K. (2010, February 18). Beyond the sugar pill: Are doctors misusing the placebo effect? Retrieved from http://blogs.scientificamerican .com/observations/2010/02/18/

beyond-the-sugar-pill-are-doctors-misusing-the-placebo-effect/

- Paper and pens
- Handouts (reproducible forms for each handout appear at the end of this section)

SUPPLEMENTAL RESOURCES:

Articles:

- Sacksteder, C., Kanazawa, A., Jacoby, M. E., & Kramer, D. M. (2000). The proton to electron stoichiometry of steady-state photosynthesis in living plants: As proton-pumping Q cycle is continuously engaged. *PNAS, 97,* 14283-14288. Retrieved from http://www.pnas.org/content/97/26/14283.full
    - o Question: What metabolic activity was being tested, and which part of an atom were the scientists testing it with?
- Eckardt, N. A. (n.d.). Plant disease susceptibility genes? *The Plant Cell, 14,* 1983–1986. Retrieved from www.plantcell.org/cgi/content/full/14/9/1983
    - o Question: Describe how *Arabidopsis* may not be affected by powdery mildew.
- Chyba, C. F. (2001). Life without photosynthesis. *Science, 292*(5524), 2026–2027. Retrieved from http://www.sciencemag.org/content/292/5524/2026.summary
    - o Question: What seems to be common in our solar system? (How are Jupiter's moons similar to Earth?)

TECHNOLOGY/MEDIA OPPORTUNITIES:

- Internet research for independent reading
- If linked with service learning, several software programs can be used

(e.g., Microsoft Publisher, iMovie, and Photo Story)

SERVICE LEARNING LINKS:

- Students make educational booklets and volunteer their time to share information and become guest speakers in other classes. For example, the articles, "A Lobster's Life: A New England Bestseller Unveils the Mysteries of America's Favorite Crustacean" and "Fixing Fish Farms: Aquaculture Has a Bad Rep, but Innovators Are Finding Healthy Ways to Return It to U.S. Waters" serve as resources that supplement a marine science course. Students also visit a biology class, share the articles, and participate in the dialogue.
- Students create elementary-level picture books, Photo Stories, or iMovies, and then teach elementary students. As an example, titles might be "What Is a Fish Farm?" or "How Do Lobsters Live?"
- Students design a pamphlet in Microsoft Publisher (with documented references) and ask permission from a local physician's office to display the material in the waiting room. For example, a pamphlet might be titled, "What Is the Placebo Effect?" Students who are fluent in other languages translate the information.

VARIATIONS:

- Encourage students to continue their service learning as a follow up to current events articles of their choice. Students can create a "*SCI-LURB* of the month": a science blurb to be displayed on the high school lobby television or school website that offers unique information to educate other students, staff, and community members. Students choose what they feel is the most interesting new information that others might also enjoy.

BONUS SCIENCE ARTICLES

Science—Biology

(Grades 11–12; Key Ideas and Details)

Sue Kennedy—Mineola High School, Garden City Park, NY

As I was preparing to become a science teacher, one piece of advice I found particularly useful was to assign my students as many science-related articles as possible. The goal is twofold: to have students keep up with current events and to increase their reading comprehension. My bonus articles help students become better readers, which moves them toward college and career readiness. Moreover, this approach piques students' interest in science because the articles are timely, relevant, and intriguing.

I like the bonus articles lesson because it does not take time away from my instruction, which is particularly important in my AP Bio class, where there is great pressure to cover content. However, I have also used bonus articles as a means of extra credit for struggling students in my general-level science classes. Because there is choice involved and because these are high-interest readings, this approach allows students to discover and make their own connections to topics in the scientific realm.

Materials Needed

- Copies of articles and/or computer access to articles:

  o Carpenter, B. (2004, August 8). Feeling the sting. Retrieved from http://www.usnews.com/usnews/culture/articles/040816/16jelly.htm
  o Lobster's life: A New England bestseller unveils the mysteries of America's favorite crustacean. (2004, August 8). Retrieved from http://www.usnews.com/usnews/culture/articles/040816/16lobster.htm
  o Querna, E. (2004, August 8). Fixing fish farms: Aquaculture has a bad rep, but innovators are finding healthy ways to return it to U.S. waters. Retrieved from http://www.usnews.com/usnews/culture/articles/040816/16aquaculture.htm
  o Harmon, K. (2010, February 18). Beyond the sugar pill: Are doctors misusing the placebo effect? Retrieved from http://blogs.scientificamerican.com/observations/2010/02/18/beyond-the-sugar-pill-are-doctors-misusing-the-placebo-effect/

- Paper and pens
- Handouts (reproducible forms for each handout appear at the end of this section)

Timing

5 class periods (This should not be conducted on consecutive days so as to allow for time for students to read outside of class)

Day 1—Introduce the Bonus Readings option and distribute articles.

Days 2–5—Take daily 5-minute quizzes on each article.

Day 1

At the start of the new school year, to introduce the concept of reading current science articles, I hand out a packet with copies of articles that cover various topics that I believe the students will find interesting. These topics are not necessarily related to my syllabus but, rather, they are high-interest because of their clear, real-life connections or their humorous approach.

Some articles are easy to read, while others are more demanding and require more effort to comprehend [R.1, R.2]. I ask the students to read the articles on their own time and give them a date for a short quiz about the articles. The Lesson Plan Template lists sample articles in the Supplemental Resources section.

THEORY LINK (Dewey): Purposeful work—articles clearly link to timely topics.

Students read the articles outside class. Because I provide not only paper copies but also links to the sites where these articles are posted, students can access the articles from anywhere—on their phones, electronic readers, laptops, and tablets [R.7].

TECH CONNECTION: Providing links allows for easy access to the articles via electronic devices.

Days 2–5

Each day, I quiz students for five minutes on a different article (**Handouts 1–4**). The quiz questions require students to summarize basic ideas from their reading. But many science topics, especially introduced in the form of opinion pieces, also spark discussion [R.6]. If students can develop and support their own opinions, I can assess that they have mastered the content knowledge based on reading the article. Students' higher-order thinking is apparent when they connect the information in the article with the required content they are learning in class [R.6, R.8, R.9].

THEORY LINK (Bloom): Students *comprehend* and *apply* their understanding to support their opinions.

As the year progresses, I give students more articles (about five) to read at once; they also get quizzed on all five articles. This allows for a more efficient system.

If students have not read the articles, their average is not affected because these are bonus quizzes. At the start of the year, 100% of students typically take advantage of this offer. This percentage does decrease as the year progresses; however, the students who keep up with the bonus article assignments usually perform better on college entrance exams because their reading skills have been honed.

Students in my class who are also involved in the Environmental Club have made trips to the local elementary schools to present some of what they have learned through coursework (including these readings). The students collaborate to

THEORY LINK (Gardner): Appeals to Interpersonal Intelligence.

create high-interest lessons for fourth graders on the ways that they can work together to improve our environment.

THEORY LINK (Dewey): Developing citizenry—students use their learning to improve their society.

CULTURAL/LINGUISTIC HIGHLIGHT: Sharing science information related to culture can lead to cross-cultural understanding.

For instance, after reading an article about environmental contamination from regular household items, my high school students taught elementary students that batteries should not go in the regular garbage. The high school students explained how our town collects batteries for free and distributed information so that the elementary students' parents could arrange for proper disposal of their batteries. Considering how many toys use batteries, the elementary school students and their parents were a great target audience for my students.

HANDOUT 1

FEELING THE STING

Reading Quiz

Name:_____

Directions: Answer the following based on "Feeling the Sting" by Betsy Carpenter.

1. 50 tons of jellyfish caused a major problem in the Philippines. What was it?

2. How are jellyfish adapted to handle oxygen-poor water and still perform aerobic respiration?

HANDOUT 2

A LOBSTER'S LIFE

Reading Quiz

Name:_____

Directions: Answer the following based on "A Lobster's Life: A New England Bestseller Unveils the Mysteries of America's Favorite Crustacean."

1. Describe a favorite new fact that you learned about lobsters from "A Lobster's Life" article.

2. Explain what Lobster Tomalley is. Should you eat it? Why or why not?

HANDOUT 3

FIXING FISH FARMS

Reading Quiz

Name:_____

Directions: Answer the following based on "Fixing Fish Farms: Aquaculture Has a Bad Rep, but Innovators Are Finding Healthy Ways to Return It to U.S. Waters" by Elizabeth Querna.

1. Why are offshore aquacultures a preferred method compared to current fish farm methods?

2. Describe *one* challenge that offshore snapper farms have to contend with because of the nature of their design.

HANDOUT 4

BEYOND THE SUGAR PILL

Reading Quiz

Name:_____

Directions: Answer the following based on "Beyond the Sugar Pill: Are Doctors Misusing the Placebo Effect?" by Katherine Harmon.

1. Define *placebo*.

2. What is a benefit of a placebo? Have placebos ever been used in surgery?

3. Describe the story that the author experienced that introduced the reader to the placebo effect.

4. Describe how "Great Expectations" was used as an analogy to describe the placebo effect.

Vocabulary Videos
Technical Subject—Computer Apps
(Grades 9–10; Craft and Structure)
Katie Sheehan—Mineola High School, Garden City Park, NY

LESSON PLAN TEMPLATE

TOPIC:

Vocabulary Videos (Grades 9–10)

TIMING:

7 class periods

CCSS STRAND:

Reading

BACKWARD DESIGN COMPONENTS:

DESIRED RESULTS/CCSS ADDRESSED:

Enduring Understandings

- Through the analysis of varied contexts, students will examine unfamiliar vocabulary and interpret or infer meaning [R.1, R.2, R.4, R.6, R.9].

Knowledge and Skills

- Students will be able to create, revise, and edit works with sufficient details and coherent structure that convey the meaning of a vocabulary word in several ways [R.4, R.5, R.6, W.3, W.5, W.6].

- Students will be able to present and explain their work and to analyze and evaluate their peers' work by posting on a webpage [R.1, R.2, R.4, R.5, R.6, R.9, W.6].

ACCEPTABLE EVIDENCE:

- Students' analysis and discussion of the creative representation of word meanings on the gotbrainy.com Word List.

- Completed vocabulary video that conveys the meaning of a vocabulary word through three different scenarios.

- Students' discussion and evaluation of each other's work.

LEARNING EXPERIENCES AND INSTRUCTION:

- Day 1—Overview of the project.

- Days 2–3—Plan and film vocabulary videos.

- Days 4–5—Edit videos in iMovie.

- Days 6–7—Share with peers.

STRATEGIES:

- Modeling

- Cooperative Learning

- Guidance and Monitoring

MATERIALS NEEDED:

- Digital video cameras

- Computers with Internet access and iMovie or other editing software

- Paper and pens

- Handouts (reproducible forms for each handout appear at the end of this section)

SUPPLEMENTAL RESOURCES:

- Howjsay.com—This website pronounces words for students

- Quizlet.com—This site has ready-made virtual stacks of SAT vocabulary flashcards

- http://theelearningcoach.com/resources/storyboard-depot/—This site offers a variety of free storyboarding templates for your students to use while planning their videos

- http://www.youtube.com/watch?v=J79_0h3ozS0&feature=related—This is one of many videos for people who are just learning iMovie

TECHNOLOGY/MEDIA OPPORTUNITIES:

- Students can also use Photo Story to create their videos with stills and captions if they do not have access to iMovie.

- Students may make a virtual stack of flashcards on quizlet.com.

SERVICE LEARNING LINKS:

- Students post these videos on a common site that is accessible to all students who are reviewing for the SAT.

- Students poll their teachers for common vocabulary words that the teachers would like to have clarified through vocabulary videos and create videos based on this poll.

VARIATIONS:

- Develop a theme or focus for the project (e.g., words commonly found in test directions, subject-specific words, commonly misused words).

- Connect with students from other school districts and initiate a vocabulary video exchange program.

- Post word of the week videos based on favorite words submitted by teachers and students.

VOCABULARY VIDEOS

Technical Subject—Computer Apps

(Grades 9–10; Craft and Structure)

Katie Sheehan—Mineola High School, Garden City Park, NY

I teach a Digital Storytelling Class. Most students enter the class with a substantial digital and technical knowledge base, so the emphasis is more on the storytelling than on the basics of digital media use. For one of the units in this class, students are required to produce a video that explains and exemplifies an SAT vocabulary word. This is an interesting and fun way to merge vocabulary development, a task that is typically dull and difficult for students, with video technology, a medium that most high school students feel is both exciting and accessible.

Note: This project is assigned after students develop some familiarity with the use of a digital camera and editing with iMovie.

Materials Needed

- Digital video cameras
- Computers with Internet access and iMovie or other editing software
- Paper and pens
- Handouts (reproducible forms for each handout appear at the end of this section)

Timing

7 class periods (lessons do not need to be conducted on consecutive days)

Day 1—Overview of the project.

Days 2–3—Plan and film vocabulary videos.

Days 4–5—Edit videos in iMovie.

Days 6–7—Share with peers.

Day 1

Students use the site gotbrainy.com for the SAT vocabulary words on which to base their films. I like this site because of its memes (memorable posters, which include powerful pictures with captions) that incorporate each of the vocabulary words listed [R.1, R.2, R.4, R.6, R.9]. Next to each word in the Word List section of gotbrainy.com is a number in parentheses. This number indicates how many memes have been posted to represent the word. I require students to select a word that has been used 10 or fewer times on the site for their project. Why? Because the students then choose words that are more esoteric and, therefore, more challenging for them.

Students review the requirements for this assignment on my website. As with all projects for my course, students will find three elements in the assignment folder: the task (**Handout 1**), the rubric by which they will be assessed (**Handout 2**), and project exemplars.

The video must be 30 seconds or longer. Within the videos, students must have at least three distinct clips (see Days 2 and 3 for examples). They can decide whether or not to include audio in the video. The goal of the video is to convey to the viewer a clear definition of the meaning of the word represented in the video [R.4, R.6, W.3]; 40% the rubric is devoted to judging how effectively the video does this.

Here is a description of a successful video for the word *vigilant*: In the first clip, a girl gently pulls her purse closer to her body as a suspicious character walks by. In the second clip, a boy looks over his shoulder repeatedly while typing his password to log in to a computer. In the third clip, a boy looks over his shoulder repeatedly at a girl who is presumably following him. Each of these clips makes the word, *vigilant,* come to life for the viewer.

Days 2–3

Students shoot their videos during the school day, using a group of peers as their actors.

Days 4–5

Students edit their videos in iMovie, and they submit them by posting the videos to my website [R.4, R.5, R.6, W.5, W.6]. During this process, I am available to critique student work and provide technical assistance.

Days 6–7

Students share their videos with their classmates and provide peer feedback based on the rubric (**Handout 2**). The class then nominates the best videos to be used as exemplars for future students [R.1, R.2, R.4, R.5, R.6, R.9, W.6].

After several years of assigning this project, I have noted a pattern: The words that are less frequently used (fewer than 10 times) and are thus candidates for the project are commonly adverbs and adjectives. Students struggle more to convey the meaning of adjectives and adverbs than they do verbs, which can typically be demonstrated through action. I use this knowledge to open a metacognitive dialogue with students, allowing them to think more deeply about their learning than they might have had they not completed a project like this. Given that

CULTURAL/LINGUISTIC HIGHLIGHT: The multimodal approach to this lesson and the emphasis on vocabulary building provide significant linguistic and content support.

THEORY LINK (Bloom): Students *apply* their understanding of the word to the process of creating the video.

THEORY LINK (Gardner): Appeals to Verbal-Linguistic, Visual-Spatial, Bodily-Kinesthetic, Interpersonal, and possibly Musical Intelligences.

DIFFERENTIATION TIP: Students may work in pairs for peer support if needed with the iMovie software.

THEORY LINK (Dewey): Purposeful work—students' work is not just submitted for a grade. It may be used in the future as an exemplar for others.

we live in an age in which students are used to viewing information on a TV, computer, tablet, or cell phone screen, I believe—and the students agree—that visual representations of vocabulary words are a particularly effective learning tool. Who knows? Someday, this project may replace the index card method of study!

CULTURAL/LINGUISTIC HIGHLIGHT: Cooperative learning opportunities can develop students' language skills and promote cross-cultural understanding.

HANDOUT 1

VOCABULARY VIDEO

Task

Overview:

Develop a video that clearly represents a vocabulary word from the gotbrainy.com Word List.

Steps:

Step 1. Visit http://www.gotbrainy.com/words and choose a word that has been used fewer than 10 times. The number of times a word has been used is listed in parentheses next to that word.

Step 2. Script at least three clips that will represent the meaning of your chosen word.

Step 3. Film your scenes*.

Step 4. Edit your videos on iMovie.

Step 5. Share your movies with the class.

---

*Your video must be a minimum of 30 seconds long and must contain at least three separate clips.

HANDOUT 2

VOCABULARY VIDEO

Rubric

_____ **Title Screen (10)**

- Clearly states the word that will be represented
- Visually appealing to the viewer

_____ **Credit Screen (10)**

- All students who worked on the video are represented
- Text is legible
- Credits roll at a pace that allows the viewer to read them easily

_____ **Appropriate Word (10)**

- Used fewer than 10 times on the gotbrainy.com Word List
- Appropriate for sharing with your teachers and peers

_____ **Video is engaging (30)**

- All material is in publishable form (thoroughly proofed and without careless errors)

_____ **Word used in the appropriate context (20)**

- All three clips demonstrate strong understanding of the word's definition.

_____ **Technical aspects (20)**

_____ **TOTAL**

Continental Drift

Science—Earth Science

(Grades 6–8; Integration of Knowledge and Ideas)

Michael Acquaro—South Woods Middle School, Syosset, NY

LESSON PLAN TEMPLATE

TOPIC:

Continental Drift (Grades 6–8)

CCSS:

Reading

TIMING:

6 class periods

BACKWARD DESIGN COMPONENTS:

DESIRED RESULTS/CCSS ADDRESSED:

Enduring Understandings

- After reading a common class text and conducting group research, students will understand the importance of evaluating the reasoning of various sources related to a scientific theory [R.7, R.8, R.9].

Knowledge and Skills

- Students will be able to build a knowledge base of continental drift and identify/define science vocabulary terms [R.1, R.2, R.4].

- Students will be able to conduct research using online databases, assess the value of their findings, and integrate the information in a written explanation [R.9, R.10, W.7, W.8].

- Students will be able to engage in the writing process to summarize articles researched, determine main ideas, and analyze the information [R.9, R.10, W.5, W.6, W.8, W.9].

ACCEPTABLE EVIDENCE:

- Textual evidence students use to support their answers to the Dynamic Earth Text-Based Reaction Questions

- Final drafts of written summaries that compare evidence gathered through team research with the information presented in the J. Tuzo Wilson article (http://www.platetectonics.com/article.asp?a=18).

LEARNING EXPERIENCES AND INSTRUCTION:

- Day 1—Read and summarize the article; highlight and define unknown vocabulary terms.

- Days 2–3—Complete Questions 1–8.

- Day 4—Conduct research on a chosen question in the computer lab.

- Day 5—Write a summary that compares evidence gathered through team research with the information presented in the J. Tuzo Wilson article (http://www.platetectonics.com/article.asp?a=18).

- Day 6—Compare research findings with classmates.

STRATEGIES:

- Guidance and Monitoring

- Discussion

- Cooperative Learning

- Writing Process

- Modeling

MATERIALS NEEDED:

- Lined paper
- Highlighters
- Pencils or pens
- Handouts (reproducible forms for each handout appear at the end of this section)

SUPPLEMENTAL RESOURCES:

- http://www.enchantedlearning.com/subjects/dinosaurs/glossary/Contdrift.shtml. This website is designed to help students learn about all aspects of science; information is kept simple and to the point.

- http://www.sciencedaily.com/releases/2012/01/120104133151.htm. This website serves as an online resource for the newest scientific research and articles.

TECHNOLOGY/MEDIA OPPORTUNITIES:

- Students conduct Internet research for complementary articles.

SERVICE LEARNING LINKS:

- Students create a visual representation of continental drift to present to younger children studying science.

- Students take part in an interdisciplinary effort with foreign language and social studies classes to improve international relations by displaying their research on continental drift at a multicultural night. Understanding that the continents were once connected may help students strengthen connections among various cultures and nationalities.

VARIATIONS:

- Students research and answer all of the questions and write a summary of the sources for classmates.

- Students receive basic notes and find the necessary evidence to support the concepts of plate tectonics, continental drift, and magnetic reversal.

CONTINENTAL DRIFT

Science—Earth Science

(Grades 6–8; Integration of Knowledge and Ideas)

Michael Acquaro—South Woods Middle School, Syosset, NY

In the days leading up to this lesson, my students and I have talked about evidence of crustal change and how deformed rock structures give us some evidence that the earth's crust is moving. At this point, we have completed a rocks and minerals unit and studied how a majority of sedimentary rocks are deposited in or near water, which causes them to form horizontally first. Students understand that if the rock layers are disturbed in any way, such as tilting, folding, or faulting, that must have happened after they were deposited.

The class has also been looking into fossil evidence. For example, we have learned that shallow water fossils are being found at great ocean depths and marine fossils of brachiopods are being found in high elevations, such as Denver, Colorado. We have discovered that the earth is broken up into sections—crust, mantel, outer core, inner core—and that the crust is broken into sections called the *lithosphere* (ridged rock material) and the *asthenosphere* (plastic-like material capable of flow). This lesson allows students to discover how all of this movement occurs and some of the evidence behind these theories of movement.

Note: At this point, all students know how to use the Internet effectively.

Materials Needed

- Lined paper
- Highlighters
- Pencils or pens
- Handouts (reproducible forms for each handout appear at the end of this section)

Timing

6 class periods

Day 1—Read and summarize the article; highlight and define unknown vocabulary terms.

Days 2–3—Complete Questions 1-8.

Day 4—Conduct research on a chosen question in the computer lab.

Day 5—Write a summary that compares evidence gathered through team research with the information presented in the J. Tuzo Wilson article.

Day 6—Compare research findings with classmates.

Day 1

During the first day, I give students the article "Continental Drift" (1996) by J. Tuzo Wilson (http://www.platetectonics.com/article.asp?a=18). I also pass out lined paper. I ask students to read the article and highlight pertinent information based on the text. They take notes by highlighting, underlining, or circling key points [R.1, R.2]. After reading the article, they share what they believe are the most important facts within the article.

On the lined paper, students list all vocabulary words they are not familiar with and use context clues and textual evidence to attempt to define the words. Examples include a combination of academic words (found across disciplines), such as *fortuitous*, *overridden*, and *condemned*, and technical terms (specialized in science), such as *uplift*, *geologist*, *geophysicist*, *paleomagnetism*, *mid-ocean ridge*, *ridge*, *postulate*, and *oceanographic*. After discussing the words with their partners, students look up the words and correct definitions as needed. As a group, we discuss the vocabulary words and how they shape the meaning of the article [R.4].

THEORY LINK (Gardner): Appeals to Verbal-Linguistic and Interpersonal Intelligences.

CULTURAL/LINGUISTIC HIGHLIGHT: Note-taking tools (highlighting, underlining, circling) can help highlight key information for students.

CULTURAL/LINGUISTIC HIGHLIGHT: Vocabulary activities and strategies (defining unfamiliar words through contextual clues and dictionary use, group discussion) provide linguistic support.

THEORY LINK (Gardner): Appeals to Verbal-Linguistic and Interpersonal Intelligences.

Days 2–3

Students respond to the Dynamic Earth Text-Based Reaction Questions (**Handout 1**), which serve as an outline of critical information [R.1, R.2, R.9]. It is important that I circulate and assist students in completing this task. Students have the original article in front of them as well as the resources of the class books, textbook, review material, and the Internet at their disposal to assist them in answering the questions. In particular, students may struggle with describing how the molten material moves (Question 2b); the idea of convection cells has been covered several times at this point, but the connection using prior knowledge may elude them.

Students may also need some guidance in responding to Question 3, which asks them to show how magnetic reversal works. I refer them to the reading and guide them by asking them step-by-step scaffolded text-based questions in order to get them to discover the answers on their own.

After students complete the questions, I collect the handout and check it for the next class period.

DIFFERENTIATION TIP: A quick review may help here. Also, students can opt to draw the movement of the molten material and provide a visual interpretation of it.

THEORY LINK (Dewey): Purposeful learning—Students learn about real-life subject matter that has relevance to their lives.

Day 4

The next day, students team up to conduct research on either (a) further supporting evidence of continental drift or (b) supporting/reasoning for magnetic reversal (**Handout 2**) [R.9, R.10, W.7]. The former group is required to find a minimum of two supporting articles; the latter, one article. The reason for the difference in resources is that magnetic reversal has fewer available articles that students will find at a suitable reading level.

As students search the Internet for different materials, we use the CARRDS method (**Handout 3**) to critically assess websites to make sure they are credible.

Through research, students gather enough information to draw conclusions regarding the processes of plate tectonics, continental drift, and paleomagnetism and connect these processes to everyday occurrences. They take notes to provide supporting evidence from their research and document their sources. Eventually, they will include a correct works-cited page [R.7, W.8].

DIFFERENTIATION TIP: Allow students to choose which topic to research.

CULTURAL/LINGUISTIC HIGHLIGHT: Cooperative learning opportunities can develop students' language skills and promote cross-cultural understanding.

THEORY LINK (Bloom): Students *evaluate* online sources.

TECH CONNECTION: This is a good opportunity to continue with the practice of evaluating online sources.

THEORY LINK (Bloom): Students *comprehend, analyze, and synthesize* the information.

Day 5

After conducting research in their separate teams, students create a written summary that compares the evidence gathered through their team research with the information presented to them in the Tuzo Wilson article. As noted, students must correctly cite their sources. I also require them to include in their summary the information that they investigated in their team research and to align that new knowledge with the Tuzo Wilson article [R.9, R.10, W.8, W.9].

Day 6

I pair students from Group A with students from Group B so they can share their written comparisons with a classmate. They read their summaries to one another and make comparisons to the original article. Within their pairs, they help to evaluate their partner's writing (**Handout 4**) and make any corrections that need to be made for their final draft [W.5].

Students then use the computer to type up their final drafts and use the spell check, grammar, and thesaurus features to polish their work [W.6]. As they work on this task, students refer to the rubric for questions about the requirements of this assignment (**Handout 5**).

THEORY LINK (Gardner): Appeals to Verbal-Linguistic and Interpersonal Intelligences.

Through this writing activity, students work on reading comprehension, editing skills, vocabulary building, and research skills. Students learn how to paraphrase information and summarize an article while using textual evidence to compare the assigned article to the one they found. Reading a classmate's summary exposes students to another point of view and prompts them to reconsider the material. Allowing the students to critique one another also gives the students a sense of ownership for their work. Throughout this process, students develop a richer understanding of how plate tectonics work and how paleomagnetism is evidence for the crustal movements of today.

TECH CONNECTION: Students can also use online sources (e.g., citationmachine.net) for questions on formatting.

HANDOUT 1

DYNAMIC EARTH TEXT-BASED REACTION QUESTIONS

1. Who was Alfred Wegener and what evidence did he use to support his theory of continental drift?

    a. Who was Alfred Wegener? _____

    b. Evidence that he used to support the theory of continental drift:

        i. _____
        _____

        ii. _____
        _____

        iii. _____
        _____

        iv. _____
        _____

        v. _____
        _____

2. The article describes mantel currents. Connect the movement of these currents to the convection currents that we spoke about in the meteorology unit.

    _____
    _____
    _____
    _____

    a. Label the diagram with arrows showing the movement of molten material based on the convection currents you just described.

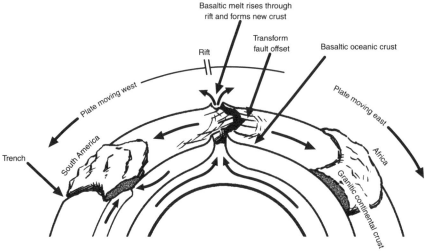

b. Describe how density plays a part in the material's movement.

_____

_____

_____

_____

3. Using evidence from the article, describe paleomagnetism and complete the diagram to illustrate magnetic reversal.

_____

_____

_____

_____

Key	
Magnetic Polarity of Bedrock	
Normal	Reversed

4. Why was magnetic reversal useful to the author for providing evidence for seafloor spreading?

_____

_____

_____

_____

5. Compare the age of the seafloor (basalt) at the coast to the age of the seafloor material (basalt) at the mid-ocean ridges.

_____

_____

_____

6. Which of the following letters represents an area that has the youngest material?

_____

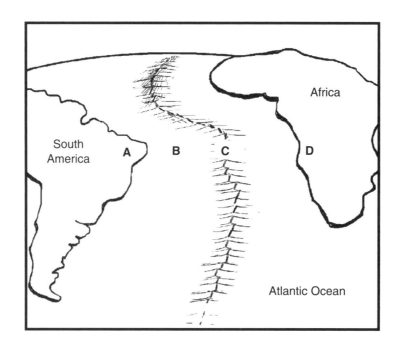

7. Using textual evidence, describe what would happen if the continents where pushed together.

_____

_____

_____

_____

8. Describe the difference between continental drift and plate tectonics with as much detail as possible.

_____

_____

_____

_____

_____

_____

HANDOUT 2

RESEARCH

Directions: Choose from one of the following topics for your follow-up research.

A. Find at least two articles that give further supporting evidence of continental drift/seafloor spreading.

Group A researches continental drift and seafloor spreading and uses online databases, such as the following:

- General OneFile
- GreenFile
- Facts on File Science Online

B. Find at least one article that supports and describes how magnetic reversal works.

Group B researches magnetic reversal and uses selected online resources, such as

- http://www.geomag.bgs.ac.uk/education/reversals.html
- http://istp.gsfc.nasa.gov/earthmag/reversal.htm
- http://www.pbs.org/wgbh/nova/earth/when-our-magnetic-field-flips.html,

Guidelines for Research:

1. Go to school home page

2. Click on library resources

3. Click on online databases

4. Enter username and password

5. Click on one of several different online databases

   a. **Examples:** General OneFile, GreenFile, Facts on File Science Online

6. After choosing your online database, enter your library card number

7. Type in your key words in the topic bar example: Process of continental drift

   a. Search through findings and read summaries to find an article that matches your topic

   b. Click on article and read

Website Suggestions:

http://www.sciencedaily.com/

http://www.gsa.gov/

http://www.infoplease.com/

http://www.usgs.gov/

http://www.ucmp.berkeley.edu/history/wegener.html

HANDOUT 3

CARRDS DEFINED

Use this to help you fill out the CARRDS web evaluation sheet on the next page.

CREDIBILITY:

Who is the author? Is there an e-mail address to contact the author (not the webmaster)? Why do you trust him or her? Example: The author of a site who is a Wikipedia author with no credentials or e-mail address is less trustworthy than the author of a weather site who is a SUNY Stony Brook professor of meteorology with a credible e-mail address.

ACCURACY:

Based on your knowledge, does the information seem accurate?
Examples:

1. Parts of this site are similar to what I already know about the topic from my textbook, so I think I can trust the information. Or

2. I don't know anything about my topic yet, so I am not sure. Or

3. This site is different from what I learned before, so I should compare it with other sources before I use it.

RELIABILITY:

Does the site present an opinion, point of view, bias? Is this opinion clearly stated? What is it?

RELEVANCE:

Does this information help to answer my question? Is it in-depth? Is it too hard, too easy, or just right? Yes or no answers are fine for the first part, then rate the level of the information.

DATE:

When was the information created? Was it revised? Are these dates meaningful in terms of subject matter? Example: This site is from 2011 and is about global warming, so it is up to date. Or this site is from 1979 and is about global warming; it may be too old and out of date.

SOURCES:

Does the site have a works cited section or a bibliography? If there are links for the sources of information, do they still work? Yes or No answers are fine. Elaborate if needed.

OVERALL THIS SITE IS (Circle One):

Useful   **Somewhat Useful**   **No Good** (If this is your answer, find a different site!)

URL_____

Name_____ Title of Site_____

USE CARRDS TO EVALUATE YOUR SOURCES

Read the definitions and instructions on the previous page.
If you still need help, ask!

Credibility:

Accuracy:

Reliability:

Relevance:

Date:

Sources:

OVERALL THIS SITE IS (Circle One):

Useful   **Somewhat Useful**   **No Good**

HANDOUT 4

PEER-EDITING WORKSHEET

Writer: _____ **Editor:** _____

		Good	Needs Improvement	Comments
1. Introduction				
a.	Is there background information that defines important vocabulary and related information?			
b.	Is the rationale for writing the summary explained?			
c.	Are the hypotheses included? (How does continental drift occur?)			
2. Writing Summary				
a.	Organization and structure very evident: major points divided into paragraphs and signaled by use of transitions.			
b.	Each paragraph has a topic sentence; sentences within each paragraph relate to each other and are subordinate to the topic.			
c.	Does the writing give textual evidence from reading to support the writer's point of view?			

		Good	Needs Improvement	Comments
3. Conclusions				
a.	Are all conclusions stated?			
b.	What were your major findings? Were the hypotheses supported?			
c.	Are the conclusions supported by references?			
4. Abstract				
a.	Is an abstract written following the outline? (75 words)			
5. Works Cited, Internal Citations				
a.	Is there a works-cited page with proper heading and MLA-style formatting?			

HANDOUT 5

CONTINENTAL DRIFT RUBRIC

1. Cover Sheet
   a. Is there a title that correctly describes the topic at hand?   0   1
   b. Are your name and the teacher's name included?   0   1
   c. Is the date this report was prepared included?   0   1

2. Introduction
   a. Is there background information defining important vocabulary and related information?   0   10   15   17
   b. Is the rationale for writing the summary explained?   0   5
   c. Are your hypotheses included? (How does continental drift occur?)   0   10

3. Writing Summary
   a. Organization and structure very evident: major points divided into paragraphs and signaled by use of transitions.   0   5
   b. Each paragraph has a topic sentence; sentences within each paragraph relate to each other and are subordinate to the topic.   0   10
   c. Does the writing give textual evidence from reading to support your assignment's point of view?   0   5   10   15

4. Conclusions
   a. Are all conclusions stated? (What were your major findings? Were your hypotheses proven true?)   0   5   10
   b. Are the conclusions supported by references?   0   5   10

5. Abstract
   a. Is an abstract written following the outline? (75 words)   0   5   10

6. Works-cited, internal citations
   a. Is there a works-cited page with proper heading and MLA-style format?   0   5

Total _____ / 100

Part II

Writing Standards for Literacy in History/Social Studies, Science, and Technical Subjects

5 The Benefits of the CCSS for the Teaching of Writing in the Content Areas

There seems to be a sort of fatality in my mind leading me to put at first my statement or proposition in a wrong or awkward form. Formerly I used to think about my sentences before writing them down; but for several years I have found that it saves time to scribble in a vile hand whole pages as quickly as I possibly can, contracting half the words; and then correct deliberately. Sentences thus scribbled down are often better ones than I could have written deliberately.

—Charles Darwin

Good news, readers! Our students are often in the same camp with Charles Darwin. Like the great thinker, scientist, and writer, our students may scribble down their ideas as furiously as they can. The trick for us as teachers is to get them to follow Darwin's next step: to "correct deliberately."

This uninhibited initial approach to writing may be beneficial for many of us. We can think freely and record our ideas without the restraints of grammar or acceptable structure. Then we can make changes in form or content. If we finish writing the draft and realize that the introduction does not correspond well to the rest of the essay, then we can write an entirely new introduction. We can cut or copy and paste and delete text, and even make track changes to record our revisions. We can save our work and revisit it a few hours later.

The Common Core State Standards (CCSS) for Literacy in History/Social Studies, Science, and Technical Subjects address the importance of both *content* and *form* to develop students' writing skills. One of the best ways to encourage students to become critical thinkers and strategic learners is to incorporate writing into the content areas (Brozo & Simpson, 2007). Nancie Atwell (1989) pointed out that although the role of language arts teachers is to guide students' development as writers, teachers of every discipline share in the responsibility of showing students how to think and write as scientists, historians, mathematicians, and literary critics.

The CCSS place a strong focus on argument writing and informative/ explanatory writing. Within both types of writing, students must provide

Table 5.1 Anchor Standards for Writing

Text Types and Purposes

1. Write arguments to support claims in an analysis of substantive topics or texts, using valid reasoning and relevant and sufficient evidence.

2. Write informative/explanatory texts to examine and convey complex ideas and information clearly and accurately through the effective selection, organization, and analysis of content.

3. Write narratives to develop real or imagined experiences or events using effective technique, well-chosen details, and well-structured event sequences.

Production and Distribution of Writing

4. Produce clear and coherent writing in which the development, organization, and style are appropriate to task, purpose, and audience.

5. Develop and strengthen writing as needed by planning, revising, editing, rewriting, or trying a new approach.

6. Use technology, including the Internet, to produce and publish writing and to interact and collaborate with others.

Research to Build and Present Knowledge

7. Conduct short as well as more sustained research projects based on focused questions, demonstrating understanding of the subject under investigation.

8. Gather relevant information from multiple print and digital sources, assess the credibility and accuracy of each source, and integrate the information while avoiding plagiarism.

9. Draw evidence from literary or informational texts to support analysis, reflection, and research.

Range of Writing

10. Write routinely over extended time frames (time for research, reflection, and revision) and shorter time frames (a single sitting or a day or two) for a range of tasks, purposes, and audiences.

evidence to support claims. In addition, students must engage in a range of writing across genres (appropriate to task, purpose, audience) and time frames (research project vs. writing on demand). The CCSS provide a balanced approach to expectations for writing that puts particular emphasis on various text types, meaning as well as form, and the role of technology in enhancing writing.

In this chapter, we introduce the CCSS Writing Standards for Literacy in History/Social Studies, Science, and Technical Subjects, Grades 6–12 and provide commentary on the value of each of the Anchor Standards for increasing students' college and career readiness. For easy reference, the CCSS Anchor Standards for Writing that we discuss throughout this chapter are listed in Table 5.1. At the end of the chapter, we go beyond the general Anchor Standards and examine the "Research to Build and Present Knowledge" grade-specific Writing Standards for Literacy in History/Social Studies, Science, and Technical Subjects, 6-12.

TEXT TYPES AND PURPOSES

In a study conducted by Partnership for 21st Century Skills (2006) of employers' perspectives of high school graduates' workforce readiness, survey results indicated that 72% of employers thought that high school graduates are deficient in writing. The Anchor Standards for "Text Types and Purposes" address the types of writing that students should be engaged in (argument, informative/explanatory, narrative) as well as the purposes for which they write (argue/persuade, inform/explain, convey experience). Many of the skills that students need to develop are transferable among text types and purposes. The CCSS for "Text Types and Purposes" are the following:

1. Write arguments to support claims in an analysis of substantive topics or texts, using valid reasoning and relevant and sufficient evidence.

2. Write informative/explanatory texts to examine and convey complex ideas and information clearly and accurately through the effective selection, organization, and analysis of content.

3. Write narratives to develop real or imagined experiences or events using effective technique, well-chosen details, and well-structured event sequences.

The CCSS call for students to become well-rounded individuals who write different types of texts (e.g., argument, informative/explanatory, narrative) for different purposes and audiences. "Writing for different purposes and audiences stimulates different kinds of thinking, such as logical thinking, exploratory thinking, aesthetic thinking, and expressive thinking" (Soven, 1999). Mastering all these kinds of thinking leads to well-rounded individuals. Dewey would certainly approve of the idea that purposeful writing provides students with real-world, experiential learning that enhances their development as learners as well as individuals.

Arguments

Stating arguments is common practice in the real world. According to the CCSS, "Arguments are used for many purposes—to change the reader's point of view, to bring about some action on the reader's part, or to ask the reader to accept the writer's explanation or evaluation of a concept, issue, or problem. An argument is a reasoned, logical way of demonstrating that the writer's position, belief, or conclusion is valid" (National Governors Association Center for Best Practices [NGA Center]/Council of Chief State School Officers [CCSSO], 2010c, p. 23). Specifically, writers of an argument should do the following:

1. Consider two or more perspectives on an issue.
2. Think critically and deeply.
3. Assess the validity of these perspectives as well as their own thinking.
4. Present the pros and cons while anticipating counterarguments.

Benjamin Bloom might note that the levels of thinking range from basic recall to the more sophisticated stage of evaluation.

Wolpert-Gawron (2011) supported the CCSS' focus on argument because of its obvious real-world application. She noted, "The focus isn't to provide evidence as the sole means to prove, but rather to make an argument and bring in evidence that one must then justify through argumentation" ("Across the Curriculum," para. 1).

Informative/Exploratory Texts

Contrary to argument, the purpose of informative/exploratory texts is to advance a reader's knowledge or comprehension about a subject. In this type of writing, students convey intricate ideas through the accurate and clear use of content. Genres include literary analyses, reports, summaries, and real workplace functional writing, such as memos, applications, and so forth (NGA Center /CCSSO, 2010c).

Narratives

As students hone their ability to write a narrative, they also develop skills for argument and informative/explanatory writing. For instance, students may strengthen their argument and informative/explanatory writing by including anecdotal evidence (a reduced-form of narrative). Also, the writing elements called for in narrative writing (effective devices, details, and logical progression of events) may transfer to sophisticated expository writing.

PRODUCTION AND DISTRIBUTION OF WRITING

According to the Partnership for 21st Century Skills (2006), 62.8% of employers surveyed reported that high school graduates' technology skills are "adequate" (p. 14). However, given that 72% of those employers stated that students are deficient in writing, students clearly need to learn how to apply their technology skills to improve their writing. The CCSS for "Production and Distribution of Writing" address the components of well-written work (development, organization, style), the process of creating high-quality work (planning, revising, editing, etc.), and using technology to publish writing:

4. Produce clear and coherent writing in which the development, organization, and style are appropriate to task, purpose, and audience.

5. Develop and strengthen writing as needed by planning, revising, editing, rewriting, or trying a new approach.

6. Use technology, including the Internet, to produce and publish writing and to interact and collaborate with others.

According to Kerr and Picciotti (2010),

Writing can serve as a means for exploring academic subject matter as well as students' own perceptions of understanding. At the same time, writing can serve another purpose: it can provide students with a means for examining discourse itself, enabling them to gain a greater awareness of—and thus control over—various discourse conventions. (p. 105)

The CCSS Anchor Standards for "Production and Distribution of Writing" guide content-area teachers as they work to develop students' understanding of content and increase students' writing skills.

To help teachers guide their students in meeting the CCSS, we have gathered some research on writing instruction. Zumbrunn and Krause (2012) interviewed experts on the teaching of writing and composed a list of best practices for teachers:

1. Effective writing instructors realize the impact of their own writing beliefs, experiences, and practices.

2. Effective writing instruction encourages student motivation and engagement.

3. Effective writing instruction begins with clear and deliberate planning, but is also flexible.

4. Effective writing instruction and practice happen every day.

5. Effective writing instruction is a scaffolded collaboration between teacher and students. (p. 347)

The researchers emphasized that teachers should also be writers. Teachers can then reflect on their own practice in order to share what works and what hinders them as writers.

Zumbrunn and Krause (2012) also highlighted the need for deliberate planning to connect classroom writing with an authentic audience; this motivates and engages students. They noted that to aid with writing every day, writing must take place across all disciplines.

In addition, Zumbrunn and Krause (2012) summarized Gibson's view in this way:

> Guided writing instruction, in which teachers guide students through the writing process with a combination of modeling, direct instruction, and guided and independent practice, is one such way that teachers can provide appropriate scaffolding for individual students to improve writing proficiency. (p. 352)

For teachers who are working to balance teaching content with teaching writing skills, Wolpert-Gawron (2011) provided a simpler starting point. She listed three areas of focus that can provide guidance to the majority of content-area teachers in their writing instruction:

The Thesis Statement/Main Topic Sentence: The thesis is the map of the essay. It not only states the argument but also gives an indication of the organization of the essay. All subjects must standardize the need to see one [thesis statement] in a student's argument regardless of the content.

Evidence: Evidence is the quote, the computation, the data, the statistics, and the findings. Evidence backs up the argument made in the thesis statement. This is the content that the teacher as subject matter expert must verify. But it doesn't end there.

Commentary: Commentary is the original thought. It doesn't just translate the evidence to the layman; it brings in a new layer to the information that brings the argument home. (para. 12)

This list clearly applies to argument, but the concept of a standard structure for writing across the content areas is beneficial for all types of writing. The more continuity that teachers can create for their students from assignment to assignment and from subject-area class to subject-area class, the more likely students are to develop positive habits for strong writing. Wolpert-Gawron's (2011) focus on thesis statement, evidence, and commentary align closely with the National Science Education States' Essential Features of Classroom Inquiry (Olson & Loucks-Hoursely, 2000)

1. Learner engages in scientifically oriented questions.

2. Learner gives priority to evidence in responding to questions.

3. Learner formulates explanations from evidence.

4. Learner connects explanations to scientific knowledge.

5. Learner communicates and justifies explanations to others. (p. 29)

A well-written response to a science-oriented question will include a thesis/topic sentence that gives a general overview of the student's response to the question and that introduces (and likely prioritizes) the evidence that will be discussed. The more detailed explanation from evidence as called for by the CCSS corresponds with Wolpert-Gawron's focus on evidence. Finally, the CCSS' requirement for students to connect and justify explanations relates to Wolpert-Gawron's emphasis on commentary.

According to Applebee and Langer (2011),

> Writing instruction 30 years ago was a simple affair: the typical assignment consisted of a few sentences setting out a topic, given in class and finished up for homework. Students were expected to write a page or less, to be graded by the teacher. Almost no class was given over to class instruction or even to introducing the assignment . . . the teacher took an average of just over three minutes to introduce the assignment, answer the inevitable procedural questions . . . , and ask the students to start writing. (p. 14)

Today's students need increased guidance in order to produce more sophisticated high-quality writing. The CCSS for Writing in the Content Areas raise the bar for our expectations of students. As teachers, we must consider how to support our students as they strive to reach the standards. Engaging students in the writing process is one clear way to do so.

A *Process Versus Product* Approach

The second Anchor Standard for "Production and Distribution of Writing" includes the major components of the writing process. The process approach, which became popular in the 1970s, focuses on a recursive series of steps— primarily planning, drafting, revising, editing, and publishing (or simply prewriting, drafting, and rewriting)—that lead to the production of good writing. Prewriting activities, such as brainstorming and outlining, allow students to articulate their thoughts and design a plan. Students conference with their peers and teacher during the rewriting stage, receive feedback, and work on editing and revising for both content and form. The goal is to eventually produce a final draft (as *final* as time permits) that effectively communicates topic and purpose to a specified audience.

This process approach replaced the product approach, which emphasized formalism, correctness, and structure. The product approach did not take into account students' meaning-making processes. Instead, it assumed that students had nothing to offer and depended on teachers to supply them with the knowledge and skills necessary to succeed academically. The expository essay was the staple of the school writing curriculum. Writing for exploration and discovery were not valued and creative (expressive, poetic) writing took a back seat.

In the product approach, students were required to write one coherent, grammatically correct draft on an assigned topic, usually in the format of an essay for a single audience—the teacher—in a single sitting. The teacher graded the essay and commented, particularly on grammar, and returned it without necessarily expecting a revised draft. There were limited opportunities for student input regarding topic, format, audience, and revision. Fortunately, this teacher-centered philosophy is contrary to the student-centered approaches that characterize much of the teaching and learning that take place in U.S. classrooms today.

The Benefits of Technology

The benefits of technology are clear regarding drafting, developing, revising, and editing, but technology offers much more than that. Technology can help students publish their writing for readers, a main component of *relevance*, which plays a great part in student engagement and motivation. For instance, students can compose or create a wiki to post information, or a blog to offer opinions on a topic. Programs like Microsoft Print Shop and Publisher provide templates and graphic development tools to help users create projects such as brochures, newsletters, and so forth.

Students routinely use technology to interact and communicate with others, and their desire to do so can be harnessed in school. Using applications such as wiki to learn collaboratively is of particular benefit to Interpersonal learners (Gardner). Students can also use social media such as a class Facebook page (monitored by the teacher) to share information about literary and informational texts and to persuade others.

As research shows, "Students are already creating and sharing content in their everyday lives when they participate in social networking sites, share their iPod or MP3 player playlists, or create YouTube videos" (State Educational Technology Directors Association, 2011, p. 25). In class, learners can create PowerPoint presentations or podcasts to review concepts or teach content to their peers. As Zumbrunn and Krause (2012) noted, the electronic sharing of information via blog, e-mail, wiki, discussion groups, and other media offers yet another valuable way for students to practice writing. When students have reflective time each day to e-mail or blog about the information they have gathered in their classes, they not only cement their learning for the day but also improve their writing skills.

RESEARCH TO BUILD AND PRESENT KNOWLEDGE

Never has the act of conducting research been easier than today with the Internet at our fingertips. If you have a question (about anything), you can google (which has become a verb) to find the answer. For instance, when you google the keyword *metaphor*, you get 33,700,000 results. However, the amount of information available to students via the Internet makes it extremely important for students to learn to assess the credibility and accuracy of each electronic source of information before integrating it into their writing. For instance, in the Continental Drift lesson in Chapter 4, as students search the internet for different materials, they use the CARRDS method (**Handout 3**) to critically assess websites to make sure they are credible.

Students also need to learn how to avoid plagiarizing. The CCSS for "Research to Build and Present Knowledge" address the need for students to make their research accurate and inclusive of varied sources.

> 7. Conduct short as well as more sustained research projects based on focused questions, demonstrating understanding of the subject under investigation.
>
> 8. Gather relevant information from multiple print and digital sources, assess the credibility and accuracy of each source, and integrate the information while avoiding plagiarism.
>
> 9. Draw evidence from literary or informational texts to support analysis, reflection, and research.

In 2009, Applebee and Langer noted that state standards and high-stakes testing are resulting in "shifting attention away from a broad program of writing instruction toward a much narrower focus on how best to answer particular types of test questions" (p. 26). They stressed the importance of writing instruction that offers a wide range of topics for exploration and that allows students to engage in the writing process. Their reasoning supports the rationale behind the CCSS:

> Although it is important for students to do well on high-stakes tests, it is our professional obligation to ensure they become the writers they will need to be as they leave our secondary schools at the cusp of lives as adults and citizens. (p. 27)

Research, it should be noted, is a key component of college and career writing. According to the CCSS, students must research and gather information from various print and electronic sources and synthesize that information coherently. They also state that research should be short term as well as long term and that students must draw evidence from informational text to support their research, analysis, and reflection. Providing supporting proof from text makes ideas and information credible and valid. Textual evidence is essential in both establishing the credibility of the writer and appealing to the reader's "self-interest, sense of identity, or emotions" (NGA Center/CCSSO, 2010c, p. 4).

The research skills required by the CCSS are a natural component of Project Based Learning (PBL).

> In Project Based Learning (PBL), students go through an extended process of inquiry in response to a complex question, problem, or challenge. . . . Rigorous projects . . . help students learn key academic content [and] practice 21st Century Skills (such as collaboration, communication & critical thinking). (PBL, n.d., "What Is PBL?" para. 1)

PBL may culminate in a written assignment, but it may also involve a multimedia product to demonstrate knowledge and understanding.

RANGE OF WRITING

It is necessary in this era of testing that students meet Standard 10:

> 10. Write routinely over extended time frames (time for research, reflection, and revision) and shorter time frames (a single sitting or a day or two) for a range of tasks, purposes, and audiences.

Students need to be able to write an essay in 20 minutes as well as produce a 10-page paper in five days.

An awareness of audience is always important. Students must understand that communicating effectively also applies to texting, e-mail, Twitter, blogging, and other electronic modes of communication. Even when the discourse style is unique to the mode, the intent still needs to be clear.

Success in the real world depends on students' ability to adjust to real-world demands. Workplace functions include completing a job application, writing a memo, and composing a strong letter or e-mail message. College expectations include writing short responses, longer responses, and completing more sustained projects (e.g., papers, reports) in various genres, including scientific or historical reports, news articles, and summaries. Students must learn to adjust their writing to the circumstance and situation, an essential aspect of college and career readiness.

A CLOSER LOOK

Let's look now at the grade-specific standards for the first set of standards under "Research to Build and Present Knowledge." Here, we can determine what students in Grades 6–12 need to know and be able to do by the end of each grade band (see Table 5.2).

In Grades 6–8, students conduct "short research projects" based on either a teacher- or a self-generated question. This research process is intended to lead the student to develop further questions, thus expanding the student's thinking along "multiple avenues of exploration." In Grades 9–10 and 11–12, the research may be "more sustained" and it may be conducted in order to "solve a problem" rather than to answer a question. The expectations regarding style and comprehension become more demanding as students are expected to "synthesize" their sources.

Regarding the gathering of sources, students in Grades 6–8 must "assess the credibility and accuracy" of both "print and digital sources" and cite their quoted or paraphrased findings, thus avoiding plagiarism. In Grades 9–10, students must find "authoritative" sources, use "advanced searches," and determine the "usefulness" of the sources for their purpose. They must also "integrate" their findings into a paper that has a "flow of ideas." These descriptors indicate higher expectations for students in Grades 9–10.

An even greater sophistication in writing is expected of students in Grades 11–12. They must assess not only the strengths but the limitations of their sources regarding their "specific task, purpose, and audience." They must also

Table 5.2 Writing Standards 6–12 for History/Social Studies, Science, and Technical Subjects

Grade 6–8 Students	Grade 9–10 Students	Grade 11–12 Students
Research to Build and Present Knowledge	*Research to Build and Present Knowledge*	*Research to Build and Present Knowledge*
7. Conduct short research projects to answer a question (including a self-generated question), drawing on several sources and generating additional related, focused questions that allow for multiple avenues of exploration.	7. Conduct short as well as more sustained research projects to answer a question (including a self-generated question), or solve a problem; narrow or broaden the inquiry when appropriate; synthesize multiple sources on the subject, demonstrating understanding of the subject under investigation.	7. Conduct short as well as more sustained research projects to answer a question (including a self-generated question), or solve a problem; narrow or broaden the inquiry when appropriate; synthesize multiple sources on the subject, demonstrating understanding of the subject under investigation.
8. Gather relevant information from multiple print and digital sources, using search terms effectively; assess the credibility and accuracy of each source; and quote or paraphrase the data and conclusions of others while avoiding plagiarism and following a standard format for citation.	8. Gather relevant information from multiple authoritative print and digital sources, using advanced searches effectively; assess the usefulness of each source in answering the research question; integrate information into the text selectively to maintain the flow of ideas, avoiding plagiarism and following a standard format for citation.	8. Gather relevant information from multiple authoritative print and digital sources, using advanced searches effectively; assess the strengths and limitations of each source in terms of the specific task, purpose, and audience; integrate information into the text selectively to maintain the flow of ideas, avoiding plagiarism, overreliance on any one source, and following a standard format for citation.
9. Draw evidence from informational texts to support analysis, reflection, and research.	9. Draw evidence from informational texts to support analysis, reflection, and research.	9. Draw evidence from informational texts to support analysis, reflection, and research.

avoid "overreliance on any one source." These expectations will support a student's transition into college and work-related writing.

The final grade-specific standard for "Research to Build and Present Knowledge" is the same at each grade level. Students are expected to "Draw evidence from informational texts to support analysis, reflection, and research."

CONCLUSION

The importance of "writing to learn" is evident. According to Heller and Greenleaf (2007):

> The real goal is to help all students master the knowledge, procedures, and skills of the academic disciplines that run the secondary school curriculum, and which serve as the gatekeeper to success in college, work, and other facets of adult life. Because literacy makes it possible for students to master the disciplines, and because each discipline requires its own kinds of literacy, the next step for those working to improve adolescent literacy instruction must be to integrate the teaching of reading and writing more fully into the academic content areas. (p. 32)

The CCSS emphasize just that.

- First, they balance the process and product approaches to writing. Students produce writing over longer time frames (projects) supported by the writing process, and over shorter time frames (writing on demand). Various genres of writing are valued. Both meaning and form are central to good writing.
- Second, the CCSS emphasize the importance of using textual evidence necessary to support a writer's analysis, reflection, and research. Students write different pieces (argument, informative/explanatory, narrative,) for various purposes and audiences and, when making claims, must provide evidence from varied sources that influence their ideas.
- Last, the CCSS incorporate the use of technology as a means to produce and publish writing independently and in collaboration. Technology enhances writing by permitting multiple modes of exploration and communication.

When we take steps to incorporate more writing into the content areas, students begin to deepen their understanding of the steps they are taking to solve problems and to learn. They expand their capacity to answer the "why," to understand the big ideas, and to see the real-world relevance of what they are learning. Through various literacy-based content activities that are purposeful and meaningful, students develop the skills required to successfully master content and increase problem-solving and critical-thinking skills.

6 Argument Writing Lessons

In this chapter, we present three lessons (one history/social studies, one science, one technical subject) that we believe are particularly effective for addressing the CCSS for Writing. These lessons involve many reading and writing skills and thus address the majority of the CCSS; however, we have designated the lessons according to the text types and purposes of their writing requirements.

The lessons in this chapter help students formulate and enhance their argument writing skills:

- History/Social Studies: Grades 6–8, "Mock Trial: Native Americans and European Colonization"
- Science: Grades 9–10, "Boyle's Law"
- Technical Subject: Grades 11–12, "Fantasy Basketball"

Within the history/social studies lesson, students write research-based Reader's Theater scripts for a mock trial in which they present evidence as to whether the Native Americans or the Europeans are more worthy of ownership of New York. For the science lesson on Boyle's Law, students examine the structure of an argument and effective rhetorical approaches in science readings. Then, they formulate their own evidence-based argument essay regarding the need for funding research on the prolonged effects of extreme pressure changes on human beings. Finally, in the fantasy basketball lesson, students are required to develop several paragraphs in which they argue to rationalize the choices that they make for their team (e.g., team name, roster of players, stadium sponsors, etc.).

In all three lessons, students learn to write for a specific task, purpose, and audience in an appropriate format. They use evidence to support their claims in a coherent way. They pursue opportunities to revisit and make improvements to their writing.

As you read through these lessons and as you develop your own lessons, we encourage you to focus on how you can best guide your students to meet the CCSS for Writing.

WRITING ANCHOR STANDARDS REFLECTIVE QUESTIONS

How does the lesson require students to do one or more of the following?

1. Write arguments to support claims using valid reasoning and relevant and sufficient evidence

2. Write informative/explanatory texts to examine and convey complex ideas and information clearly and accurately

3. Write narratives to develop real or imagined experiences or events using effective technique, well-chosen details, and well-structured event sequences

4. Produce clear and coherent writing appropriate to task, purpose, and audience

5. Develop and strengthen writing as needed by planning, revising, editing, rewriting, or trying a new approach

6. Use technology, including the Internet, to produce and publish writing and to collaborate with others

7. Conduct short as well as more sustained research projects based on focused questions

8. Gather relevant information from multiple print and digital sources, assess the sources, and synthesize the information without plagiarizing

9. Draw evidence from literary or informational texts to support analysis, reflection, and research

10. Write routinely over extended time frames and shorter time frames for a range of tasks, purposes, and audiences

LESSON DESIGN REFLECTIVE QUESTIONS

1. How does the lesson require close and multiple readings of grade-level complex text?

2. How does my questioning require students to use the text as support for their interpretations/arguments?

3. How does the lesson incorporate varied thinking skills (e.g., read, summarize, analyze, interpret)? (Bloom)

4. How does the lesson include the three components of Backward Design: (a) desired results, (b) acceptable evidence, and (c) learning experiences?

5. How do I differentiate instruction, materials, and expectations for this particular lesson so that all students can be successful?

6. How does the lesson provide opportunities for technology/media use?

7. How does the lesson include research-based instructional strategies to promote effective teaching?

8. How does the lesson present opportunities for interdisciplinary connections?

9. How does the lesson provide opportunities for students with varied Multiple Intelligences to be successful? (Gardner)

10. How do I present the lesson in a way that encourages students to see the value of what they are learning (e.g., service learning, college- and career-readiness skills)? (Dewey)

Mock Trial: Native Americans and European Colonization
History/Social Studies—U.S. History
(Grades 6–8; Argument)
Jessica Kuehn—Waverly Park School, Lynbrook, NY

LESSON PLAN TEMPLATE

TOPIC:

Native Americans and European
Colonization (Grades 6–8)

TEXT TYPES AND PURPOSES:

Argument

CCSS STRAND:

Writing

TIMING:

12 class periods

BACKWARD DESIGN COMPONENTS:

DESIRED RESULTS/CCSS ADDRESSED:

Essential Understandings

- After conducting research that includes multiple historical perspectives, students will understand the importance of evidence to support an argument [W.1, W.7, W.8, W.9].

Knowledge and Skills

- Students will be able to create and present arguments based on an analysis of a novel to support their viewpoint [R.6, W.1].

- Students will be able to research and analyze documents and media and select and synthesize appropriate evidence to support arguments in a speech [R.1, R.2, R.7, W.1, W.8].

- Students will be able to write a research-based Reader's Theater script on a historical point of view and revise as needed to strengthen it [W.2, W.4, W.5, W.6].

- Students will be able to argue, defend, and evaluate arguments during a mock trial [W.1, W.8].

ACCEPTABLE EVIDENCE:

- Textual evidence students use to complete the Examining Perspectives Organizer

- Graphic Research Organizer used as an outline for the student research

- Trial Preparation Web that focuses on identifying main topics

- Reader's Theater on a historical point of view

- Mock trial arguing, defending, and evaluating arguments

LEARNING EXPERIENCES AND INSTRUCTION:

- Day 1—Overview of the mock trial; introduction to project.

- Days 2–4—Research selected topic and begin writing a speech for mock trial.

- Day 5—Consult with lawyers about posing an effective argument and courtroom expectations.

- Days 6–8—Find documents to support arguments. Create a PowerPoint slideshow and a script for research-based Reader's Theater.

- Days 9–10—Stage and film the research-based Reader's Theater scripts to be shared at the trial.

- Day 11—Participate in co-counsel strategy meeting with cultural experts.

- Day 12—Engage in mock trial.

STRATEGIES:

- Modeling
- Discussion
- Cooperative Learning
- Writing Process

MATERIALS NEEDED:

- Yolen, J. (1992). *Encounter*. San Diego, CA: Harcourt Brace Jovanovich.
- A variety of resource materials from both viewpoints, including political cartoons, documents, photographs, paintings, and songs
- Lawyer's advice—lawyer serves as guest speaker in person, via Skype, or responds to interview questions via e-mail
- Video camera
- PowerPoint
- Paper and pens
- Handouts (reproducible forms for each handout appear at the end of this section)

SUPPLEMENTAL RESOURCES:

- Native North Americans—The Effects of Colonization (http://www .funsocialstudies.learninghaven.com /articles/natives2.htm)
- European Colonization of the United States (http://www.youtube.com /watch?v=Z3mu47IfTXg)

TECHNOLOGY/MEDIA OPPORTUNITIES:

- Contact local politicians to speak.
- Contact local newspapers for publicity.
- Create video clips of the Reader's Theater scripts.
- Construct a PowerPoint slideshow organizing the evidence for the trial.

SERVICE LEARNING LINKS:

- Students show their mock trial to younger children and discuss the importance of understanding both sides of an issue before making a judgment (empathy training).

VARIATIONS:

- Create a mock trial on a different issue.
- Ask other students to be the jurors.

MOCK TRIAL: NATIVE AMERICANS AND EUROPEAN COLONIZATION

History/Social Studies—U.S. History

(Grades 6–8; Argument)

Jessica Kuehn—Waverly Park School, Lynbrook, NY

Throughout this American history unit, students explore the following essential question: "Based on their contributions, were the Native Americans or the Europeans more worthy of ownership of New York?" As informed citizens who seek to be college and career ready, students must be able to consider a situation from different perspectives and make a judgment based on evidence. This all-encompassing question encourages students to look at history through different lenses.

The interdisciplinary project described in this lesson combines reading, writing, social studies, art, music, physical education, and technology. Students must research and gather information about the Native Americans and Europeans and think critically to support their case. The culmination of this unit is a mock trial in which students present their findings.

For the trial, each student is assigned the role of a lawyer or an expert witness. During the trial, the lawyers must submit evidence to support their arguments. Evidence may come in the form of a political cartoon, document, painting, video clip, photograph, or live demonstration. The expert witnesses write a Reader's Theater script based on the cultural contributions of their assigned group—Native Americans or Europeans—and perform a Reader's Theater. The verdict is delivered by the jurors (parents); they are encouraged to vote for the side that makes the best arguments.

Materials Needed

- Yolen, J. (1992). *Encounter.* San Diego, CA: Harcourt Brace Jovanovich.
- A variety of resource materials from both viewpoints, including political cartoons, documents, photographs, paintings, and songs
- Lawyer's advice—lawyer serves as guest speaker in person, via Skype, or responds to interview questions via e-mail
- Video camera
- PowerPoint
- Paper and pens
- Handouts (reproducible forms for each handout appear at the end of this section)

Timing

12 class periods

Day 1—Overview of the mock trial; introduction to project.

Days 2–4—Research selected topic and begin writing a speech for mock trial.

Day 5—Consult with lawyers to learn about posing an effective argument and courtroom expectations.

Days 6–8—Continue researching documents to support arguments. Create a PowerPoint slideshow and a script for research-based Reader's Theater.

Days 9–10—Stage and film research-based Reader's Theater scripts to be shared at the trial.

Day 11—Participate in co-counsel strategy meeting with expert witnesses.

Day 12—Engage in mock trial.

Day 1

After my students and I take turns reading aloud *Encounter* by Jane Yolen, we discuss looking at a situation from different perspectives. *Encounter* is the story of Columbus's "discovery" of the New World written from the perspective of a young Taino boy. The boy warns his people against the strangers who arrive in their land and who eventually end up colonizing them and destroying their culture [R.6]. Students examine both perspectives—the European and Native American—and provide evidence from the book on the Examining Perspectives Organizer (**Handout 1**) to support why they believe each group was doing the right or wrong thing [R.1, W.1].

After students share their text-based arguments with the class, they discuss how supporting evidence in an argument relates to the courtroom. I present them with the idea of conducting a mock trial in which they will take on the roles of lawyers and expert witnesses. The essential question the students will debate is this: "Based on their contributions, were the Native Americans or the Europeans more worthy of ownership of New York?" I give them a side (colonist or Native American), and they select either the role of a lawyer or of an expert witness on a specific cultural contribution. Even though some students initially complain when they are assigned a side with which they do not agree, I tell them that lawyers must develop empathy for their clients and the necessary argument skills to convince a jury of the validity of their cases.

The cultural contributions include philosophies, literature, economy and natural resources, games and sports, and music and arts. I provide a jury summons for students to give to their parents to inform them about the upcoming mock trial (**Handout 2**).

CULTURAL/LINGUISTIC HIGHLIGHT: Exploring matters from different perspectives and reading literature that involves characters from different cultures can lead students to become self-aware and understand other cultures.

THEORY LINK (Bloom): Students *comprehend, analyze, argue,* and *critique* characters and events in the story that are reflected in history.

CULTURAL/LINGUISTIC HIGHLIGHT: Graphic organizers help highlight key information and scaffold learning for diverse learners.

Days 2–4

For the next three days, we shift our focus to nonfiction related to the main idea of *Encounter*, the conflict between colonists and Native Americans regarding ownership of New York. Students use a graphic organizer (**Handout 3**) to guide their research as lawyers or expert witnesses and to begin constructing arguments with supporting evidence [W.1, W.7, W.8, W.9]. I provide textbooks, picture books, websites, and video clips from my resource collection, and they use these to gather information. Based on their research, students begin writing a speech that they will share on the day of the mock trial [W.1, W.8].

 THEORY LINK (Gardner): Appeals to Verbal-Linguistic Intelligence.

Day 5

A lawyer comes in as a guest speaker to discuss how to use evidence to support an argument, when to present that evidence, what attire is appropriate for a courtroom, and what presentation skills are most effective. Students take the opportunity to ask any questions pertaining to the trial. If a lawyer cannot be present, you can use Skype, which can be projected on a screen. An alternative is to elicit from students a list of related questions, have a lawyer answer them, and then share the answers with the students. Students can also volunteer to interview a lawyer that they know in person, over the phone, or via e-mail and share the information with the class.

 CULTURAL/LINGUISTIC HIGHLIGHT: Graphic organizers help highlight key information and scaffold learning for diverse learners.

THEORY LINK (Dewey): Purposeful learning—students are making connections to real life and developing their speaking and listening skills in the presence of an authentic audience.

Days 6–8

With the lawyer's input in mind, students continue their research by identifying and analyzing political cartoons, documents, photographs, paintings, and songs [R.7]. Teachers may wish to preselect the evidence options, offering students a chance to analyze those options and select which one best supports their case. I give students the opportunity to find evidence by looking at documents from prior document-based questions, textbooks, and online resources.

As students select appropriate pieces of evidence to support their area of expertise for the mock trial, I remind them that it is vital that the supporting evidence supports their arguments or main points.

I also explain to students that the evidence can be used twofold: It can support one point or refute the opposing counsel's point. Students conference with me and make adjustments to their speeches to enhance them [W.5]. Each side collaborates to create a PowerPoint slideshow to organize their evidence [W.6].

 CULTURAL/LINGUISTIC HIGHLIGHT: Cooperative learning opportunities can develop students' language skills and promote cross-cultural understanding.

 TECH CONNECTION: Students can also use Prezi software to create their presentation.

Days 9–10

Students write scripts based on their research [W.2]. They develop dialogue that conveys the facts and details that would persuade viewers to align with their group's perspective. For example, the games and sports group may demonstrate how lacrosse, a popular sport among students, was invented by the Native Americans. This could serve as one supporting detail in the argument that it is unfair to take land away from the people who have added to the value of recreation time by teaching colonists a new game that would be passed down from generation to generation.

After developing their scripts, students perform them through a Reader's Theater, incorporating relevant props and using the location of their choice to enhance their meaning.

Students use appropriate expression and fluency when performing Reader's Theater. We film these scripts and use them as supporting evidence during the mock trial. Students do an amazing job!

Day 11

Expert witnesses collaborate with their lawyers to identify the main points of each team member's individual arguments. They discuss the cohesiveness of their arguments and make sure that no information is missing. The closing lawyers must ensure that their arguments will not include any new evidence that is not also discussed during the trial. To avoid this issue, students use the Trial Preparation Web (**Handout 4**) to arrange their evidence and the Opening and Closing Arguments Organizer (**Handout 5**) to plan their opening and closing remarks [R.2, W.4].

Day 12

Students take on an active role as lawyers and expert witnesses within the mock trial. For each side, there are opening lawyers, philosophy experts, literature experts, economy and natural resources experts, games and sports experts, music and art experts, and closing lawyers. Students must dress professionally as if they were really in a courtroom. The principal takes on the role of the judge. Parents act as jurors for the case, and they deliver the verdict using their Jury Duty Ballot (**Handout 6**). An alternative approach is for the teacher to serve as judge and other invited teachers, aides, or students in the school to act as jurors. At the end of the lesson, I use a rubric in two ways: for students to reflect on their work and to evaluate themselves and for me to evaluate students for a final grade (**Handouts 7 and 8**).

As a result of this mock trial, students are able to closely read texts and documents. This purposeful reading challenges learners to think critically

DIFFERENTIATION TIP: Students who are talented or interested in costume design or "stage design" can be assigned to work on this area.

THEORY LINK (Gardner): Appeals to Interpersonal Intelligence.

TECH CONNECTION: Students can take turns filming the mock trial. The teacher can guide them to develop skills in using this medium.

CULTURAL/LINGUISTIC HIGHLIGHT: Allowing students to act out parts gives them opportunities to practice their vocabulary and oral skills as well as demonstrate their knowledge in an alternative way.

THEORY LINK (Gardner): Appeals to Visual-Spatial Intelligence.

THEORY LINK (Dewey): Purposeful learning—students assume real-life roles and make real-world applications.

and analytically when reading, and it aligns with the CCSS, which ask the same. It is essential for students to be able to master informational texts. By the end of this experience, students are able to take information and analyze it with the goal of supporting their arguments.

DIFFERENTIATION TIP: You can differentiate text complexity according to the needs of your students.

HANDOUT 1

EXAMINING PERSPECTIVES ORGANIZER

The Europeans

The Europeans believed that they were doing the right thing when they . . .

_____

_____

The Europeans believed that this was right because . . .

_____

_____

_____

I think that the Europeans were wrong to . . .

_____

_____

I think that this was wrong because . . .

_____

_____

_____

EXAMINING PERSPECTIVES ORGANIZER

The Native Americans

The Native Americans believed that they were doing the right thing when they . . .

_____

_____

The Native Americans believed that this was right because . . .

_____

_____

_____

I think that the Native Americans were wrong to . . .

_____

_____

I think that this was wrong because . . .

_____

_____

_____

HANDOUT 2

NATIVE AMERICANS AND EUROPEAN COLONIZATION

Jury Duty Summons

Jury Duty Summons

You are hereby summoned to serve as a **TRIAL JUROR** commencing on:

___/___/___ at ___:___

_____(name of school) Courthouse, ___ Floor, Room ___

You will be serving on the trial that will decide the following question:

Based on their contributions, were the Native Americans or the Europeans more worthy of ownership of New York?

VERY IMPORTANT: You must complete, detach, and send back within five days of receipt.

JUROR CONFIRMATION FORM

I, juror, _____, am:

(Check one)

_____ able to fulfill my responsibilities as an informed U.S. citizen.

_____ not able to fulfill my responsibilities as an informed U.S. citizen. Failure to obey this summons without a justifiable excuse is a crime that, upon conviction, is punishable by a fine not more than a big hug to your child.

HANDOUT 3

NATIVE AMERICANS AND EUROPEAN COLONIZATION

Research Graphic Organizer

Name: _____   Date: _____

Mock Trial Research

Cultural Contribution_____

Contribution	Supporting Information	Sources (e.g., books, websites, videoclips, etc.)

HANDOUT 4

TRIAL PREPARATION WEB

Lawyer Representing: _____

(Indicate: *Native Americans* or *Colonists*)

	Philosophy Evidence	
Games and Sports Evidence		Economy and Natural Resources Evidence
	Opening Statement (Introduce the main idea that you want the jury to believe)	
Oral Traditions Evidence		Music and Art Evidence
	Closing Statement (Close with some key pieces of evidence that you want the jury to remember as they deliberate)	

HANDOUT 5

OPENING AND CLOSING ARGUMENTS

Lawyer Representing: _____

(Indicate: *Native Americans* or *Colonists*)

Opening Argument:

1. What are the basic facts of the case that you want the jury to understand?

2. What witnesses will you bring to the stand to support your case?

3. What should the jury keep in mind as they listen to these witnesses?

Closing Argument:

1. What are some key pieces of evidence that you want the jury to remember as they deliberate?

2. How does this evidence support your main argument(s) in the case?

3. If a jury member can only remember one idea from the witnesses, what would it be?

HANDOUT 6

NATIVE AMERICANS AND EUROPEAN COLONIZATION

Jury Duty Ballot

As an impartial **TRIAL JUROR**, it is your duty to decide the winner of the trial based on the arguments presented. You are answering the essential question:

Based on their contributions, were the Native Americans or the European settlers more worthy of ownership of New York?

Check Only **ONE**:

☐	Native Americans	☐	Colonists

HANDOUT 7

NATIVE AMERICANS AND EUROPEAN COLONIZATION

Mock Trial Self-Reflection Rubric (for Student Use)

Name _____

	1	2	3	4
Presentation Skills	One or more members of the team had a presentation style that did not keep the attention of the audience.	Team sometimes used gestures, eye contact, tone of voice, and a level of enthusiasm in a way that kept the attention of the audience.	Team usually used gestures, eye contact, tone of voice, and a level of enthusiasm in a way that kept the attention of the audience.	Team consistently used gestures, eye contact, tone of voice, and a level of enthusiasm in a way that kept the attention of the audience.
Information	Information had several inaccuracies OR was usually not clear.	Most information presented in the debate was clear and accurate, but was not usually thorough.	Most information presented in the debate was clear, accurate, and thorough.	All information presented in the debate was clear, accurate, and thorough.
Evidence	Not every point was supported.	Every major point was supported with facts, documents, and/or examples, but the relevance of some was questionable.	Every major point was adequately supported with relevant facts, documents, and/or examples.	Every major point was well supported with several relevant facts, documents, and/or examples.
Reader's Theater Script	Reader's Theater script was not relevant to arguments.	Reader's Theater script included some inaccuracies and missing information.	Reader's Theater script adequately supported the arguments made.	Reader's Theater script clearly supported the arguments made.

Total Score: _____

Strengths:

_____

_____

_____

_____

_____

I need to work on:

_____

_____

HANDOUT 8

NATIVE AMERICANS AND EUROPEAN COLONIZATION

Mock Trial Rubric (for Teacher Use)

Name _____

	1	2	3	4
Presentation Skills	One or more members of the team had a presentation style that did not keep the attention of the audience.	Team sometimes used gestures, eye contact, tone of voice, and a level of enthusiasm in a way that kept the attention of the audience.	Team usually used gestures, eye contact, tone of voice, and a level of enthusiasm in a way that kept the attention of the audience.	Team consistently used gestures, eye contact, tone of voice, and a level of enthusiasm in a way that kept the attention of the audience.
Information	Information had several inaccuracies OR was usually not clear.	Most information presented in the debate was clear and accurate, but was not usually thorough.	Most information presented in the debate was clear, accurate, and thorough.	All information presented in the debate was clear, accurate, and thorough.
Evidence	Not every point was supported.	Every major point was supported with facts, documents, and/or examples, but the relevance of some was questionable.	Every major point was adequately supported with relevant facts, documents, and/or examples.	Every major point was well supported with several relevant facts, documents, and/or examples.
Reader's Theater Script	Reader's Theater script was not relevant to arguments.	Reader's Theater script included some inaccuracies and missing information.	Reader's Theater script adequately supported the arguments made.	Reader's Theater script clearly supported the arguments made.

Total Score: _____

Strengths:

_____

_____

_____

_____

_____

Student needs to work on:

_____

_____

Boyle's Law
Science—Chemistry
(Grades 9–10; Argument)
Maria Haralampopoulos and Niki Meleties—
Long Island City High School, Long Island City, NY

LESSON PLAN TEMPLATE

TOPIC:

Boyle's Law—The Inversely Proportional Relationship Between Pressure and Volume on a Confined Gas

CCSS STRAND:

Writing

TEXT TYPES AND PURPOSES:

Argument

TIMING:

3 class periods

BACKWARD DESIGN COMPONENTS:

DESIRED RESULTS/CCSS ADDRESSED:

Enduring Understandings

- Based on their scientific reading and their lab experience, students will understand the connection between the evidence-based approach of the scientific process and the process of constructing an effective written argument [W.1, W.4, W.9].

Knowledge and Skills

- Students will be able to closely read complex informational texts to determine central ideas and what the article says explicitly as well as interpret words and phrases as they are used in a text [R.1, R.2, R.4, R.10].

- Students will be able to *observe*, *chart*, *analyze*, and *synthesize* information presented in diverse ways [R.7].

- Students will be able to write clear and coherent text-based responses to informational sources and synthesize these sources into an argument that supports a claim with clear reasons and sufficient evidence [W.1, W.4, W.9].

ACCEPTABLE EVIDENCE:

- Class discussions

- Completion of Demonstration Observation Sheet, questions on Robert

Boyle reading, and "The Other Final Frontier" Article; Simulation Summary; and Group Graph Activity

- Argument essay on the importance of continuing funding for research on prolonged human exposure to extreme pressure changes and what the long-term benefits of this research will be

LEARNING EXPERIENCES AND INSTRUCTION:

- Day 1—Introduce topic.

- Day 2—Work on qualitative and quantitative analysis through simulation and graph activities.

- Day 3—Complete reading and writing assignment; write an argument essay.

STRATEGIES:

- Modeling

- Cooperative Learning

MATERIALS NEEDED:

- Vacuum pump

- Marshmallow

- Flask

- Syringes

- Calculators

- Projector/SMART Board

- Paper and pens

- Handouts (reproducible forms for each handout appear at the end of this section)
- Videos:
  - http://www.youtube.com /watch?v=LfCOnGHheok
  - http://www.ehow.com/ video_4993625_equalize-ear-pressure-scuba-diving.html
  - http://intro.chem.okstate. edu/1314F00/Laboratory/GLP.htm
- Article:
  - Hellwarth, B. (2012, January 21). The other final frontier. *New York Times*. Retrieved from http://www.nytimes .com/2012/01/22/opinion/sunday /the-other-final-frontier.html

SUPPLEMENTAL RESOURCES:

- Zumdahl, S., & Zumdahl, S. (2010). *Chemistry*. Belmont, CA: Brooks Cole.
- Dictionary.com, LLC. (2012). Thesaurus .com. Retrieved from http://thesaurus .com/

TECHNOLOGY/MEDIA OPPORTUNITIES:

- Through the use of the Internet, students can enhance their understanding of the physical behavior of gas particles by looking at different videos and simulations.
- Students with disabilities who need assistive technology can use the computer to take notes, complete handouts, and write the essay.
- A projector and SMART Board or whiteboard can be used to display visuals.

SERVICE LEARNING LINKS:

- The pressure demonstration with the marshmallow is always fun for students to see. Students use this and other experiments that stand out to them to excite younger students about science during a class visit or a science night for elementary school students.
- Students make posters that remind scuba divers of the importance of paying attention to air pressure. These posters are displayed at local scuba-diving schools or at resorts that offer this activity.
- If students do not live in an area that offers scuba diving classes or the actual scuba experience, they correspond with peers who live in an area that does offer this sport. This exchange allows them to share their safety tips and learn much more about sciences connected to water.
- Students develop argument essays based on other science topics that are important to them (e.g., recycling, global warming, nutrition, etc.) and post them on a website or share them with the community through a science newsletter to be distributed at local stores, banks, or libraries.

VARIATIONS:

- This lesson plan can be modified to create lesson plans for the other gas laws, such as Charles's Law and Guy-Lussac's Law.
- To make the assignment more challenging, students can perform more difficult math problems involving different mathematical conversions.

BOYLE'S LAW

Science—Chemistry

(Grades 9–10; Argument)

*Maria Haralampopoulos and Niki Meleties—
Long Island City High School, Long Island City, NY*

> *Science is a way of thinking more than a body of knowledge.*
>
> Sagan

This lesson expands how students view the natural phenomena in their surroundings through complex literacy tasks [W.1, R.10]. Students watch a simple video of a scuba diver and then partake in a scientific inquiry-based lesson in which they explore the inversely proportional relationship of pressure and volume of a confined gas, which is also known as Boyle's Law. The lesson is designed to elicit the relationship of the two variables from the students themselves. Students explore the importance and relevance of Boyle's Law, consider its contribution to the development of the kinetic molecular theory, and gain a better understanding of particle behavior.

This lesson is part of the larger unit, The Physical Behavior of Matter. As a result of this lesson, students learn to think about everyday phenomena like scientists. The lesson also incorporates modeling, cooperative learning, literacy in science, quantitative and qualitative analysis, videos, demonstrations, and technology—as well as links to other sciences—so students can transfer their knowledge to other applications and situations.

Materials Needed

- Vacuum pump
- Marshmallow
- Flask
- Syringes
- Calculators
- Projector/SMART Board
- Paper and pens
- Handouts (reproducible forms for each handout appear at the end of this section)
- Videos:
  - http://www.youtube.com/watch?v=LfCOnGHheok
  - http://www.ehow.com/video_4993625_equalize-ear-pressure-scuba-diving.html
  - http://intro.chem.okstate.edu/1314F00/Laboratory/GLP.htm
- Hellwarth, B. (2012, January 21). The other final frontier. *New York Times*. Retrieved from http://www.nytimes.com/2012/01/22/opinion/sunday/the-other-final-frontier.html

Timing

3 class periods

Day 1—Introduce topic.

Day 2—Work on qualitative and quantitative analysis through simulation and graph activities.

Day 3—Complete reading and writing assignment; write an argument essay.

Day 1

Students view a scuba-diving video (http://www.youtube.com/watch?v=LfCOnGHheok) and answer questions regarding the need for a scuba diver to equalize pressure (**Handout 1**) [R.1].This leads to an inquiry-based discussion. Students consider the effects of increasing pressure on the human body, specifically the lungs, and we discuss different ways to overcome this problem (e.g., scuba tank). Students formulate a hypothesis regarding the relationship between pressure and volume [R.2]. To follow up on students' hypotheses, we perform two demonstrations, one using a syringe and another using a marshmallow in a flask with a vacuum attachment. In the first demonstration, the syringe is used to demonstrate the inversely proportional relationship between pressure and volume. As we press down on the plunger of the syringe, thereby increasing the pressure, it can be clearly seen that the volume of the gas decreases.

In the second demonstration, when the marshmallow is placed in the flask and the air pressure is decreased by applying the vacuum (less air, less pressure), the marshmallow expands, demonstrating that by decreasing pressure, the volume of a gas increases. After completing the demonstration observation sheet, the students identify the inversely proportional relationship between pressure and volume.

Students read an article about the life and contributions of Robert Boyle and answer questions based on the article [R.1] (**Handout 2**). The vocabulary words in the article are listed in the handout and added to the word wall that lists the definitions of key academic words and science words covered in the lesson [R.4] (**Handout 3**).

CULTURAL/LINGUISTIC HIGHLIGHT: Visual representations deepen students' comprehension of content and language.

Students play a short game in which they kinesthetically act like gas particles being affected by pressure. When I shout out that the air pressure is increasing, they come closer together so that the space they occupy decreases (volume). When I shout out that the air pressure is decreasing, they spread apart. The day's lesson concludes with discussion and a short video that explains ways to equalize ear pressure during scuba diving (http://www.ehow.com/video_4993625_equalize-ear-pressure-scuba-diving.html).

CULTURAL/LINGUISTIC HIGHLIGHT: Word walls provide linguistic support to students and help develop and expand their vocabulary.

Day 2

Students perform a qualitative analysis of Boyle's Law by engaging in an interactive, online simulation with a guiding question activity (http://intro .chem.okstate.edu/1314F00/Laboratory/GLP.htm) (**Handout 4**). They observe, chart, and analyze how volume changes with varying pressures and write a summary of the relationship between the two variables [R.2, R.7, W.9]. Students then work on a group activity in which they create a graph, analyze the graph, and make predictions through discussion (**Handout 5**) [R.7]. In addition, through quantitative analysis, students come up with the mathematical expression of Boyle's Law ($p1v1=p2v2$).

 CULTURAL/LINGUISTIC HIGHLIGHT: Cooperative learning opportunities can develop students' language skills and promote cross-cultural understanding.

Day 3

Students complete a reading and writing assignment on "The Other Final Frontier," a scientific current events article (**Handout 6**) [R.1]. We tell students that as they read, they should consider the questions they will need to answer postreading and focus on the vocabulary words and what they mean. We discuss the responses and vocabulary at the end of the activity in class and add the new words to the word wall. After the content-based discussion of the article, students focus on the elements of the argument in the article:

- What evidence is provided to support the writer's claim?
- How is counterargument addressed?
- What effective vocabulary strengthens the voice of the writer?

Students write an argument essay as a final project (**Handout 7**) in which they argue why it is important that the funding for research on prolonged human exposure to extreme pressure changes continues and what the long-term benefits of this research will be [W.1, W.4, W.9]. As they work, they aim to meet the criteria we have mapped out on a rubric (**Handout 8**).

In their essays, students provide both background and other relevant information. They discuss the relationship between pressure and volume as well as the health effects of being exposed to extreme pressure changes over prolonged periods of time. They provide counterarguments and a rebuttal. We require students to use evidence from various sources and include at least five vocabulary words in their body paragraphs.

This essay assignment aligns with the higher-level thinking demanded by the CCSS. It requires that students think deeply and critically about the effects of scientific research on real-life issues, analyze and evaluate evidence to defend their position, assume a stand, and provide convincing arguments from outside sources to support their claims. They engage in purposeful learning as they write about a topic that concerns them and their fellow human beings and, therefore, think like scientists as well as concerned, compassionate citizens.

HANDOUT 1

DEMONSTRATION OBSERVATION SHEET

I. Watch the scuba diving video (http://www.youtube.com/watch?v=LfCOnGHheok) and respond to the following questions:

1. Why do scuba divers need to equalize their pressure as they dive deeper into the water?

2. Why do you think this is necessary?

II. Draw and write observations of the syringe demonstration:

1. What is inside the "empty" syringe?

2. How can we increase the pressure?

3. How does the volume of the gas (air) change as we increase the pressure?

4. How are pressure and volume related?

5. Will the number of gas molecules change? Why or why not?

6. Draw two boxes and a representation of the gas molecules initially and after increasing pressure.

Before   After

III. Flask with Vacuum Pump Attachment Containing a Marshmallow Demonstration

1. How can we decrease the pressure in the flask?

2. What happens to the marshmallow as we apply the vacuum? Why does this happen?

3. Why do you think a marshmallow and not a gummy bear was used for this demonstration?

4. Draw the shape of the marshmallow before and after the application of the vacuum pump.

Marshmallow   Marshmallow
Before Vacuum   After Vacuum
Is Applied   Is Applied

HANDOUT 2

ROBERT BOYLE ARTICLE

Directions: Read the article about the life and contributions of Robert Boyle (1627–1691) and answer the following questions. Key words in the article are listed below:

theory

scientific method

procedure

apparatus

observations

hypothesis

vacuum pump

pressure

proportionally

volume

particles

element

corpuscular theory

ROBERT BOYLE

Robert Boyle (January 25, 1627–December 30, 1691) is considered one of the fathers of modern chemistry because he revolutionized the scientific process. In Boyle's day, scientists made up a **theory** and then judged how facts and observations fit that theory. Boyle's approach was the opposite. He observed the facts first and then developed a theory to explain those facts.

Other scientists agreed with Boyle's approach, and they formed a group to discuss their new ideas. They called themselves the Invisible College. In 1663, the king chartered the group, which was then called the Royal Society. The motto of the Royal Society was "Nullius in Verba." This means "nothing in words." According to this motto, all science should be based on experiments rather than on theory.

Boyle's adherence to logic and empirical data established him as the founder of the modern **scientific method**. Beginning in 1664, Boyle spent 14 years at Oxford running a research lab. He not only recorded the **procedure**, **apparatus**, and **observations** of his experiments, he published this information so that other scientists could repeat the experiments and compare results. If similar results were obtained each time another scientist repeated the experiment, then the **hypothesis** tested was strengthened. If the results differed, scientists knew they needed to alter the original hypothesis. This approach was the basis for the scientific method.

Among many of Boyle's scientific accomplishments, the **vacuum pump** is the most important piece of equipment that he developed. Boyle created this device with the help of his assistant, Robert Hooke. The vacuum pump allowed Boyle to experiment and discover Boyle's Law. This law of inverse proportionality explains the behavior of gasses. When **pressure** increases **proportionally**, gas **volume** decreases proportionally. For instance, if the pressure on a quantity of gas is doubled, the volume of that gas is reduced by half. This realization helped Boyle understand that if gas could be compressed, it must be made up of tiny **particles** separated by space. This understanding led him to define the modern idea of an "**element**" and to develop a universal "**corpuscular theory**" of chemistry.

In 1680, Boyle was elected president of the Royal Society. He declined this honor because he thought the presidential oath conflicted with his religious beliefs. With or without the title of president, it is clear that Boyle was a leader in the world of science.

Directions: Answer the following questions in complete sentences.

1. Robert Boyle is known as one of the fathers of chemistry. In what ways did he contribute to the development of modern-day scientific inquiry?

2. How did Boyle's approach differ from previous methods?

3. Explain the importance of the motto of the Royal Society—"Nullius in Verba" ("nothing in words").

4. What other contributions to science did Robert Boyle make?

5. Based on the article, what is Boyle's Law?

References

Robert Boyle: Mighty chemist. (n.d.). Retrieved from http://www.woodrow.org/teachers/ci/1992/boyle.html

Robert Boyle Biography. (n.d.). Retrieved from http://www.bookrags.com/biography/robert-boyle-wsd/

HANDOUT 3

WORD WALL

pressure	corpuscular theory
volume	element
directly proportional	thermonuclear device
inversely proportional	standard temperature and pressure
confined gas	atmospheric pressure
constant	Sealab
kinetic molecular theory	bends
particle behavior	exotic gas mixtures
physical behavior of matter	aquanauts
kinesthetic	newfangled diving methods
equalize	submarines
qualitative analysis	acidification
quantitative analysis	herbivore diversity
interpolation	degrading reefs
vacuum pump	Remotely Operated Vehicles (R.O.V.'s)
procedure	*Okeanos Explorer*
apparatus	sentient human
observations	"the silent world"

HANDOUT 4

PRESSURE AND VOLUME SIMULATION

Purpose:

To explore the relationship between pressure and volume of gases when the temperature and the number of gas molecules remains constant.

Procedure:

Log on to the Online Interactive Gas Law Simulation website http://intro.chem.okstate .edu/1314F00/Laboratory/GLP.htm. Explore the site and collect data points about the relationship between pressure and volume. Please collect a minimum of 10 points and record your data in Table 1.

OBSERVATIONS

1. What happens to the particles in the container as the variables of pressure and volume change? Please be specific.

2. What other observations were you able to make?

Table 1

Volume	Pressure

3. Data Analysis: Based on the data collected, what is the relationship between volume and pressure?

HANDOUT 5

GROUP GRAPH ACTIVITY AND BOYLE'S LAW

Directions: In groups, respond to the following questions using the following website: http://intro.chem.okstate.edu/1314F00/Laboratory/GLP.htm

Boyle's Law

Pressure Exerted on a Gas P atm (y-axis)	Volume of Gas V mL (x-axis)	P×V
0.5	2,000	0.5 × 2,000 = 1,000
1	1,000	
2		
4		
8		
16		

1. Fill in the missing information.

2. Graph P versus V using an appropriate scale.

3. Describe the shape of the graph using complete sentences.

4. a. From the graph, obtain P when V is 200 mL.
   b. From the graph, obtain V when P is 1,500 mL.

5. What is the conclusion we can draw for the last column of the table (P × V)? Write your answer using complete sentences.

HANDOUT 6

THE OTHER FINAL FRONTIER

Directions: Read the article "The Other Final Frontier" by Ben Hellwarth (http://www
.nytimes.com/2012/01/22/opinion/sunday/the-other-final-frontier.html), and answer the
questions that follow. Focus on the vocabulary words listed below and try to figure out their
meaning. We will discuss these vocabulary words and their definitions along with your
responses after you complete this activity.

- Sealab
- bends
- exotic gas mixtures
- aquanauts
- newfangled diving methods
- submarines
- *Aquarius*
- acidification
- herbivore diversity
- degrading reefs
- Remotely Operated Vehicles (R.O.V.'s)
- *Okeanos Explorer*
- a sentient human
- "the silent world"

Questions:

1. What are some of the dangers to the human body as a result of being exposed to
   extreme pressure changes during prolonged periods of time, either through deep sea or
   outer space exploration?

2. What are some of the valuable scientific and technological advances that can be made
   by our government by investing in research in this area?

3. What does the term *aquanaut* imply?

4. In what ways did the purpose of and research initially conducted at Sealab change over
   time, in comparison to the modern day *Aquarius* and *Oceanus Explorer?*

5. Do you agree with the author that the benefits of deep-sea exploration outweigh those
   of space exploration? Please provide supporting facts.

HANDOUT 7

Final Assignment: Argument Essay on a Current Science Topic

Overview:

A large portion of the funds spent by our government on deep sea and outer space exploration programs goes toward researching the issue of prolonged human exposure to extreme pressure changes. Given the current state of our economy, many argue that the economic burden on the already overtaxed American citizen outweighs the benefits of the research conducted.

Directions:

Write an essay arguing why it is important that the funding for research on prolonged human exposure to extreme pressure changes continues and what the long-term benefits of this research will be.

Include the following in your essay:

1. Introduction (1 paragraph)—State your thesis and the main idea of your essay. Provide both background and relevant information. Make sure to discuss the relationship between pressure and volume as well as the health effects of being exposed to extreme pressure changes over prolonged periods of time.

2. Body paragraphs (2-3 paragraphs)—Use evidence from various sources (e.g., readings, videos) from class to support your thesis statement. Include at least five vocabulary words in your body paragraphs.

3. Counterargument and rebuttal (1 paragraph)—Mention the arguments from the other side of the issue and briefly refute the other side's statements.

4. Conclusion (1 paragraph)—Summarize your thesis statement and the main points of your essay.

HANDOUT 8

ARGUMENT ESSAY RUBRIC

	Excellent *90–100%*	*Good* *80–89%*	*Fair* *70–79%*	*Poor* *Below 70%*
Introduction (20 points)	Well-developed introductory paragraph that includes thesis statement, background, and relevant information.	A somewhat well-developed introductory paragraph that includes a thesis statement, background, and relevant information.	Introductory paragraph includes neither a strong thesis statement nor background and relevant information.	A poorly developed introductory paragraph that is missing required information.
Body paragraphs and counter-argument (50 points)	Main points are well developed with strong supporting evidence. Refutation paragraph acknowledges the opposing view by summarizing its main points. This is followed by a strong rebuttal. At least five vocabulary words are used.	The main points are present but may lack details, evidence, and support. Refutation paragraph acknowledges the opposing view but doesn't summarize points. The rebuttal is adequate. Three or four vocabulary words are used.	May be lacking enough main points as well as development and evidence. Refutation paragraph missing and/or vague. Rebuttal is weak. Two vocabulary words are used.	Lacking main points, or all main points argued lack development. Refutation paragraph missing and/or vague. Rebuttal is ineffective or nonexistent. One vocabulary word is used.
Conclusion (20 points)	A coherent conclusion that summarizes the main points of the essay in a fresh and powerful way.	A coherent conclusion that relates to the introduction.	Conclusion simply restates the introduction.	Weak or irrelevant conclusion.
Spelling, grammar, and sentence structure (10 points)	Spelling, grammar, and sentence structure are correct.	Shows few spelling, grammar, and sentence structure errors.	Shows many errors in spelling, grammar, and sentence structure.	Many errors in spelling, grammar, and sentence structure make the paper difficult to read.

Fantasy Basketball
Technical Subject—Sports Marketing
(Grades 11–12; Argument)
Rory Block—Mineola High School, Garden City Park, NY

LESSON PLAN TEMPLATE

TOPIC:

Fantasy Basketball (Grades 11–12)

CCSS STRAND:

Writing

TEXT TYPES AND PURPOSES:

Argument

TIMING:

14 class periods

BACKWARD DESIGN COMPONENTS:

DESIRED RESULTS/CCSS ADDRESSED:

Enduring Understandings

- Through the creation of a fantasy basketball team, students will develop an understanding of the ways that society, the economy, and current events influence business choices.

Knowledge and Skills

- Students will be able to develop and analyze information related to their business choices and to rationalize their choices in well-written paragraphs [R.1, R.7, W.1, W.4, W.7, W.8, W.9, W.10].

- Students will be able to discuss the effects that current events might have on their choices and to produce a written reflection based on the discussion [W.1, W.8, W.9].

ACCEPTABLE EVIDENCE:

- Well-written rationales (in paragraph and proposal form) for the team name, team logo, team uniform, team sponsorship, and team giveaway

- Participation in class discussion and presentations regarding business choices and research that supports said choices

LEARNING EXPERIENCES AND INSTRUCTION:

14 class periods (lessons do not need to be conducted on consecutive days)

- Day 1—Project overview. Choose teams.

- Day 2—Decide team location. Develop a team name.

- Days 3–4—Develop a team logo. Submit a paragraph rationale for the logo. Share the logo with peers, and gather peer feedback.

- Days 5–9—Draft professional players for teams by using the NBA website for player statistics.

- Day 10—Compose a team roster with player statistics and the team logo.

- Days 11–12—Write a proposal for the company that should sponsor and share a name with the team stadium. Design a team uniform. Revise based on peer feedback.

- Days 13–14—Decide and write a rationale for team giveaways.

STRATEGIES:

- Guidance and Monitoring

- Discussion

- Cooperative Learning

MATERIALS NEEDED:

- Art supplies

- Access to NBA Website (http://www
.nba.com/)

- Sample proposal for a flexible work
schedule (http://specialchildren.about
.com/od/familyissues/a/flextimememo
.html)

- Paper and pens

- Handouts (reproducible forms for each
handout appear at the end of this
section)

SUPPLEMENTAL RESOURCES:

- *Sports Illustrated* articles

- Fantasy basketball 101: The basics
(n.d.). Retrieved from http://basketball
.about.com/od/fantasygames/a/fantasy
-basketball-101.htm

TECHNOLOGY/MEDIA OPPORTUNITIES:

- NBA Website www.nba.com

- Clipart or Google images for logo design

SERVICE LEARNING LINKS:

- Students apply their management skills
by volunteering to help with the school
or local athletic league.

- Students transfer their design and
marketing skills to a campaign for social
change related to a topic that most
interests them.

VARIATIONS:

- This lesson can be adapted for any
professional sport, including the WNBA
and other professional women's teams.
A discussion may ensue regarding
gender inequities in professional sports.

- Students could hold a logo contest for
their school team.

FANTASY BASKETBALL

Technical Subject—Sports Marketing

(Grades 11–12; Argument)

Rory Block—Mineola High School, Garden City Park, NY

Basketball season can get pretty exciting in my Sports Marketing class thanks to the BBA (Block Basketball Association). Fantasy leagues for all professional sports have gained popularity over the past few years. Watching how my students invest their time and effort into this project helps me better appreciate this phenomenon. Though enjoyable, this project is certainly not all fun and games. As part of the BBA, students must hone their analytical, argument, and presentation skills.

Materials Needed

- Art supplies
- Access to NBA Website (http://www.nba.com/)
- Sample proposal for a flexible work schedule (http://specialchildren .about.com/od/familyissues/a/flextimememo.html)
- Paper and pens
- Handouts (reproducible forms for each handout appear at the end of this section)

Timing

14 class periods (lessons do not need to be conducted on consecutive days)

Day 1—Project overview. Choose teams.

Day 2—Decide team location. Develop a team name.

Days 3–4—Develop a team logo. Submit a paragraph rationale for the logo. Share the logo with peers and gather peer feedback.

Days 5–9—Draft professional players for teams by using the NBA website for player statistics.

Day 10—Compose a team roster with player statistics and the team logo.

Days 11–12—Write a proposal for the company that should sponsor and share a name with the team stadium. Design a team uniform. Revise based on peer feedback.

Days 13–14—Decide and write a rationale for team giveaways.

Day 1

On the first day of this project, I give a general overview of the BBA, explaining that the students will be required to create a team, draft players, and promote their team throughout the basketball season. I also stress the fact that this is a project that will yield several grades over the course of the next four months. If time allows, I show samples of student work from previous years.

Once the students have a general understanding of the BBA, I require the class to form eight teams of approximately four students each. When forming the teams, I stress the importance of having a person with basketball knowledge who can serve as team captain. In addition, I remind them that they will also need group members who are talented artists, who are strong arguers, and who are tech savvy.

 THEORY LINK (Gardner): Appeals to Multiple Intelligences.

 CULTURAL/LINGUISTIC HIGHLIGHT: Cooperative learning opportunities can develop students' language skills and promote cross-cultural understanding.

 THEORY LINK (Gardner): Appeals to Verbal-Linguistic Intelligence.

Day 2

On the second day, I distribute information on television markets and population counts for U.S. cities (**Handout 1**). Each student group must pick a city that does not have a basketball team. Based on the group's choice, students must develop a team name. I advise students to employ alliteration based on the team's location. For example, students have had teams such as Kentucky Colonels, Pittsburg Panthers, Vegas Vipers, and Kansas City Cougars.

As students work to create their group's team name, I remind them that this name will shape much of their future work, such as the design of the team logo, uniforms, and promotional materials, so they must choose wisely. At the end of the period, each group submits a brief paragraph providing evidence to support their reasoning for choosing their team location and their team name [W.1, W.4, W.7, W.10].

Days 3–4

For the next two days, groups create a logo for their team. This must be appropriate—meaning no weapons, no sexually suggestive imagery, and no prejudiced imagery. The logo should be designed to look good in various sizes (billboards, jerseys, key chains, etc.). I tell students that their best bet is to use the computer to help them with their logo design. To make impressive-looking logos, students can combine images from clipart and images available online and then infuse these images with team colors.

 TECH CONNECTION: Students may use computer art programs to enhance their work.

 THEORY LINK (Dewey): Developing citizenry— Students must communicate respectfully and effectively.

Some strong artists opt to draw their logos. This is acceptable; however, I warn them that the time limits for this element of the project may not allow for a polished product. The groups present their logos (along with a rationale for the chosen logo) to other peer groups for evaluation and feedback [W.1, W.4, W.7, W.10]. Sometimes their peers are more critical than I am!

Days 5–9

The next few days are dedicated to drafting players. As a class, we look over the players from that year's NBA teams by using the NBA website, which I project in front of the room. Students in each group take on the role of general manager by considering the number of points, rebounds, and assists each player has [R.1, R.7]. They know that they need to draft four guards, four forwards, and two centers.

It takes several days to draft all the teams, and students can get heated when the players that they want are taken by another team. I do my best to handle this with humor, and I try to remind students that this is the way things work. Sometimes you get what you want. Sometimes you don't. Overall, this is an exciting time in class. Each

TECH CONNECTION: If students have their own laptops or other devices with Internet access, they may research their choices beyond the NBA site.

Friday, following this draft, students submit their lineup for the week. They choose two guards, two forwards, and a center from their roster whose statistics they will follow for the week. Each Thursday is Transaction Thursday. Students have the opportunity to trade, waive, or assign a medical exemption to their players.

Day 10

Students create a roster that includes the team logo and information on each of the drafted players, including height, weight, position, and where they played the previous year [R.1, R.7, W.8, W.9].

THEORY LINK (Gardner): Appeals to Visual-Spatial Intelligence.

Days 11–12

Students work in their groups to write a proposal for who should get naming rights to their team arena. I tell them to find a company that is well-known and well-connected to their geographic area. Students must submit a proposal stating their choice of sponsor and providing evidence to support that choice. I provide a sample proposal as a guide (http://specialchildren .about.com/od/familyissues/a/flextimememo .html). This proposal is meant to be simple enough to follow and is deliberately not related to sports so as to avoid limiting students' voices in their own works.

THEORY LINK (Bloom): Students *analyze* and *evaluate* the company and *apply* findings to their argument.

Once they choose their sponsor, the students design a uniform (jersey and shorts) with the team logo, a player's name and number, and a representation of their sponsor. These are taped to the board for peer evaluation. Students consider neatness, balance, and clear basketball references, and—of course—the rationale provided by the designers [W.1, W.4, W.7, W.10].

Days 13–14

Students must decide what kinds of giveaways they are going to use at their home games (bobble heads, mugs, key chains, etc). Again, they must submit a paragraph explaining their choice [W.1, W.4, W.7, W.10].

Throughout this process, much of our reading and discussion relate back to the BBA. Students discuss current events in sports and how such events might influence their team. To ensure understanding, students write a brief reflection on these discussions [W.1, W.8, W.9]. For instance, the popularity of Jeremy Lin sparked great class discussion. Students considered how Lin's popularity might influence demand for tickets, TV ratings, public relations, and more.

THEORY LINK (Bloom): Students *comprehend* and *apply* their understanding of the articles to their teams.

This project gives a greater meaning to class readings and enhances students' decision-making and argument skills. Students are highly motivated to provide a strong rationale for each choice that they make throughout the unit. They know that they have to convince both their peers and me that they have made wise decisions regarding their teams. Best of all, it is so fun that students forget that they are working!

HANDOUT 1

TELEVISION MARKETS AND CITY POPULATION INFORMATION

2011 Rank	Designated Market Area (DMA)	No. of TV Households
1	New York	7,384,340
2	Los Angeles	5,613,460
3	Chicago	3,484,800
4	Philadelphia	2,949,310
5	Dallas–Ft. Worth	2,588,020
6	San Francisco-Oakland–San Jose	2,502,030
7	Boston (Manchester)	2,366,690
8	Washington, DC	2,359,160
9	Atlanta	2,326,840
10	Houston	2,215,650
11	Detroit	1,845,920
12	Seattle-Tacoma	1,818,900
13	Phoenix	1,812,040
14	Tampa–St. Petersburg	1,806,560
15	Minneapolis–St. Paul	1,728,050
16	Miami–Ft. Lauderdale	1,621,130
17	Denver	1,566,460
18	Cleveland–Akron	1,485,140
19	Orlando-Daytona Beach	1,453,170
20	Sacramento-Stockton-Modesto	1,387,710
21	St. Louis	1,243,490
22	Portland, OR	1,182,180
23	Pittsburgh	1,165,740
24	Raleigh–Durham	1,150,350
25	Charlotte	1,136,420
26	Indianapolis	1,089,700

(Continued)

(Continued)

2011 Rank	Designated Market Area (DMA)	No. of TV Households
27	Baltimore	1,085,070
28	San Diego	1,075,120
29	Nashville	1,014,910
30	Hartford–New Haven	996,550
31	Kansas City	931,320
32	Columbus, OH	930,460
33	Salt Lake City	917,370
34	Milwaukee	902,190
35	Cincinnati	897,890
36	San Antonio	881,050
37	Greenville–Spartanville–Asheville	846,030
38	West Palm Beach–Ft. Pierce	794,310
39	Grand Rapids–Kalamazoo	720,150
40	Las Vegas	718,990
41	Oklahoma City	718,770
42	Birmingham	717,530
43	Harrisburg–Lancaster–Lebanon–York	716,990
44	Norfolk–Portsmouth–Newport News	709,730
45	Austin	705,280
46	Greensboro–High Point	695,100
47	Albuquerque–Santa Fe	691,450
48	Louisville	670,880
49	Memphis	662,830
50	Jacksonville	659,170

Source: http://www.sportstvjobs.com/resources/local-tv-market-sizes-dma.html

TEAMS/TELEVISION MARKETS

1. **NEW YORK**: Knicks, Nets, Rangers, Islanders, Devils, Giants, Jets, Mets, Yankees

2. **LOS ANGELES**: Dodgers, Anaheim, Clippers, Lakers, Kings, Ducks

3. **CHICAGO**: Cubs, White Sox, Bulls, Bears, Blackhawks

4. **PHILADELPHIA**: Flyers, Sixers, Phillies, Eagles

5. **BOSTON**: Red Sox, Patriots, Celtics, Bruins

6. **SAN FRANCISCO–OAKLAND–SAN JOSE**: 49ers, Raiders, A's, Giants, Golden State Warriors, San Jose Sharks

7. **DALLAS–FT. WORTH**: Cowboys, Mavericks, Stars, Rangers

8. **WASHINGTON, DC**: Redskins, Capitals, Wizards (Nationals)

9. **ATLANTA**: Braves, Falcons, Hawks, Thrashers

10. **DETROIT**: Pistons, Red Wings, Lions, Tigers

11. **HOUSTON**: Astros, Rockets, Texans

12. **SEATTLE–TACOMA**: Supersonics, Mariners, Seahawks

13. **TAMPA–ST. PETERSBURG**: Lightning, Buccaneers, Devil Rays

14. **MINNEAPOLIS–ST. PAUL**: Twins, Vikings, Timberwolves, Wild

15. **PHOENIX**: Diamondbacks, Cardinals, Coyotes, Suns

16. **CLEVELAND–AKRON**: Indians, Cavaliers, Browns

17. **MIAMI–FT. LAUDERDALE**: Dolphins, Marlins, Heat, Panthers

18. **DENVER**: Broncos, Nuggets, Avalanche, Rockies

19. **SACRAMENTO: STOCKTON–MODESTO**: Kings

20. **ORLANDO–DAYTONA BEACH–MELBOURNE**: Magic

21. **ST. LOUIS**: Blues, Rams, Cardinals

22. **PITTSBURGH**: Pirates, Steelers, Penguins

23. **BALTIMORE**: Orioles, Ravens

24. **PORTLAND, OR**: Trailblazers

25. **INDIANAPOLIS**: Colts, Pacers

26. **SAN DIEGO**: Padres, Chargers

27. **HARTFORD & NEW HAVEN**:

28. **CHARLOTTE**: Bobcats, Panthers

29. **RALEIGH–DURHAM (Fayetteville)**: Hurricanes

30. **NASHVILLE**: Titans, Predators

31. **KANSAS CITY**: Chiefs, Royals

32. **MILWAUKEE**: Brewers, Bucks, Packers

33. **CINCINNATI**: Bengals, Reds

34. **COLUMBUS, OH**: Blue Jackets

35. **GREENVILLE–SPARTA–ASHEVILLE**:

36. **SALT LAKE CITY**: Jazz

37. **SAN ANTONIO**: Spurs

38. **GRAND RAPIDS–KALAMAZOO**:

39. **WEST PALM BEACH–FT. PIERCE**:

40. **BIRMINGHAM**:

41. **NORFOLK–PORTSMOUTH–NEWPORT NEWS**:

42. **HARRISBURG–LANCASTER**:

43. **NEW ORLEANS**: Hornets, Saints

44. **MEMPHIS**: Grizzlies

45. **OKLAHOMA CITY**:

46. **BUFFALO**: Sabres, Bills

47. **ALBUQUERQUE–SANTA FE**:

48. **GREENSBORO–SALEM**:

49. **PROVIDENCE–NEW BEDFORD**:

50. **LOUISVILLE**:

51. **LAS VEGAS**:

52. **JACKSONVILLE**: Jaguars

Source: Adapted from http://en.wikipedia.org/wiki/List_of_professional_sports_teams_in_the_United_States_and_Canada

TOP 50 CITIES IN THE U.S. BY POPULATION AND RANK

The table below lists the largest 50 cities in the United States based on population and rank for the years 1990, 2000, 2005, and 2010.

	4/1/2010 Census Population	7/1/2005 Population Estimate	4/1/2000 Census Population	4/1/1990 Census Population	Numeric Population Change 1990–2000	Percentage Population Change 1990–2000	Size Rank 1990	Size Rank 2000	Size Rank 2005	Size Rank 2010
New York, NY	8,175,133	8,143,197	8,008,278	7,322,564	685,714	9.4	1	1	1	1
Los Angeles, CA	3,792,621	3,844,829	3,694,820	3,485,398	209,422	6.0	2	2	2	2
Chicago, IL	2,695,598	2,842,518	2,896,016	2,783,726	112,290	4.0	3	3	3	3
Houston, TX	2,099,451	2,016,582	1,953,631	1,630,553	323,078	19.8	4	4	4	4
Philadelphia, PA	1,526,006	1,463,281	1,517,550	1,585,577	−68,027	−4.3	5	5	5	5
Phoenix, AZ	1,445,632	1,461,575	1,321,045	983,403	337,642	34.3	10	6	6	6
San Antonio, TX	1,327,407	1,256,509	1,144,646	935,933	208,713	22.3	9	9	7	7
San Diego, CA	1,307,402	1,255,540	1,223,400	1,110,549	112,851	10.2	6	7	8	8
Dallas, TX	1,197,816	1,213,825	1,188,580	1,006,877	181,703	18.0	8	8	9	9
San Jose, CA	945,942	912,332	894,943	782,248	112,695	14.4	11	11	10	10
Jacksonville, FL	821,784	782,623	735,617	635,230	100,387	15.8	15	14	13	11
Indianapolis, IN	820,445	784,118	781,870	741,952	49,974	6.7	13	12	12	12
San Francisco, CA	805,235	739,426	776,733	723,959	52,774	7.3	14	13	14	13
Austin, TX	790,390	690,252	656,562	465,622	190,940	41.0	25	16	16	14
Columbus, OH	787,033	730,657	711,470	632,910	78,560	12.4	16	15	15	15
Fort Worth, TX	741,206	624,067	534,694	447,619	87,075	19.5	29	27	19	16
Charlotte, NC	731,424	610,949	540,828	395,934	144,894	36.6	33	26	20	17

(Continued)

(Continued)

	4/1/2010 Census Population	7/1/2005 Population Estimate	4/1/2000 Census Population	4/1/1990 Census Population	Numeric Population Change 1990–2000	Percentage Population Change 1990–2000	Size Rank 1990	Size Rank 2000	Size Rank 2005	Size Rank 2010
Detroit, MI	713,777	886,671	951,270	1,027,974	−76,704	−7.5	7	10	11	18
El Paso, TX	649,121	598,590	563,662	515,342	48,320	9.4	22	23	21	19
Memphis, TN	646,889	672,277	650,100	610,337	39,763	6.5	18	18	17	20
Baltimore, MD	620,961	635,815	651,154	736,014	−84,860	−11.5	12	17	18	21
Boston, MA	617,594	559,034	589,141	574,283	14,858	2.6	20	20	24	22
Seattle, WA	608,660	573,911	563,374	516,259	47,115	9.1	21	24	23	23
Washington, DC	601,723	550,521	572,059	606,900	−34,841	−5.7	19	21	27	24
Nashville-Davidson, TN[a]	601,222	549,110	545,524	510,784	59,107	11.6	26	22	28	25
Denver, CO	600,158	557,917	554,636	467,610	87,026	18.6	28	25	25	26
Louisville-Jefferson County, KY[b]	597,337	556,429	256,231	269,063	12,832	−4.8	58	67	26	27
Milwaukee, WI	594,833	578,887	596,974	628,088	−31,114	−5.0	17	19	22	28
Portland, OR	583,776	533,427	529,121	437,319	91,802	21.0	27	28	30	29
Las Vegas, NV	583,756	545,147	478,434	258,295	220,139	85.2	63	32	29	30
Oklahoma City, OK	579,999	531,324	506,132	444,719	61,413	13.8	30	29	31	31
Albuquerque, NM	545,852	494,236	448,607	384,736	63,871	16.6	40	35	33	32

	4/1/2010 Census Population	7/1/2005 Population Estimate	4/1/2000 Census Population	4/1/1990 Census Population	Numeric Population Change 1990–2000	Percentage Population Change 1990–2000	Size Rank 1990	Size Rank 2000	Size Rank 2005	Size Rank 2010
Tucson, AZ	520,116	515,526	486,699	405,390	81,309	20.1	34	30	32	33
Fresno, CA	494,665	461,116	427,652	354,202	73,450	20.7	48	37	36	34
Sacramento, CA	466,488	456,441	407,018	369,365	37,653	10.2	37	40	37	35
Long Beach, CA	462,257	474,014	461,522	429,433	32,089	7.5	32	34	34	36
Kansas City, MO	459,787	444,965	441,545	435,146	6,399	1.5	31	36	40	37
Mesa, AZ	439,041	442,780	396,375	288,091	108,284	37.6	53	42	41	38
Virginia Beach, VA	437,994	438,415	425,257	393,069	32,188	8.2	39	38	42	39
Atlanta, GA	420,003	470,688	416,474	394,017	22,457	5.7	38	39	35	40
Colorado Springs, CO	416,427	369,815	360,890	281,140	79,750	28.4	54	48	49	41
Omaha, NE	408,958	414,521	390,007	335,795	54,212	16.1	47	44	43	42
Raleigh, NC	403,892	–	–	–	–	–	–	–	–	43
Miami, FL	399,457	386,417	362,470	358,548	3,922	1.1	46	47	45	44
Cleveland, OH	396,815	452,208	478,403	505,616	–27,213	–5.4	23	33	39	45
Tulsa, OK	391,906	382,457	393,049	367,302	25,747	7.0	44	43	46	46
Oakland, CA	390,724	395,274	399,484	372,242	27,242	7.3	35	41	44	47
Minneapolis, MN	382,578	372,811	382,618	368,383	14,235	3.9	43	45	48	48
Wichita, KS	382,368	353,823	344,284	–	–	–	–	50	51	49
Arlington, TX	365,438	362,805	332,969	261,721	71,248	27.2	62	54	50	50

Source: Top 50 Cities in the U.S. by Population and Rank (n.d.).

a. Nashville–Davidson city is consolidated with Davidson County.

b. Louisville and Jefferson County merged in Jan. 2003. Figures prior to 2003 are for Louisville city only.

185

7 Informative/ Explanatory Writing Lessons

In this chapter, we present three lessons (one social studies, one science, one technical subject) that we believe are particularly effective for addressing the CCSS for Writing. These lessons involve many reading and writing skills and thus address the majority of the CCSS; however, we have designated the lessons according to the text types and purposes of their writing requirements.

The lessons in this chapter help students formulate and enhance their informative/explanatory writing skills:

- Technical Subject: Grades 6–8, "Math in Everyday Life"
- Science: Grades 9–10, "Earth Day"
- History/Social Studies: Grades 11–12, "Montgomery Bus Boycott"

For the math lesson, students must write a shopping instruction manual that helps the shoppers in their lives calculate the best bargain for their dollar. To do this, students must present a clear explanation of proportions, percent, and unit rate.

In the science lesson, students develop a newspaper article about the history of Earth Day based on class instruction and a Directed Reading and Thinking Activity (DRTA).

For the Civil Rights Movement lesson, students also write a newspaper article, but in this case, their sources include not only class instruction and readings but a documentary as well.

In all three lessons, students learn to write for a specific task, purpose, and audience in an appropriate format. They write to explain information that they have gathered and report it in a coherent way. They are given opportunities to revisit and make improvements to their writing.

As you read through these lessons and as you develop your own lessons, we encourage you to focus on how you can best guide your students to meet the CCSS for Writing.

WRITING ANCHOR STANDARDS REFLECTIVE QUESTIONS

How does the lesson require students to do one or more of the following?

1. Write arguments to support claims using valid reasoning and relevant and sufficient evidence

2. Write informative/explanatory texts to examine and convey complex ideas and information clearly and accurately

3. Write narratives to develop real or imagined experiences or events using effective technique, well-chosen details, and well-structured event sequences

4. Produce clear and coherent writing appropriate to task, purpose, and audience

5. Develop and strengthen writing as needed by planning, revising, editing, rewriting, or trying a new approach

6. Use technology, including the Internet, to produce and publish writing and to collaborate with others

7. Conduct short as well as more sustained research projects based on focused questions

8. Gather relevant information from multiple print and digital sources, assess the sources, and synthesize the information without plagiarizing

9. Draw evidence from literary or informational texts to support analysis, reflection, and research

10. Write routinely over extended time frames and shorter time frames for a range of tasks, purposes, and audiences

LESSON DESIGN REFLECTIVE QUESTIONS

1. How does the lesson require close and multiple readings of grade-level complex text?

2. How does my questioning require students to use the text as support for their interpretations/arguments?

3. How does the lesson incorporate varied thinking skills (e.g., read, summarize, analyze, interpret)? (Bloom)

4. How does the lesson include the three components of Backward Design: (a) desired results, (b) acceptable evidence, and (c) learning experiences?

5. How do I differentiate instruction, materials, and expectations for this particular lesson so that all students can be successful?

6. How does the lesson provide opportunities for technology/media use?

7. How does the lesson include research-based instructional strategies to promote effective teaching?

8. How does the lesson present opportunities for interdisciplinary connections?

9. How does the lesson provide opportunities for students with varied Multiple Intelligences to be successful? (Gardner)

10. How do I present the lesson in a way that encourages students to see the value of what they are learning (e.g., service learning, college- and career-readiness skills)? (Dewey)

Math in Everyday Life
Technical Subject—Math
(Grades 6–8; Informative/Explanatory)
Katherine O'Sullivan—Bay Shore Middle School, Bay Shore, NY

LESSON PLAN TEMPLATE

TOPIC:

Math in Everyday Life (Grades 6–8)

CCSS STRAND:

Writing

TEXT TYPES AND PURPOSES:

Informative/Explanatory

TIMING:

5 class periods

BACKWARD DESIGN COMPONENTS:

DESIRED RESULTS/CCSS ADDRESSED:

Enduring Understandings

- Through the close examination of several texts and through the application of math to common tasks, students will understand the importance of math in everyday life and how to explain their understanding to others in writing [R.1, R.10, W.2, W.4].

Knowledge and Skills

- Students will read an article for information and central ideas and compare that information with their textbook and teacher instruction on proportions, percent, and unit price [R.1, R.2, R.4, R.6, R.8, R.9].

- Students will apply an understanding of proportions, percent, and unit rate by writing an explanatory instruction manual for finding the best price [W.2, W.4, W.5, W.7, W.9].

ACCEPTABLE EVIDENCE:

- Answers to guiding questions for "Kindle vs. Nook vs. iPad: Which e-book reader should you buy?"

- Completed math word problems related to grocery prices based on proportions, percent, and unit rate

- Completed Shopping Instruction Manual that includes an explanation of unit pricing and a discussion of the importance of understanding the concept, real-world examples of finding the best price, and a conclusion

LEARNING EXPERIENCES AND INSTRUCTION:

5 class periods (lessons do not need to be conducted on consecutive days)

- Days 1–2—Read the article and answer response questions.

- Day 3—Lesson on proportions, percent, and unit rate.

- Day 4—Apply understanding of proportions, percent, and unit rate to grocery store pricing.

- Day 5—Write shopping instructional manual based on proportions, percent, and unit rate.

STRATEGIES:

- Guidance and Monitoring

- Modeling

- Discussion

- Writing Process

MATERIALS NEEDED:

- Articles:

  o Falcone, J. (2012, August 7). Kindle vs. Nook vs. iPad: Which e-book reader should you buy? Retrieved from http://news.cnet.com/

8301-17938_105-20009738-1/kindle
-vs-nook-vs-ipad-which-e-book
-reader-should-you-buy/

- Sohn, E. (2003, October 7). It's a math world for animals. Science News for Kids. Retrieved from http://www.sciencenewsforkids.org/2003/10/its-a-math-world-for-animals-2

- Computer access to grocery store websites or printed versions of grocery store circulars

- Paper and pens

- Handouts (reproducible forms for each handout appear at the end of this section)

SUPPLEMENTAL RESOURCES:

- Ratios, proportions, and percents. (n.d.). Pete's PowerPoint Station. Retrieved from http://math.pppst.com/ratio-proportion-percent.html

- Ratio, proportion, unit rate, percent: 7 questions (2009, September 9.) Retrieved from http://en.allexperts.com/q/Algebra-2061/2009/9/Ratio-proportion-unit-rate.htm

- Ratios, proportions, and percents: Unit rate and equivalent rates. (n.d.). Retrieved from http://www.ixl.com/math/grade-6/unit-rates-and-equivalent-rates

- Ratios and percent. (n.d.). Retrieved from http://www.shmoop.com/ratios-percentages/unit-rate.html

TECHNOLOGY/MEDIA OPPORTUNITIES:

- Student can explore various websites to consider pricing for other items of interest.

- Students may post their instruction manual online.

SERVICE LEARNING LINKS:

- Students share their shopping manuals with the local soup kitchen or food pantry to encourage them to get the most for their dollar when shopping.

- Students use their understanding of proportions, percent, and unit rate to get the best prices for food at their next school event.

VARIATIONS:

- Compare the pricing of food at fast-food restaurants.

- Apply the lesson to lumber and costs for housing renovations.

MATH IN EVERYDAY LIFE

Technical Subject—Math

(Grades 6–8; Informative/Explanatory)

Katherine O'Sullivan—Bay Shore Middle School, Bay Shore, NY

In my math classes, students frequently ask, "Why do I have to learn this?" Students don't inherently understand that math is important in their daily lives or realize that we constantly use math to make decisions and solve problems. By incorporating articles related to math into my curriculum, I show my students how people use the skills that I am teaching in my class.

Materials Needed

- Articles:

    o Falcone, J. (2012, August 7). Kindle vs. Nook vs. iPad: Which e-book reader should you buy? Consumer Reports.org. Retrieved from http://news.cnet.com/8301-17938_105-20009738-1/kindle-vs-nook-vs-ipad-which-e-book-reader-should-you-buy/

    o Sohn, E. (2003, October 7). It's a math world for animals. Science News for Kids. Retrieved from http://www.sciencenewsforkids.org/2003/10/its-a-math-world-for-animals-2

- Computer access to grocery store websites or printed versions of grocery store circulars
- Paper and pens
- Handouts (reproducible forms for each handout appear at the end of this section)

Timing

5 class periods (lessons do not need to be conducted on consecutive days)

Days 1–2—Read the article and answer guiding questions.

Day 3—Lesson on proportions, percent, and unit rate.

Day 4—Apply understanding of proportions, percent, and unit rate to grocery store pricing.

Day 5—Write shopping instructional manual based on proportions, percent, and unit rate.

Days 1–2

When I begin teaching proportions, percent, and unit rate, I share an article titled "Kindle vs. Nook vs. iPad: Which e-book reader should you buy?" This article describes the general information that consumers should consider when deciding on an e-book reader. It is an excellent introduction to proportions, percent, and unit rate.

TECH CONNECTION: Use an LCD projector to show the article to the class while reading aloud.

THEORY LINK (Bloom): Students *apply* their understanding of the reading to answer the math questions.

We read the article together, and students answer comprehension and discussion questions (**Handout 1**). Some of these questions require computation. Thus, they help students develop the skills they need to answer word problems [R.1, R.2, R.4, R.8, R.10].

Day 3

Based on the previous day's article, I teach students a lesson on proportions, percent, and unit rate. We read through word problems, determine what is being compared, and set up proportions (e.g., $\frac{3}{5} = \frac{x}{75}$). Students practice setting up and solving these equations.

If time allows, I share an excerpt from an additional article titled "It's a Math World for Animals" by Emily Sohn (http://www.sciencenewsforkids .org/2003/10/its-a-math-world-for-animals-2/). At the end of the article, Sohn describes how dogs make judgments regarding which plate of food to choose based on the amount of food on the plate. A pattern developed in the experiment implies that dogs are able to assess proportions.

THEORY LINK (Gardner): Appeals to Logical-Mathematical, Visual-Spatial, and Naturalist Intelligences.

Day 4

Now it is time for students to create their own examples of proportions. By using circulars from the local grocery stores or by accessing similar advertisements via the Internet, students go shopping! They compare prices of related items and determine which unit rate is most cost-efficient [R.1, R.2, R.4, R.6, R.9]. For example, students can compare the cost of a king-sized chocolate bar with a bag of fun-sized chocolate bars. Students have to find the unit rate for each item to determine which is the better buy. In addition, students may compare the way that stores structure their sales. For example, one store may have a sale on containers of strawberries that involves an offer of "buy one get one free," while another may offer two containers for $5. Which is the better buy? At the end of the period, students submit four examples of price evaluation based on proportions (**Handout 2**).

For homework, students compare pricing on items on the Kate's Kitchen menu (**Handout 3**).

DIFFERENTIATION TIP: The number of examples required may be adapted based on students' skill level.

CULTURAL/LINGUISTIC HIGHLIGHT: Cooperative-learning opportunities can develop students' language skills and promote cross-cultural understanding.

Day 5

To show that they understand how to use proportions and unit pricing to evaluate cost-effectiveness, students write a shopping instruction manual for the person in their family who does the shopping (**Handout 4**).

THEORY LINK (Dewey): Purposeful work—students' work will not only earn a grade; it will help the shopper.

The requirements for the instruction manual include an introduction, a "How To" component, an attention-grabbing example, and a summary. In the introduction, students must explain to the reader how an understanding of unit pricing relates to finding the best price [W.2, W.4]. For the next component ("How To"), students explain how to set up and solve proportions and how to analyze said proportions based on either the size or weight of the desired item. To further clarify the explanation, students must include an attention-grabbing example [W.7, W.9]. The final component is the conclusion in which students sum up their ideas and thank the reader.

Students share their instruction manuals with an adult in the building (teacher, administrator, teacher's aide) to ensure that their presentation is clear [W.5]. The adult-reviewer completes a brief response (**Handout 5**) that is part of the rubric for this assignment (**Handout 6**).

In addition, I encourage the students to go shopping with the person who usually shops for them and to share a story of how they helped that shopper make good decisions based on proportions and unit pricing.

The creation of an instruction manual works very well as a writing-based summative evaluation of student learning because when students can explain their steps to another individual, it shows me that they have mastered the content. When students actually shop with the person who usually does the shopping for them, it further increases their understanding of the application of math skills to everyday life and it deepens their appreciation for the person who helps care for them.

THEORY LINK (Gardner): Appeals to Bodily-Kinesthetic, Interpersonal, and Logical-Mathematical Intelligences.

HANDOUT 1

ARTICLE READING QUESTIONS

"Kindle vs. Nook vs. iPad: Which e-book reader should you buy?"

John P. Falcone

1. If you are strictly interested in reading books and newspapers, which type of device is best for you? Cite evidence from the text to support your answer.

2. Why is it important to consider the weight of the device in your decision-making process?

3. What are the benefits of getting a device with e-ink?

4. Why would a user store information in "the cloud"?

5. According to the article, how can you "borrow" books for free on your device?

6. Why don't the e-book readers all offer the same types of service?

7. If the Apple I-Pad 2 weighs approximately 1.34 lbs and is 10 inches in length × 0.3 inches in depth × 1.3 inches wide, what is the weight per cubic inch?

8. If T-Mobile offers 3G service for $50 per month, how much would that cost per day for the month of January?

9. Using evidence from the text, construct an argument that you would use to convince your parent/guardian to get you an e-reader or a tablet. If you are convincing enough, it might pay off for you. ☺

Source: http://news.cnet.com/8301-17938_105-20009738-1/kindle-vs-nook-vs-ipad-which-e-book-reader-should-you-buy/

HANDOUT 2

GROCERIES PRICE EVALUATION

Name _____

Date _____

Directions: Choose four items that you wish to purchase from the circular. Find the unit rate of the items. Find the same four items from an additional circular. Find the unit rate of the newly found items. Compare the unit rates of each to determine which store offers the "better buy" for each item.

1. Store:_____   Store:_____

Item:_____   Item:_____

Cost:_____   Cost:_____

Work Space: Work Space:

Which store offers the better buy?_____

2. Store:_____   Store:_____

Item:_____   Item:_____

Cost:_____   Cost:_____

Work Space: Work Space:

Which store offers the better buy?_____

3. Store:_____   Store:_____

Item:_____   Item:_____

Cost:_____   Cost:_____

Work Space: Work Space:

Which store offers the better buy?_____

4. Store:_____   Store:_____

Item:_____   Item:_____

Cost:_____   Cost:_____

Work Space: Work Space:

Which store offers the better buy?_____

Based on all of the information computed above, which store offers the better buy?

HANDOUT 3

KATE'S KITCHEN PRICE EVALUATION

Name _____

Date _____

Directions: Choose three items from Kate's Kitchen menu that come in various sizes (French fries, onion rings, soda, etc.). Find the unit price for each item and choose which would be the better buy.

Menu Item	Size	Price
Large Soda	24 oz	$2.29
Medium Soda	16 oz	$1.79
Small Soda	8 oz	$1.29
Large French Fries	16 oz	$1.65
Small French Fries	10 oz	$0.99
Large Onion Rings	16 oz	$1.85
Small Onion Rings	10 oz	$1.15
Large Burger	½ lb beef	$2.89
Small Burger	¼ lb beef	$1.65
Large Bag Cookies	8 cookies	$3.29
Individual Cookies	2 cookies	$1.00

1. Menu Item:_____   Menu Item:_____

   Better Buy: _____

2. Menu Item: _____   Menu Item:_____

   Better Buy: _____

3. Menu Item: _____   Menu Item:_____

   Better Buy: _____

4. Menu Item:_____   Menu Item:_____

   Better Buy: _____

HANDOUT 4

SHOPPING INSTRUCTION MANUAL

Overview:

Now that you have a strong understanding of proportions and unit pricing, develop an instruction manual for the shopper in your life. Be sure to be informative and to appeal to the shopper's interests and values. Also, make your work visually attractive.

Manual Requirements:

The instruction manual contains the following segments:

1. **Introduction/Overview**—explain to the reader why it is important to understand unit pricing in order to be a highly effective shopper.

2. **How To**—explanation of how to compare like items using proportions and unit pricing. This should include how to set up proportions, how to solve the proportions, and how to compare the results (bigger is not always better!). When it comes to cost, you want the lower number. When it comes to weight, you want the higher number.

3. **An Attention-Grabbing Example**—from the grocery store or Kate's Kitchen menu.

4. **Conclusion**—sum up what you have taught and thank your personal shopper.

Process Requirements:

1. Refer to our unit notes in your manual.

2. Share with an adult in the school for feedback.

HANDOUT 5

SHOPPING INSTRUCTION MANUAL

Feedback Form

Based on this manual, do you understand how to compare like items using proportion and unit pricing?   Yes   No (circle one)

What is the most effective component of this manual?

What (if anything) needs clarification?

Additional Comments:

HANDOUT 6

SHOPPING INSTRUCTION MANUAL

Rubric

_____ **Introduction/Overview (20 Points)**—explain to the reader why it is important to understand unit pricing in order to be a highly effective shopper.

_____ **How To (40 Points)**—explain how to compare like items using proportions and unit pricing. This should include how to set up proportions, how to solve the proportions, and how to compare the results (bigger is not always better!). When it comes to cost, you want the lower number. When it comes to weight, you want the higher number.

_____ **An Attention-Grabbing Example (20 Points)**—from the grocery store or Kate's Kitchen menu.

_____ **Conclusion (10 Points)**—sum up what you have taught and thank your personal shopper.

_____ **Adult Feedback Form (10 Points)**—completed by an adult in the school.

Revisions are made based on feedback (if needed).

Earth Day
Science—Earth Science
(Grades 9–10; Informative/Explanatory)
Silke Jacobs—Boardman Elementary School, Oceanside, NY

LESSON PLAN TEMPLATE

TOPIC:

Earth Day (Grades 9–10)

CCSS STRAND:

Writing

TEXT TYPES AND PURPOSES:

Informative/Explanatory

TIMING:

3 class periods

BACKWARD DESIGN COMPONENTS:

DESIRED RESULTS/CCSS ADDRESSED:

Enduring Understandings

- Through research that includes the examination of multiple print and digital sources, students will understand how accurately and concisely communicating complex ideas can inform others and spark and support social change [W.2, W.7, W.8, R.1, R.2, R.3, R.7].

Knowledge and Skills

- Through a close reading of the text, students will be able to analyze and summarize the content and structure of text and integrate the content in a graphic organizer [R.1, R.2, R.3, R.4, R.7].

- Students will be able to use various sources to convey information clearly and accurately by writing an explanatory text using technology [W.1, W.4].

- Students will be able to engage in the writing process in order to produce strong writing [W.5, W.6].

ACCEPTABLE EVIDENCE:

- The responses to the Directed Reading and Thinking Activity (DRTA), a tool that guides students' comprehension during reading

- Graphic organizer with topic sentences representing text summary and structure

- Written newspaper article on the topic of Earth Day

LEARNING EXPERIENCES AND INSTRUCTION:

- Day 1—Introduce the topic and complete DRTA.

- Days 2–3—Complete the Graphic Organizer representing text summary and structure and compose a newspaper article on the topic.

STRATEGIES:

- Guidance and Monitoring

- Cooperative Learning

- Writing Process

MATERIALS NEEDED:

- Paper and pens

- Markers

- Handouts (reproducible forms for each handout appear at the end of this section)

SUPPLEMENTAL RESOURCES:

- Excerpts from *Silent Spring* by Rachel Carson, an important nonfiction work that influenced environmental awareness in the second half of the 20th century.

- It began with Silent Spring and an oil spill. (2010, April 22). CBS News. Retrieved from http://www.cbc.ca /news/world/story/2010/04/21/earthday -thoughts.html
- Water Planet Challenge (www .waterplanetchallenge.org)—a website that offers resources to help improve the health of the environment

TECHNOLOGY/MEDIA OPPORTUNITIES:

- Students can use Inspiration software to develop their own graphic organizer.

SERVICE LEARNING LINKS:

- Students present the newspaper articles to the school on Earth Day.

- Students partner with environmental clubs at the college level or in the community to distribute their newsletter to the public at a college campus Earth Day event or at a community Earth Day event.
- Students research and develop an environmental movement by crafting their message based on Rachel Carson and any other powerful writer whom they encountered during their research.

VARIATIONS:

- Students calculate their ecological footprint at earthday.org and write a journal entry on at least two things they can change in their daily lives to have less impact on the environment.

EARTH DAY

Science—Earth Science

(Grades 9–10; Informative/Explanatory)

Silke Jacobs—Boardman Elementary School, Oceanside, NY

Over the past decades, Earth Day and the environmental movement have increasingly gained attention in the public eye. With issues such as global warming taking center stage in politics, it is important to familiarize our students with movements such as Earth Day. The story of Earth Day also shines light on important historical influences, as well as on advances in technology and research that have helped create the environmental movement as we experience it today. This topic is an excellent opportunity to expose students to real-world issues through a cross-curricular approach in our high school classrooms. The use of an elaborate, step-by-step editing process for this writing assignment helps the students understand, apply, and eventually internalize the different stages of explanatory writing.

Materials Needed

- Paper and pens
- Markers
- Handouts (reproducible forms for each handout appear at the end of this section)

Timing

3 class periods

Day 1—Introduce the topic and complete Directed Reading and Thinking Activity.

Days 2–3—Complete a graphic organizer representing text summary and structure, and compose a newspaper article on the topic.

Day 1

During the first 15 minutes of Day 1, I introduce students to the topic of environmentalism. In a *Find Someone Who* activity (**Handout 1**), students walk around the room and find classmates who affirmatively answer specific questions about their behavior. Following this activity, we discuss some of the statements as a class, and students decide whether certain activities are good or bad for the environment.

After this introductory activity, the class completes a DRTA activity with a text on the origin and

THEORY LINK (Gardner): Appeals to Bodily-Kinesthetic and Naturalist Intelligences.

CULTURAL/LINGUISTIC HIGHLIGHT: The "Find Someone Who" activity develops students' oral skills and establishes peer relations.

history of Earth Day (**Handout 2**). I set the tone by reading the first paragraph aloud, after which students have several minutes to individually answer questions based on the reading and come up with a question of their own based on the paragraph.

We discuss the answers to the teacher-constructed questions, and students share the questions that they constructed. The rest of the reading is done in a similar manner, with the students alternately reading out loud, reading individually, or working in groups on the remaining paragraphs [R.1, R.4, R.7].

Days 2–3

Having completed the Earth Day reading the day before, students are ready to analyze and summarize the components of the text. Students work in groups to paraphrase each paragraph into one sentence. Then, students write their summary sentences on a group poster, which they present to the class. Students then organize the sentences in the Graphic Organizer (**Handout 3**) [R.2, R.3].

When the graphic organizer templates are complete, I assign different roles to the group members. Each group has the following roles:

- Scribe
- Reader
- Leading presenter
- Timekeeper

Students refer to the contents of the graphic organizer and additional resources on Earth Day, such as the CBC News article (http://www.cbc.ca/news/world/story/2010/04/21/earthday-thoughts.html), to draft a newspaper article on the history of Earth Day. As they write, they use the Newspaper Article Assignment/Draft Organizer (**Handout 4**) and the Newspaper Article Template (**Handout 5**) [W.1, W.4, W.7, W.8]. According to the rubric (**Handout 7**), the article must contain two relevant illustrations with accompanying captions for all required elements of the newspaper article.

After they have each completed their first draft, students engage in the editing process. Students use a rubric check (**Handout 6**) to check whether or not all necessary elements are present and identify the aspects of their writing that need additional attention. They revise their drafts based on teacher and peer feedback and compose their final version in a Microsoft Office Publisher template [W.2, W.4, W.5, W.6]. This kind of work, when done over time, helps young writers become independent.

THEORY LINK (Gardner): Appeals to Verbal-Linguistic Intelligence.

CULTURAL/LINGUISTIC HIGHLIGHT: DRTA provides linguistic support and scaffolds comprehension.

CULTURAL/LINGUISTIC HIGHLIGHT: Graphic organizers help highlight key information and scaffold learning.

CULTURAL/LINGUISTIC HIGHLIGHT: Cooperative learning opportunities can develop language skills and promote cross-cultural understanding.

CULTURAL/LINGUISTIC HIGHLIGHT: Templates help scaffold learning.

TECH CONNECTION: Students research online sources to use in their articles.

THEORY LINK (Bloom): Students *comprehend*, *analyze*, and *evaluate* texts and *synthesize* the information in a newspaper article.

HANDOUT 1

FIND SOMEONE WHO . . .

Directions: Walk the classroom and write down the names of classmates who . . .

1. Care deeply about the environment: _____

2. Know what Earth Day is: _____

3. Use pesticides at home: _____

4. Think that war is a more important issue than the environment: _____

   _____

5. Want to climb Mount Everest: _____

6. Recycle regularly at home: _____

7. Have thrown garbage out of a car window: _____

8. Know someone who owns a hybrid vehicle: _____

HANDOUT 2

EARTH DAY READING—DRTA

On April 22, 1970, approximately 20 million people took to the streets in a political movement called "Earth Day." This grassroots demonstration was the idea of a man who is considered the Father of Earth Day, Senator Gaylord Nelson. Nelson wanted to create a protest similar to the antiwar protests of the 1960s but in relation to environmental concerns. The senator and his fellow organizers of Earth Day chose a date in April because this is a time when schools and colleges are in session, and they really wanted students to be involved in Earth Day. Considering the number of people involved across the nation (many of them students), they made an excellent choice.

Earth Day had a strong impact on politicians. Before 1970, environmentalism was not a major concern in Washington, D.C. After Earth Day, the U.S. Environmental Protection Agency (EPA) was established along with the Clean Air Act, Clean

1. **What do you think this reading is going to be about?**

2. **Who is known as the father of Earth Day?**

3. **The Earth Day demonstration was modeled after protests against what major war?**

4. **Why was Earth Day held in April?**

5. **How did the political climate of that time influence the Earth Day movement?**

6. **My question:**
   _____
   _____

Michigan Bald Eagle Sightings Indicate Remarkable Comeback for America's Favorite Bird of Prey

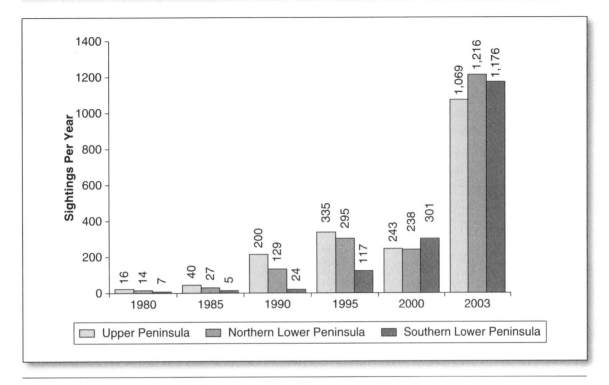

Source: Michigan Department of Natural Resources

Water Act, and Endangered Species Act. In addition, the United States and Canada agreed to restore the Great Lakes. Also, the car industry took on new EPA requirements by building cars with catalytic converters that allowed the cars to run on unleaded gasoline. Another major government decision was the banning of DDT, a pesticide that is harmful to the environment. Many believe that because of this ban, the bald eagle was saved from extinction in the United States.

Unfortunately, the effect of the first Earth Day was not long lasting. During the 1970s people were more concerned about issues related to the Vietnam War and civil rights. The media gave more attention to these issues than to environmental issues. Earth Day wasn't officially held again until 1980. Approximately 3 million people took part in the 10th anniversary of the first Earth Day. Although that was impressive, it took another 10 years for Earth Day to become an annual event extending across the globe. In 1990, approximately 200 million people worldwide took part in Earth Day.

7. **Name two things that were accomplished in the United States because of the first Earth Day.**

8. **How can the Endangered Species Act benefit the environment?**

9. **Look at the figure above and reread the last sentence of the paragraph. How can environmental policy and legislation influence the survival of a species?**

10. **My question:**
   _____
   _____

11. **When did Earth Day become recognized as a major event around the world?**

The worldwide Earth Day in 1990 inspired several events. An international team of mountain climbers cleaned up two tons of garbage left by previous climbers on Mount Everest. Two years later, the UN held an Earth Summit in Rio de Janeiro where the environment was considered the most important topic on the world agenda. Over 100 leaders discussed climate change and made plans for sustainable development in the 21st century.

With the expanded popularity of Earth Day comes the risk of this movement losing the power of its meaning. It is estimated that over 1 billion people have taken part in Earth Day. Do all participants understand the original purpose of this day, or has it just become a trend? In 1990, an Earth Day concert in Central Park created so much waste that eco-conscious individuals were left to wonder how the concert could have been attended by people who understood the meaning behind the event. It is important to remember the vision that Senator Nelson had in 1970 when we celebrate Earth Day. This is a day dedicated to inspiring political change to protect our planet.

12. **How can you explain the fallback of Earth Day's popularity in the 1970s?**

13. **Why is it important that nations from all over the world work together on the environmental issue?**

14. **My question:**

     _____

     _____

15. **What, besides good intentions, do we need to make progress?**

16. **What does the author mean when he calls Earth Day a "trend"?**

REFERENCES

Earth day and EPA history. (n.d.). Environmental Protection Agency. Retrieved from http://www.epa.gov/earthday/history.htm

Earth Day: The history of a movement. (n.d.). Earth Day Network. Retrieved from http://www.earthday.org/earth-day-history-movement

Nelson, G. (n.d.). How the first earth day came about. Retrieved from http://earthday.envirolink.org/history.html

HANDOUT 3

PRE-PLANNER FOR GRAPHIC ORGANIZER

Directions: Reread the text and summarize each paragraph in one sentence. Your summary sentence should contain the most important information in the paragraph. Then, write your summary in the graphic organizer on the following page.

Paragraph 1:

_____

Paragraph 2:

_____

Paragraph 3:

_____

Paragraph 4:

_____

GRAPHIC ORGANIZER

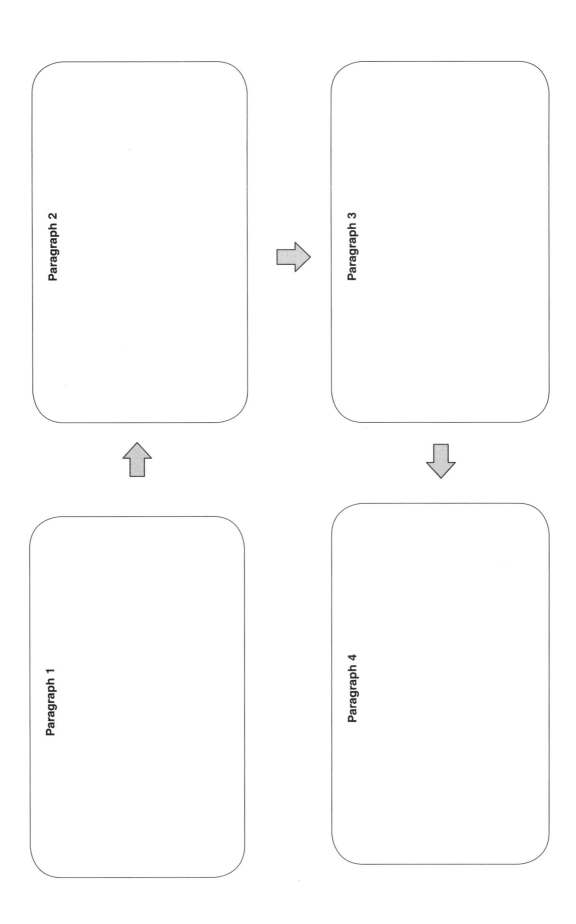

Paragraph 1

Paragraph 2

Paragraph 3

Paragraph 4

HANDOUT 4

NEWSPAPER ARTICLE ASSIGNMENT

Write a newspaper article about Earth Day and its history based on what you have learned. You can use outside sources.

Review the parts of a newspaper article below to help you accomplish this task. Before you start writing, organize your thoughts on the draft page.

In a newspaper article, the opening, or first paragraph contains most of the important information. This information includes *who, what, when, where, why,* and *how* (5Ws + 1H). Newspaper writers put the most important information at the beginning because many people do not read an entire newspaper article.

Most newspaper articles contain five parts:

Headline:	This is a short, attention-getting statement about the event. It is the title of the article.
Byline:	This tells who wrote the story.
First paragraph:	This is also called the *lead paragraph.* It contains all the who, what, when, where, why, and how aspects of the article. The writer finds the answers to these questions and writes them into the opening sentences of the article.
Second paragraph:	After the lead paragraph has been written, the writer decides what other facts or details the reader might want to know. As a writer, you try to make sure that the article contains enough information to answer any additional questions a reader might have.

Newspaper Article Draft

Headline:

Byline:

Lead paragraph: Who:

                                         What:

                                         When:

                                         Where:

                                         Why:

                                         How:

Second paragraph: Detail 1:

                                         Detail 2:

                                         Detail 3:

HANDOUT 5

NEWSPAPER ARTICLE TEMPLATE

Newspaper Title	Today's Date
Byline	
Advertisement	
Headline	

Paragraph 1

Illustration 2

Illustration 1

Paragraph 2

HANDOUT 6

PEER-EDITING WORKSHEET

Category	Check	Suggestions or Comments
Does the newspaper article have a headline?		
Does the lead paragraph contain the main facts of the article (the 5 *Ws* + *How*)?		
Does the second paragraph contain supporting details?		
Does the article contain two relevant illustrations with accompanying captions?		
Is the language of the article clear?		
Does the writer use appropriate punctuation?		

HANDOUT 7

EARTH DAY NEWSPAPER ARTICLE RUBRIC

CATEGORY	3 Excellent	2 Satisfactory	1 Needs Improvement
Headline	My title (called the headline) is relevant, catchy, and set in large type.	My title (called the headline) is somewhat relevant and set in large type.	My title (called the headline) is not relevant, not set in large type, and/or missing.
Pictures	I have used at least two pictures with captions.	I have two pictures, but only one contains a caption.	I have only one picture containing a caption or missing a caption.
Lead Paragraph	The lead paragraph of my newspaper article (the first paragraph) summarizes the main facts of the article and is concise and clear.	The lead paragraph of my newspaper article (the first paragraph) summarizes some of the main facts of the article.	The lead paragraph of my newspaper article does not contain the main facts of the article.
Second Paragraph	The remainder of my article contains a supporting paragraph that goes into more detail about the topic, including quotes and interesting facts.	The remainder of my article contains a supporting paragraph that goes into more detail about the topic, but I have not included quotes and only a few interesting facts.	The remainder of my article contains a supporting paragraph but with details that do not clearly relate to the topic. It does not include quotes and interesting facts.
Language	I have used clear and simple language. My writing is easy to follow.	I have used some clear and simple language. The organization of my writing is not always logical.	I need to work on keeping my language clear and simple. My writing is hard to follow.
Grammar	My writing has limited spelling and grammar errors. I follow punctuation rules and conventions.	My writing contains a number of spelling, grammar, and punctuation errors.	The spelling, grammar, and punctuation errors in my writing inhibit the reader's comprehension.

Montgomery Bus Boycott

History/Social Studies—U.S. History

(Grades 11–12; Informative/Explanatory)

Peggy Hyland—Cardinal Spellman High School, Bronx, NY

LESSON PLAN TEMPLATE

TOPIC:

Montgomery Bus Boycott (Grades 11–12)

CCSS STRAND:

Writing

TEXT TYPES AND PURPOSES:

Informative/Explanatory

TIMING:

4 class periods

BACKWARD DESIGN COMPONENTS:

DESIRED RESULTS/CCSS ADDRESSED:

Enduring Understandings

- Students will understand the importance of the fundamentals of journalistic principles—objectivity and the accurate representation of information and how journalism informs people about important events, including the context, the people involved, the actions of those involved, and the reasoning behind set actions [W.2, W.4, W.5, W.6, W.8].

Knowledge and Skills

- Students will be able to research and gather information from multiple sources, assess the relevance and accuracy of each, and integrate the information [R.7, R.9, W.8].

- Students will be able to convey information clearly and accurately by writing an explanatory text using technology [W.2, W.4].

- Students will be able to engage in the writing process to produce strong writing [W.4, W.5, W.6].

ACCEPTABLE EVIDENCE:

- Completed Viewing Guide based on the PBS documentary, *Eyes on the Prize*

- Final draft of a newspaper article that describes the events surrounding the Montgomery Bus Boycott

LEARNING EXPERIENCES AND INSTRUCTION:

- Day 1—Fill out the Anticipation Guide; view segment from the PBS documentary, *Eyes on the Prize*; take notes using the Viewing Guide; and read and analyze a newspaper article.

- Day 2—Write a first draft of a newspaper article and act as editor on a fellow classmate's work. Check for spelling and grammar errors and any signs of bias.

- Day 3—Make any necessary changes; publish article.

- Day 4—Share articles and review the Anticipation Guide.

STRATEGIES:

- Discussion

- Writing Process

MATERIALS NEEDED:

- Hampton, H. (Producer), & Vecchione, J. (Director). (1987). *Eyes on the prize*. [DVD]. United States: Blackside.

- A current newspaper article

- Microsoft Publishing

- Paper and pens

- Handouts (reproducible forms for each handout appear at the end of this section)

SUPPLEMENTAL RESOURCES:

- The website, Beforetheboycott.com (the National Civil Rights Museum), with an interactive e-learning activity about the Montgomery Bus Boycott.

- Website that accompanies the *Eyes on the Prize* documentary (http://www.pbs.org/wgbh/amex/eyesontheprize). It includes additional video clips and primary sources.

TECHNOLOGY/MEDIA OPPORTUNITIES:

- See Supplemental Resources.

- Students look up visuals on the Internet to accompany their newspaper articles.

SERVICE LEARNING LINKS:

- Students submit their work to a local newspaper with an additional written component comparing the historical importance of these acts of civil disobedience to more modern examples such as the Occupy Wall Street Movement.

VARIATIONS:

- Students write two separate editorials about the boycott: one written from the viewpoint of an African American in 1950s Alabama and the other from the viewpoint of a White segregationist in the 1950s.

- Students write a speech as Rosa Parks addressing the people of Alabama explaining why she felt compelled to take the actions that she did.

MONTGOMERY BUS BOYCOTT

History/Social Studies—U.S. History

(Grades 11–12; Informative/Explanatory)

Peggy Hyland—Cardinal Spellman High School, Bronx, NY

One of the most pivotal of the events during the African American struggle for civil rights is the Montgomery Bus Boycott of 1955–56. In the following lesson, this important event in our country's history serves as the basis for a newspaper article-writing assignment completed by the students.

In the modern age, many students are visually driven. The PBS documentary *Eyes on the Prize* (1987), a comprehensive 14-hour examination of the African American struggle for civil rights throughout the 1950s and 1960s, allows students to "witness" these events. The series contains hours of news footage of historical events from this era, as well as interviews with many of the major participants in these events. The various elements of the documentary are quite powerful, depicting the depths of racial hatred and violence that existed in the segregated South during this time. As students watch portions of the documentary, they are able to see these events unfold before their eyes, which has a far greater impact than merely reading about these same incidents.

Materials Needed

- Hampton, H. (Producer), & Vecchione, J. (Director). (1987). *Eyes on the prize.* [DVD]. United States: Blackside.
- A current newspaper article
- Microsoft Publishing
- Paper and pens
- Handouts (reproducible forms for each handout appear at the end of this section)

Timing

4 class periods

Day 1—Fill out the Anticipation Guide; view segment from the PBS documentary, *Eyes on the Prize*; take notes using the Viewing Guide; and read and analyze a newspaper article.

Day 2—Write a first draft of a newspaper article and act as editor on a fellow classmate's work. Check for spelling and grammar errors and any signs of bias.

Day 3—Make any necessary changes; publish article.

Day 4—Share articles and review the Anticipation Guide.

CULTURAL/LINGUISTIC HIGHLIGHT: The Anticipation Guide activates schema as students anticipate the ideas in a content selection and make connections to what they already know.

THEORY LINK (Gardner): Appeals to Visual-Spatial Intelligence.

CULTURAL/LINGUISTIC HIGHLIGHT: Visual representations deepen comprehension of content and language.

THEORY LINK (Gardner): Appeals to Verbal-Linguistic Intelligence.

CULTURAL/LINGUISTIC HIGHLIGHT: The Viewing Guide helps highlight key information and scaffold learning.

DIFFERENTIATION TIP: Teachers can offer articles of varying reading difficulty for analysis to individual students or groups of students according to reading level.

TECH CONNECTION: This is an excellent opportunity to discuss how to conduct effective Internet research.

Day 1

Prior to starting the lesson, the students complete an Anticipation Guide (**Handout 1**) regarding the subject matter of the video and students' understanding of journalistic writing. Next, the students view a 15-minute clip from *Eyes on the Prize* (1985) depicting the Montgomery Bus Boycott.

I give them a Viewing Guide (**Handout 2**) to assist them with taking notes that will later serve as the basis for their newspaper article.

Students answer *who, when, where, what, why,* and *how* (the 5 *Ws* + 1 *H*) questions in which they record the names of all important people mentioned in the video (who), the dates that these events took place (when), the location of the events (where), the reasons that these events took place (why), and facts of what occurred (how).

Next, I provide students with a current newspaper article and ask them to identify the 5 *Ws* + 1 *H* from their reading.

The class then reviews the article's elements together. For homework, students conduct their own online research at Civil Rights Movement Veterans (http://www.crmvet.org) and Civil Rights Special Collection (http://www.teachersdomain.org/special/civil/) to find two additional sources in preparation to write an article as if they were a reporter during the time of the Montgomery Bus Boycott [W.8].

Day 2

Students prepare to write an article reporting the events of the Montgomery Bus Boycott [W.2, W.4]. They use their notes from the viewing guide and their additional research to begin writing a first draft of their articles using the template (**Handout 3**). Each article must include a brief, eye-catching headline; an appropriate date; an introductory paragraph that introduces the topic by providing the necessary historical background information; and the body of the article (2-3 paragraphs), which answers the 5 *Ws* + 1 *H*. Not only do students reference the information obtained through watching the film, but also they are responsible for gathering additional information from two print or online sources of their choice. I ask students to fact-check their article for historical accuracy and proofread for grammar and spelling. Students also include appropriate photographs, artwork, or both.

Each student swaps his or her article with another student, and they act as editors of each other's work. I give them a checklist to assist in editing (**Handout 4**).

As peers evaluate each other's work, I instruct them to search for any bias in their classmate's article. *Can the author's opinions be determined based on his or her writing?* Very often, student journalists will not be as able to identify bias in their own writing, but they can do so in each other's writing.

Day 3

When the students have made changes based on their peers' advice, they then publish their articles using Microsoft Publishing [W.5, W.6]. I give them a rubric (**Handout 5**) to guide their efforts.

Day 4

Students share their articles with the class. At the conclusion of the experience, the students revisit the Anticipation Guide (**Handout 1**) and reflect on their initial opinions in regard to the provided statements.

This lesson is multifaceted. First, it serves as an informative and motivating introduction to our unit on the Civil Rights Movement. The evocative imagery of the documentary draws the students into the topic on an emotional, human level. "Witnessing" these events makes students connect to the material in a more meaningful way, which inspires their journalistic writing. As students focus on the basics of the writing process to construct their articles, they also develop a greater understanding of the Montgomery Bus Boycott. Furthermore, they learn the fundamentals of journalistic principles, such as accurate representation of facts and objectivity.

THEORY LINK (Gardner): Appeals to Visual-Spatial Intelligence.

CULTURAL/LINGUISTIC HIGHLIGHT: Templates provide scaffolded linguistic support.

THEORY LINK (Gardner): Appeals to Interpersonal Intelligence.

THEORY LINK (Dewey): Purposeful learning— Students write for a real audience.

THEORY LINK (Bloom): Higher-level thinking is required to check for historical accuracy and bias in the article.

TECH CONNECTION: Students learn how to use Microsoft Publishing to publish their own articles.

HANDOUT 1

ANTICIPATION GUIDE—MONTGOMERY BUS BOYCOTT NEWSPAPER ARTICLE

Read each statement below and then use the first column to write whether you agree or disagree with each statement. After you have viewed the documentary *Eyes on the Prize* and composed your newspaper article, use the second column to reflect on whether or not your opinions have changed.

STATEMENT	AGREE OR DISAGREE	REFLECTION
1. The Montgomery Bus Boycott was intended to end racial segregation on city buses.		
2. African Americans were the only group to participate in the bus boycott.		
3. Martin Luther King Jr. was very influential to those participating in the boycott.		
4. Rosa Parks played the most important role in the bus boycott.		
5. The bus boycott was successful in meeting all of its goals.		
6. The Civil Rights Movement would never have happened if not for the Montgomery Bus Boycott.		
7. It is important to properly cite all sources and quotes when writing a newspaper article.		
8. Journalists should always give their opinions on the news events they are covering.		

HANDOUT 2

VIEWING GUIDE FOR "EYES ON THE PRIZE"

As you watch a video clip on the Montgomery Bus Boycott, use this sheet to take notes about how the events you are watching unfold. Remember that you are acting as a journalist and will be responsible for reporting on these events when you write your newspaper article. The more complete and accurate your notes are, the more successful you will be as a reporter.

<u>WHO</u>: *Record the names of all important people mentioned in the video.*

_____

_____

_____

<u>WHEN</u>: *Record the dates that these events took place.*

_____

<u>WHERE</u>: *Record the location (city and state) where these events took place.*

_____

<u>WHAT, WHY, and HOW</u>: *Record what events took place, why they happened, and how they happened.*

_____

_____

_____

_____

_____

_____

_____

_____

Hampton, H. (Producer), & Vecchione, J. (Director). (1987). *Eyes on the prize.* [DVD]. United States: Blackside.

HANDOUT 3

WORKSHEET FOR CREATING YOUR NEWSPAPER ARTICLE

1. *Write a headline.* Your headline should be brief, eye-catching, and give the reader an indication of your article's subject matter.

   _____

2. *Date your article appropriately.* Remember that you are writing this article as if you were a reporter during the time of the Montgomery Bus Boycott. What is an appropriate date for your article?

   _____

3. *Write an introductory paragraph.* Your article's first paragraph should introduce the topic by providing any necessary historical background information. Put the event that you will be describing in its context.

   _____

   _____

   _____

   _____

   _____

   _____

   _____

   _____

   _____

4. *Write the body of your article (2-3 paragraphs).* Use the film and two additional sources to write the paragraphs and answer the questions: Who? What? Where? When? Why? How?

   Remember to always write in the third person (*he, she, it,* or *they*).

   _____

   _____

   _____

   _____

   _____

   _____

   _____

   _____

   _____

   _____

   _____

5. *Proofread your article.* As well as checking for spelling and grammar errors, review your article for any signs of *bias* (a tendency to believe that some people, ideas, etc., are better than others, which usually results in treating some people unfairly). Remember that your article should be purely factual and contain no sign of your opinion of the people or events involved. If you used direct quotes, check to make sure the person(s) were quoted accurately.

6. *Add appropriate photographs and/or artwork.* Make sure that you caption photographs properly, listing the people and places pictured accurately. Also, be sure to properly credit the photographer responsible.

Congratulations! You are officially a journalist.

HANDOUT 4

EDITOR'S CHECKLIST

Use the following checklist to help you edit your classmate's newspaper article.

1. Is the headline appropriate in length and topic?   Yes or No

2. Does the headline capture the reader's attention?   Yes or No

3. Does the first paragraph introduce the topic of the article?   Yes or No

4. Does the article address the 5 Ws + 1 H of the event?   Yes or No

5. Does the article have proper spelling usage?   Yes or No

6. Does the article have proper grammar usage?   Yes or No

7. Does the article present the events in an unbiased way?   Yes or No

8. Is the article accompanied by appropriate photos and/or artwork?   Yes or No

9. Are all photographs and/or artwork captioned properly?   Yes or No

10. Is the article historically accurate?   Yes or No

If you circled "NO" for any of the above questions, use the space below to explain what edits are necessary.

_____

_____

_____

_____

_____

_____

_____

Rubric for Newspaper Article

Categories	4 Excellent	3 Good	2 Poor	1 Needs Major Revision
Headline	The headline is appropriate in length and topic. It catches the reader's attention.	The headline is either too long or short but is appropriate and catches the reader's attention.	The headline does not appropriately address the topic OR does not catch the reader's attention.	The headline is not appropriate in length or topic and does not catch the reader's attention.
Introductory Paragraph	The first paragraph introduces the topic of the article in a clear and well-written manner.	The first paragraph adequately introduces the topic of the article.	The first paragraph inadequately introduces the topic of the article.	The first paragraph is confusing, unfocused, or unclear.
Body of Article— who, what, where, when, why, and how (the 5 *Ws* + 1 *H*)	The article adequately addresses the 5 *Ws* + 1 *H* of the event.	The article adequately addresses 4 of the 5 *Ws* + 1 *H*.	The article adequately addresses 3 of the 5 *Ws* + 1 *H*.	The article adequately addresses only 1 or 2 of the 5 *Ws* + 1 *H*.
Spelling and Grammar	Few to no spelling or grammar errors are present in the article.	There are some spelling or grammar errors present in the article, but they do not impact the clarity of the writing.	There are several spelling or grammar errors present in the article, and they impact the clarity of the writing.	There are many spelling or grammar errors present in the article, and they severely impact the clarity of the writing.
Objectivity	The article shows no signs of bias in any area.	The article shows minimal signs of bias.	The article shows several signs of bias.	The article is written as an editorial with more opinions than facts.
Photographs and/ or Artwork	The article is accompanied by two or more appropriate photographs and/or pieces of artwork that are properly captioned.	The article is accompanied by one appropriate photograph and/or piece of artwork that is properly captioned.	The article is accompanied by photographs and/or pieces of artwork, but the connection is unclear or the images are improperly captioned.	The article is accompanied by photographs and/or artwork that are inappropriate or improperly captioned.
Sources	The article includes information from the film and two additional sources.	The article includes information from the film and one additional source.	The article includes only information from the film.	The article includes minimal information from only one print source.

8 Ensuring Success With the CCSS for Literacy in the Content Areas

WHAT ARE BEST PRACTICES FOR ADDRESSING THE CCSS FOR LITERACY IN THE CONTENT AREAS?

Adolescents today are not necessarily reading and writing at levels that support their understanding of the types of complex texts to which they are exposed in history/social studies, science, and technical subjects. In a typical school day, students go from one subject class to another and engage in reading from a variety of content-specific texts and writing in a number of ways. They read journal articles, primary and secondary sources, trade books, technical reports, math problems, and so forth. They write essays, articles, arguments, letters, narratives, lab reports, formulas, and mathematical proofs. They access print and electronic sources to acquire and use new content information. Yet these students may not be engaged in reading and writing strategies and activities that will help them understand and learn complex subject matter. We believe, as the Common Core State Standards (CCSS) posit, that it is the teacher's role to recognize that reading and writing are inseparable from subject area instruction and that the teacher must present research-based literacy strategies and activities that will bring all students to the levels necessary for college, career, and life.

In its Adolescent Literacy Position Statement, the International Reading Association (2012) proposes that content-area teachers must provide instruction in the multiple literacy strategies that students will need to meet the demands of the specific discipline. The lessons discussed in this book aim to develop students' literacy skills in alignment with the CCSS and research about best practices. Specifically, the reading lessons require students to

- do close reading of a range of complex texts and identify main ideas and details,
- focus on vocabulary and structure, and
- analyze, synthesize, and evaluate knowledge and ideas.

You can easily see how students are operating on different levels of Bloom's Taxonomy as they know, comprehend, apply, analyze, synthesize, and evaluate content. The lessons "Nationalism: The Good, the Bad, the Ugly" (Chapter 3) and "Bonus Science Articles" (Chapter 4) both require students to read a variety of literary and/or informational works, both digital and print, to determine and analyze the key ideas in these texts. "Social Causes of New Imperialism" (Chapter 3) and "Vocabulary Videos" (Chapter 4) help students interpret, analyze, and evaluate the structure of a work. "Vietnam: The Human Face in an Inhumane Time" (Chapter 3) and "Continental Drift" (Chapter 4) require students to delineate and analyze ideas in several texts on the same theme or topic.

In addition to the fact that these lessons address common reading and/or writing standards, they also share several key research-based content literacy strategies and activities proven effective in classroom instruction because they promote students' engagement with and understanding of texts. Specifically, the reading and writing strategies and activities used in these lessons increase students' background development, textual comprehension, and vocabulary knowledge. These best practices are many, but the ones we want to highlight here include summarizing, note taking, graphic organizers, guided reading, predictions/anticipation guides, vocabulary building, and multimodal learning opportunities.

> **Summarizing** aids in comprehension and retention of information. It involves identifying, paraphrasing, and synthesizing main ideas into a coherent retelling. For example, "Bonus Science Articles" requires students to read and summarize articles on timely science topics. "Continental Drift" calls for students to take things a step further by summarizing articles and comparing their summaries with evidence gathered through research. In "Nationalism: The Good, the Bad, the Ugly," students summarize the main ideas of two presidential speeches in order to confirm understanding before they engage in a full-class discussion.

> **Note taking** helps organize information for comprehension and study purposes. There are many forms of note taking that include graphic organizers—such as the Cornell note taking strategy, the two-column method, and the outline format—as well as highlighting, annotating, and so on. In "Social Causes of New Imperialism" (Chapter 3) students engage in a note taking session to enable their analysis of Kipling's poem. They use a graphic organizer that categorizes the causes of New Imperialism into economic, political/military, social, and science and invention; the social causes are further categorized into nationalism, Social Darwinism and the White man's burden.

In "Montgomery Bus Boycott" (Chapter 7) students take notes on a viewing guide as they watch a passage from the documentary *Eyes on the Prize*.

Graphic organizers illustrate hierarchical and/or linear relationships among ideas and concepts to promote comprehension and build on students' background knowledge. In addition to note-taking graphic organizers discussed above, there are numerous other overviews, such as the Venn diagram, story map, and word web that could be used to support students' content literacy. In "Earth Day" (Chapter 7), students complete a graphic organizer representing text summary and structure and use it to compose a newspaper article on the topic. In "Mock Trial: Native Americans and European Colonization" (Chapter 6), students complete a structural overview that guides their research on Native Americans and European colonization and helps them present and defend arguments during a mock trial.

Guided reading aids students' comprehension and motivates students to read a content-area text. Guided reading can take the form of questions or directions that call attention to particular parts of a text. In the "Continental Drift" and "Boyle's Law" (Chapter 6) lessons, students read articles and answer questions that are text dependent. Providing evidence-based responses is a key practice that the CCSS emphasize. "Earth Day" provides a structured Directed Reading Thinking Activity (DRTA) with a text on the origin and history of Earth Day in which students individually answer questions based on the reading and come up with their own questions.

Predictions/Anticipation guides activate schema as students anticipate the ideas in a content selection and make connections to what they already know. In "Earth Day," students are introduced to the topic of environmentalism by discussing statements with their classmates using the Find Someone Who activity. In "Montgomery Bus Boycott," students complete an anticipation guide on the topic, making inferences before reading and then referring to the text after reading to substantiate whether or not their predictions were accurate. In that particular lesson, after students view the documentary *Eyes on the Prize* and compose their newspaper article, they reflect on whether or not their opinions have changed. This reflection or self-questioning also develops students' metacognitive skills.

Vocabulary building is essential to comprehension. Word knowledge helps students connect concepts with meaning. In "Vocabulary Videos," students plan and film videos in which they visually represent new vocabulary words. This activity deepens their understanding of the vocabulary, which leads to increased textual comprehension. In "Boyle's Law," a word wall is used to depict the academic and technical vocabulary in the lesson. Students are thus exposed to these words multiple times and can see the connections among the words. They can learn the associative meanings of words and connect new words to known words, thereby building on prior word knowledge.

Multimodal learning opportunities allow for the use of multiple media (sounds, visuals, graphics, text) in order to interpret and produce meaning. Such opportunities appeal to diverse learning styles and intelligences. They can be extremely motivating and engaging for content learning. In "Vietnam: The Human Face in an Inhumane Time," students experience the Vietnam War through Photo Story, a news report, music videos, songs, artifacts, and dialogue writing. "Math in Everyday Life" (Chapter 7) appeals to logical-mathematical learners as well as to kinesthetic learners. It encourages students to go shopping and find the unit price for each item and choose which would be the better buy. Then, they write a shopping instructional manual based on proportions, percent, and unit rate.

In addition to the strategies and activities mentioned above, students also engage in meaningful research in which they organize and outline content and synthesize information from various sources. They are required to think critically about the information and evaluate sources. "Continental Drift," for example, includes a web evaluation activity that requires students to assess the credibility, accuracy, reliability, and relevance of the online sources that they use for their research. In "Fantasy Basketball" (Chapter 6) students draft professional players for teams by critically examining player statistics on an NBA website.

It is important to note that all the literacy strategies and activities discussed above benefit all learners but especially English language learners and struggling learners. These lessons provide content support necessary for *all* students to achieve success. Our annotations—Differentiation Tip and Cultural/Linguistic Highlight—emphasize literacy support or offer additional suggestions for making appropriate curricular and instructional adaptations for students.

Another point we want to make is that although these strategies should be taught, they should not take the place of teaching texts. Learners need to use strategies to better understand texts and become stronger readers and writers. However, close reading of texts should be the main focus, with strategies used as training wheels added to assist. The ultimate goal is that eventually the training wheels are taken off and students are able to engage in independent meaning making (McTighe, as cited in Varlas, 2012).

Although we highlight here the CCSS for Literacy (reading and writing standards), we do not want to preclude the other English Language Arts (ELA) standards—Speaking and Listening and Language—that are evident in all the lessons in this book. In terms of speaking and listening, students listen to audio, make presentations, debate in a mock trial, and discuss content in small and large groups, among other things. In terms of language, as discussed above, students develop their vocabulary and write and refine their writing to reflect conventions of standard English.

SUCCESS STORIES INVOLVING CONTENT-AREA TEACHERS WORKING TOGETHER

The CCSS for Literacy provide wonderful opportunities for content teachers to collaborate with ELA and reading teachers on literacy-rich curricula. To show how this may be done, the following section provides specific examples of interdisciplinary content-area units that have been taught successfully.

History/Social Studies (Grade 9)

When ninth graders at Mineola High School took on a gradewide read of *Briar Rose*, a novel in which author Jane Yolen (1992) uses the metaphor of the fairytale *Sleeping Beauty* to represent the events of the Holocaust, the ninth-grade history teachers saw a great opportunity for an interdisciplinary project. To help students review for their final history exam, they asked students to create their own fairy tale retellings of historical events that they had studied during the year. Topics included the Neolithic Revolution, Early River Civilizations, Rise of Empires, Religion, Silk Road, Indian Ocean trade, Muslim Expansion, Protestant Reformation, Medieval Europe, Dark Ages, Bubonic Plague, Hundred Years War, Rise of Monarch, West African Civilizations, and East Africa.

Students used a graphic organizer to help them organize key ideas and details. In groups of three or seven, they demonstrated understanding of craft and structure by including fairy tale elements such as good and evil characters, castles, royalty, magic, a problem and solution, and things happening. The creation of these historical fairy tales involved both narrative and informative/explanatory writing. Students worked together through the writing process to create their final products. They used technology to create their books and search for appropriate images online. They also used Internet sources to support and increase their knowledge and understanding of their chosen topic.

The books were a great success. One group of students continued with the *Sleeping Beauty* metaphor but applied it to the Black Plague in Europe. Another group compared *Beauty and the Beast* with the story of Helen of Troy. The most popular story metaphor was *The Three Little Pigs*. Students used this story frame to explain World War II. The wolf was compared with the Nazis. The homes of the first two pigs represented European Nations destroyed by the Nazis, and the third pig represented the Allied Forces who defeated the wolf. Another group compared the three little pigs to the Americas of the 1400s. Each pig represented a different civilization, the Incas, the Aztecs, and the Mayans. The wolf was the Spanish Conquistador, trying to take over. Not only did students enjoy the process of creating the books, but also, in presenting their work and listening to others' presentations, students reviewed a great deal of the material for their final exam. This is an excellent example of how literacy instruction can support students' content knowledge.

Science (Grade 11)

Environmental Science teacher Don Leopardi worked with Maureen Connolly to develop a unit based on Rachel Carson's (1962) *Silent Spring*. Students discussed the key ideas and details of the scientific content of *Silent Spring* in Leopardi's science class. In Maureen's English class, they completed a rhetorical analysis of the craft and structure of the work. They also created an online chart of challenging vocabulary words that contained (a) the student-selected vocabulary word, (b) the context as it was used by Carson, (c) a definition of the word, and (d) a famous quote that included the word.

Following their reading of *Silent Spring*, students took part in two different debates regarding Carson's ideas. First, students debated Carson's claim that humankind is engaged in a "war against nature." They considered whether or not they agreed that targeting certain things for destruction (or at least control) means that we are at war with nature. Students also considered what has changed since Carson wrote *Silent Spring* in 1962. They argued about whether the natural environment has improved or declined and if we are now more concerned with the effect we have on nature—or less concerned. These debates were heated. Students used their knowledge of Carson's work and also information gleaned from current science and political articles.

After the debate, students viewed two TED Talks (see ted.com), Mark Bitman's *What's Wrong With What We Eat?* (http://www.ted.com/talks/ann_cooper_talks_school_lunches.html) and *Ann Cooper Talks School Lunches* (http://www.ted.com/talks/mark_bittman_on_what_s_wrong_with_what_we_eat.html). These talks gave students a new perspective on how their eating habits affect the environment and their own health and well-being. Based on what they learned through each of these sources, along with their exploration of a website for the Meatless Monday international campaign, students developed a two-page proposal to the school principal, the district superintendent, and the head of food services asking for the cafeteria to offer more meat-free options and requesting permission to start a Meatless Monday campaign in the school. They developed flyers explaining the simple campaign to their peers. The flyers included the following:

- At least two facts about how going meatless can improve personal health and the environment
- A quote from one of the sources they had read or viewed
- An eye-catching visual

The writing for this project combined argument (the proposal) with informative/explanatory (the flyer). Students went through painstaking revision and editing during the writing process because they were well aware of the pressures of their audience. Yes, the superintendent and the principal would be judging their writing, but perhaps worse, their own peers would be judging their flyers!

As an extension of this unit, students planned to research powerful videos that could be shown in the cafeteria to make a strong case for Meatless Monday. They expressed an interest in showing the removal of clogged arteries from a man's heart or some of the cruelty that cattle endure. Of course, finding the balance between powerful and nauseating would be a challenge!

Technical Subjects—Math (Grade 7)

Upon learning about the new CCSS for Literacy, math teacher Katherine O'Sullivan, who also has a master's degree in Reading, worked to create several lessons that incorporate literacy skills. First, she searched for one- to two-page readings related to math. She discovered *Fractals, Googols, and Other Mathematical Tales* by Theoni Pappas (1993), an excellent resource for this purpose. One of Katherine's favorite readings from the book, "The Day the Number Line Fell Apart," serves as a great introduction to classifying. In the story, the different types of real numbers must decide where they should be placed on the number line. They also problem solve what to do when two numbers share the same value, eventually deciding to share the position on the number line.

Katherine read the story to students and then asked them to place values on the number line and answer three questions relating to the reading. The questions involved Tier 2 vocabulary such as *ascending/descending, increasing/decreasing* and how they relate to math.

Next, students worked in heterogeneous groups of three to four to define and discuss more content-specific Tier 3 vocabulary terms such as *rational, irrational, integer, whole number,* and *counting number.* The students then discussed with one another how to apply this vocabulary to each given value, sorting them into a Venn diagram. If the numbers were rational, the students decided whether or not to continue classifying them into any additional subgroups. On the following day, each group presented its Venn diagram while the class compiled a master Venn diagram that consisted of all the groups' values, checking each other's answers and discussing their rationale using the Tier 2 and Tier 3 vocabulary terms.

This is just one example of the way that literacy strategies can be applied to math-related readings, including the use of guiding questions to clarify basic comprehension, the examination of Tier 2 and Tier 3 words, and the organization of ideas in Venn diagrams. There are several other readings in *Fractals, Googols, and Other Mathematical Tales* (Pappas, 1993) that Katherine uses to reinforce her teaching over the course of the year. She also brings in newspaper and magazine articles that are linked to statistics. While the *Fractals, Googols, and Other Mathematical Tales* are written as entertaining teaching tools, the articles also provide real-world application of the math skills students are developing.

ACCESSING SUPPORT THROUGH TECHNOLOGY

The following is a list of 20 websites that we have found especially useful to our teaching. Some of these sites are helpful for developing lesson plans, and many offer teacher-created lesson plans. These sites allow for collaboration with teachers near and far who post their successful lessons.

Other sites on our list offer expert information from journalists, scientists, historians, and other academics and professionals. This is the beauty of the web. Most of us would never have the opportunity to collaborate with such experts if not for the Internet. Other websites on our list offer far more than just learning resources; they open a door to educational communities (e.g., research, online discussions, opportunities for advocacy and face-to-face interactions at conferences, workshops, and meetings). We organize this list into three sections:

- **Organization/Experts** includes sites that help you connect with professional organizations.

- **Content/Skills Support** includes sites that are focused on content-area information and innovative teaching approaches.
- **Tools** includes some of our favorite ways to organize and present information for teachers and students.

Organizations/Experts

1. ASCD (www.ascd.org)

This site, sponsored by ASCD (formerly the Association for Supervision and Curriculum Development) offers resources to educators throughout more than 145 different countries. With a membership of over 150,000, the networking opportunities via ASCD are varied and powerful. According to the mission statement, "ASCD is a membership organization that develops programs, products, and services essential to the way educators learn, teach, and lead."

What we like about it . . .

- Connection to ASCD Professional Interest Communities: These member-initiated groups are designed to unite people around a common area of interest in the field of education.
- Connection to ASCD Connected Communities: These groups, defined by geographic boundaries, help bring together groups of individuals concerned with improving teaching and learning.
- Provides links to publications, including *Education Leadership* and *Educational Update* along with full-length books.

2. Association for Middle Level Education (www.nmsa.org)

This site, sponsored by Association for Middle Level Education (formerly, National Middle School Association), promotes the development of more effective schools. The organization, according to a self-published position paper states the following: "Our message is for schools to be academically excellent, developmentally responsive, and socially equitable for every adolescent."

What we like about it . . .

- Connection to MiddleTalk listserv.
- Provides advocacy opportunities.
- Provides links to publications, including *Middle School Journal* and *Middle Ground* along with full-length books.

3. Teaching Channel (teachingchannel.org)

This site offers a wealth of information to teachers. Watch videos; download resources; read a blog. Whatever you choose to do, it is sure to leave you inspired!

What we like about it . . .

- Clearly organized: You can search based on subject area, grade level, or education topics.
- Includes engaging and mostly brief videos: You can watch something in 5 to 10 minutes and walk away with a new approach for your classroom.

- Offers the opportunity to join a teachers' network.
- Provides a workspace on which you can save interesting videos and articles, a means for scheduling implementation of new teaching methods in your electronic planner, and alerts for postings by teachers whose ideas you like.

4. College Board (collegeboard.org)

The CCSS are meant to prepare students for college. The College Board website provides information and resources that may help you and your students work to meet this goal.

What we like about it . . .

- Provides timely articles on education.
- Includes information about AP and SAT preparation and testing that may be applied to your lesson plans in order to increase rigor regarding literacy skills.
- Offers opportunities for professional development via summer institutes and conferences.

5. Project Based Learning (PBL) (pbl-online.org)

According to their main page, "You'll find all the resources you need to design and manage high quality projects for middle and high school students" at this site.

What we like about it . . .

- Provides guidance for planning your own PBL.
- Includes a PBL library of projects developed by fellow teachers. You can post your own as well.
- Provides research on the benefits of PBL and best practices with PBL.

6. Reading Quest (readingquest.org)

Reading Quest is designed to assist social studies teachers with helping their students increase their comprehension through the use of suggested reading strategies.

What we like about it . . .

- The strategies page is the best part of this site. Instructions for 28 reading strategies and handouts (when applicable) are available here.
- Provides frameworks for choosing comprehension strategies.
- Includes links to other resources.

7. Educational Technology Guy (http://educationaltechnologyguy.blogspot.com/)

This blog was created by David Andrade, a physics teacher and educational technology consultant. Andrade describes the blog as a place where he "explore[s] free educational technology resources, ways to integrate technology into the classroom, professional development, project-based learning, and tips and resources for new teachers."

What we like about it . . .

- Links to excellent, free resources: See Andrade's list of favorites.
- Discussion of timely topics such as Science, Technology, Engineering, Math (STEM) and PBL.
- Links to personal learning networks.

Content/Skills Support

8. Primary Source (primarysource.org)

According to their main page, "Primary Source promotes history and humanities education by connecting educators with people and cultures throughout the world." This site provides a strong rationale for global education, and it provides the means to support teachers' efforts to help their students think and act as global citizens. Though it appears to be social studies based, the site has many links to topics related to science and technology.

What we like about it . . .

- Provides opportunities to connect online with teachers throughout the world.
- Includes a vast array of resources organized into categories: books, children's books, websites, oral histories, films and video, and curriculum guides.
- Offers opportunities for professional development via summer institutes and international conferences.

9. CultureGrams (culturegrams.com)

This online database requires a subscription, but it is worth getting your library to fund it. CultureGrams offers "an insider's" perspective on daily life and culture, including history, customs, and lifestyles of the world's people.

What we like about it . . .

- Provides a variety of sources ranging from print to photos to videos.
- Interviews with adults and children to represent ways of life throughout the world.
- Information is organized into World Edition, States Edition, Provinces Edition, and Kids Edition for easy searching based on topic and reading level.
- Printer-friendly format.
- Opportunities to organize information into tables.

10. Technology Entertainment Design (TED) (www.ted.com)

The tagline for this site is "riveting talks by remarkable people, free to the world." Whether you are looking to develop a basic understanding of a topic that is foreign to you or to learn more about a topic that *is* familiar to you, this is a great resource. Videos are under 20 minutes.

What we like about it . . .

- Information is organized according to theme and interest level (most viewed, most e-mailed, "jaw-dropping", etc.).

- Offers interactive opportunities through blogging and through Ted Conversations. This link allows users to post questions, comments, or debates. Other users then respond.
- Translations of talks are available.

11. National Public Radio (www.npr.org)

This site includes a vast collection of nonfiction in written and audio form. *What we like about it . . .*

- Provides information on the latest headlines.
- *This American Life*: This show features eye-opening stories about everyday lives of Americans.
- Storycorps: This is a venue for recording stories about loved ones that might otherwise be lost.
- *Science Friday*: Provides a link to interesting topics such as space, body and brain, biology, nature, physics and chemistry, engineering, gadgets, food, energy, ethics, and more.

12. This I Believe (www.thisibelieve.org)

This site is an archive of over 90,000 essays written around the theme of core values or beliefs. Many are available as podcasts. In addition, the site offers grade-level appropriate curriculum guides for infusing This I Believe in your curriculum. *What we like about it . . .*

- Provides podcasts that you can use for students to practice listening and note-taking skills.
- Includes curriculum guides.
- Provides a forum for publishing essays.
- You may even be able to get the executive producer of *This I Believe* to visit your school!

13. Brainpop (www.brainpop.com)

This site offers information on a variety of content areas and seems to cover almost every topic within content areas with numerous examples, facts, and ideas to browse. The site is student-centered, with bright colors and an engaging organization. *What we like about it . . .*

- Students like the explanatory videos (though some are a bit basic for more mature students).
- Brainpop Educators allows you to access lesson plans by grade level and subject area. At this time, the site has over 135,000 members and 850 free resources.

14. Go to Service Learning (http://gotoservicelearning.org)

This site provides teacher-developed service-learning lessons sorted by content, themes, grade level, target populations, duration, setting, and place of impact. *What we like about it . . .*

- Because of the excellent search parameters, finding lessons that fit your needs is extremely easy.

- The common template for all lessons includes Essential Questions, Service-Learning Themes, Curriculum Connections, Stages of Service Learning, Assessment and Evaluation.

15. Public Broadcasting Service Teachers (www.pbs.org/teachers)

PBS Teachers provides pre-K–12 educational resources, including lesson plans, classroom teaching activities, on-demand videos, and interactive games.
What we like about it . . .

- Thousands of classroom resources are available that are suitable for a wide range of subjects and grade levels.
- Resources are broken down according to grade level, subject, media type, and PBS programming.
- These resources are tied to PBS's on-air and online programming (e.g., *NOVA, Nature*), allowing for multiple opportunities for multimedia assignments.
- Offers video products on education topics.
- Educators may participate in online discussions and blogs.

16. Water Planet Challenge (waterplanetchallenge.org)

The mission of this website is to "improve the health of the environment in your community and around the world." The information and content presented relate to science, civics and advocacy, research, and technology.
What we like about it . . .

- Excellent curriculum guides and educator resources.
- Connections to teacher grants.
- Links to interactive web pages and interesting videos.
- "Take Action" tab that clearly lays out each of the five stages of service learning.

17. Landmark Cases (landmarkcases.org)

This site represents the combined efforts of Street Law, Inc. and the Supreme Court to share information about landmark Supreme Court cases with students.
What we like about it . . .

- Provides clearly organized background of the case.
- Explains both sides of the issue at hand and provides links to articles and other case-related resources.
- Differentiated instructional materials for highest reading level, for average reading level, and for diverse students.
- Suggested teaching strategies for each case.
- Includes a discussion of legal concepts covered in the cases.

Tools

18. Quizlet (Quizlet.com)

This site provides interactive studying methods for students. You can choose from resources that are already available or upload your own information.

What we like about it . . .

- Allows you to create your own stack of electronic flashcards or pull cards from other teachers.
- Includes a timed memory matching game.
- Allows you to create your own quiz or test online from the study material. Quizlet grades it for you!

19. Prezi (prezi.com)

This is an excellent alternative to PowerPoint. Prezis are fun to watch as they zoom from topic to topic. When signing up on the site, you create a profile in which to share your own Prezis.

What we like about it . . .

- Provides many ways for you and your students to be creative as you design presentations. From Pan and Zoom options to Storyline options, the choices and combinations feel endless.
- Allows you to check out other people's Prezis. Click on those represented under "Prezis we like."
- Download the Prezi app to your iPad or iPhone to take your Prezis anywhere!

20. Mind 42 (mind42.com)

This site allows you to create a web representation of your thoughts. It's a great tool for students and teachers alike.

What we like about it . . .

- Enables you to design your own web, adding notes and attachments as you go along.
- Allows you to create mind maps alone or have group members sign in to add to one common map.
- Opportunities for sharing/publishing mind maps.

TEN TIPS FOR GETTING TO THE HEART OF THE COMMON CORE FOR LITERACY IN THE CONTENT AREAS

The following is a list of famous quotations that we offer as the basis for guidance for getting to the core of the CCSS for Literacy in the Content Areas.

1. "You can do anything, but not everything."—American author and consultant, David Allen (1945–)

Even though the standards are clear, coherent, and focused, they can still feel overwhelming. Try to begin by aligning at least some of your units with the CCSS or focus on a few key features of the standards instead of trying to incorporate all of them at once.

2. "Try to learn something about everything and everything about something."—English biologist, Thomas Henry Huxley (1825–1895)

At first, try to understand at least the gist of all the standards and then gradually focus closely on teaching a few standards very well. In the same way, focus on depth rather than breadth of content, as the CCSS advocate.

3. "The artist is nothing without the gift, but the gift is nothing without work."—French author, Emile Zola (1840–1902)

As educators, you have the gift of imparting content knowledge to students; that is what makes you and your profession special and valued. However, it requires hard work to help your students be ready for college, career, and life beyond school.

4. "The mistakes are all waiting to be made."—Chessmaster Savielly Grigorievitch Tartakower (1887–1956) on the game's opening position

Mistakes are inevitable, and unless you attack the CCSS head on, you will not know if and how you can be successful. Success is waiting for you; try to attain it without worrying about misunderstanding or misaligning with the CCSS.

5. "Research is what I'm doing when I don't know what I'm doing."—German American rocket scientist, Wernher von Braun (1912–1977)

Engage in research about the CCSS and designing CCSS-based lessons in order to become informed. In your content classes, have your students conduct research using traditional and online means so that they can learn more about the content topics under study.

6. "The real voyage of discovery consists not in seeking new lands but seeing with new eyes."—French author, Marcel Proust (1871–1922)

As we have stressed in this book and in our other book, *Getting to the Core of ELA*, you do not necessarily need to design brand-new lessons to align with the CCSS. The real journey of CCSS implementation lies in seeing the curriculum you already have through the lens of the CCSS and then doing some tweaking or refocusing or realigning.

7. "In the long history of humankind (and animal kind, too) those who learned to collaborate and improvise most effectively have prevailed."—English naturalist, Charles Darwin (1809–1822)

It is not only important to work together with your colleagues; you must also be flexible in the classroom and recognize when you need to improvise to adapt your lessons to best meet your students' needs.

8. "Have a vision. Be demanding."—American statesman, Colin Powell (1937–)

The CCSS help you clearly determine what students must learn. As these standards take hold in schools across the country, students may feel overwhelmed. Help your students understand the need for the rigorous work that is being demanded of them. Teach your students the skills to succeed. Keep the bar high.

9. "Education is all a matter of building bridges."—American author, Ralph Ellison (1914–1994)

The CCSS allow for teachers throughout the United States to build bridges by collaborating with each other and aligning student learning. We encourage you to help your students recognize how the skills they develop and the knowledge they obtain through meeting the CCSS can help them to be better national and global citizens.

10. "This book fills a much-needed gap."—American classical scholar, Moses Hadas (1900–1966) in a review

We believe that this book addresses the needs of content educators who must understand what the CCSS for Literacy are, how the standards benefit skills development, and how to incorporate the standards in classroom instruction.

CONCLUSION

The best advice that we can give comes in the words of the theorists to whom we have connected our work throughout this book. John Dewey reminded us that "Arriving at one goal is the starting point for another" (as cited in Casil, 2006, p. 6). It is not enough to be satisfied with yourself as a great teacher of content. As Gardner wrote, "A lot of knowledge in any kind of an organization is what we call task knowledge. These are things that people who have been there a long time understand are important, but they may not know how to talk about them" (as cited in Koch, 1996, p. 60).

You must learn to guide your students through learning the material about which you are so passionate. You must learn to impart your "task knowledge" to them in a way that they can understand and use it as well. As Bloom (1976) noted, "What any person in the world can learn, *almost* all persons can learn if provided with appropriate prior and current conditions of learning" (p. 7).

If you help your students develop their literacy skills, you will give them the tools they need to be successful in your content-area course and in all courses of study that they pursue. As educators, if you can metaphorically carry these ideas with you as you apply the CCSS to your teaching, you are bound to be successful. More literally, you can carry the CCSS around with you via the CCSS app on your smartphones. If you are planning a lesson and you want to see how it aligns with the CCSS, just check yourself against the standards listed by checking the app. And while you have that phone out, please visit us at the Corwin website (www.corwin.com) to access handouts from this book and to share your success stories!

References

ACT, Inc. (2010). *A first look at the common core and college and career readiness.* Retrieved from http://www.act.org/research/policymakers/pdf/FirstLook.pdf

Adams, M. J. (2010–2011, Winter). Advancing our students' language and literacy. *American Educator,* pp. 3–11.

Alvermann, D., & Moore, D. (1991). Secondary school reading. In R. Barr, M. Kamil, P. Mosenthal, & P. D. P. Pearson (Eds.), *Handbook of reading research* (Vol. II, pp. 1013–46.). New York: Longman.

Applebee, A. N., & Langer, J. A. (2009). What is happening in the teaching of writing? *English Journal, 98*(5), 18–28.

Applebee, A. N., & Langer, J. A. (2011). A snapshot of writing instruction in middle schools and high schools. *English Journal, 100*(6), 14–17.

Artley, S. (1944). A study of certain relationships existing between general reading comprehension and reading comprehension in a specific subject matter area. *Journal of Educational Research, 37,* 464–473.

Atwell, N. (1989). *Coming to know: Writing to learn in the intermediate grades.* Portsmouth, NH: Heinemann.

Beck, I. L., McKeown, L. L., & Kucan, L. (2002). *Bringing words to life: Robust vocabulary instruction.* New York: Guilford Press.

Bird, J. (2006). *Literature circles and reading in science.* Clark University, Worchester, MA. Retrieved from www.upcsinstitute.org/DMSFiles/LitCirclesinSci.pdf

Bloom, B. S. (1956). *Taxonomy of educational objectives, handbook I: The cognitive domain.* New York: David McKay.

Bloom, B. S. (1976). *Human characteristics and school learning.* New York: McGraw-Hill.

Brozo, W. G., & Simpson, M. L. (2007). *Content literacy for today's adolescents: Honoring diversity and building competence* (5th ed.). Upper Saddle River, NJ: Merrill/Prentice Hall.

Burke, J. (2010). *What's the big idea? Question-driven units to motivate reading, writing, and thinking.* Portsmouth, NH: Heinemann.

Carson, R. (1962). *Silent spring.* Boston, MA: Houghton Mifflin.

Casil, A. S. (2006). *John Dewey: The founder of American liberalism.* New York: Rosen.

Dalton, J., & Smith, D. (1986). *Extending children's special abilities: Strategies for primary classrooms.* Melbourne, Victoria, Australia: Curriculum Branch, Schools Division.

D'Arcangelo, M. D. (2002). The challenge of content-area reading: A conversation with Donna Ogle. *Educational Leadership, 60*(3), 12–15.

Dewey, J. (1916). *Democracy and education: An introduction to the philosophy of education.* New York: Free Press.

Dewey, J. (1938). *Experience and education.* New York: Collier.

Dieker, L. A., & Little, M. (2005). Not just for reading teachers anymore. *Intervention in School and Clinic, 40*(5), 276–283.

Falcone, J. P. (2012, March 13). Kindle vs. Nook vs. iPad: Which e-book reader should you buy? *CNET News.* Retrieved from http://news.cnet.com

Gamoran, A., Wisconsin Center for Education Research, Committee on Science, Space, and Technology. (2011). *Written testimony of Adam Gamoran before the U.S. House of Representatives.* Retrieved from http://science.house.gov/sites/republicans .science.house.gov/files/documents/hearings/101211_Gamoran.pdf

Gardner, H. (1983). *Frames of mind: The theory of multiple intelligences.* New York: Basic Books.

Giouroukakis, V., & Connolly, M. (2012). *Getting to the core of English language arts, grades 6–12: How to meet the Common Core State Standards with lessons from the classroom.* Thousand Oaks, CA: Corwin.

Griggs, M. C., Daane, Y. J., & Campbell, J. R. (2003). *The nation's report card.* Washington, DC: U.S. Department of Education.

Hampton, H. (Producer), & Vecchione, J. (Director). (1987). *Eyes on the prize* [DVD]. United States: Blackside.

Hayslip, L. L. (1989). *When heaven and earth changed places.* New York: Plume.

Heller, R., & Greenleaf, C. L. (2007). *Literacy instruction in the content areas: Getting to the core of middle and high school improvement.* Alliance for Excellent Education. Retrieved from http://www.all4ed.org/files/LitCon.pdf

Hellwarth, B. (2012, January 21). The other final frontier. *New York Times.* Retrieved from http://www.nytimes.com/2012/01/22/opinion/sunday/the-other-final-frontier.html

International Reading Association. (2012). *Adolescent literacy position statement.* Retrieved from http://www.reading.org/Libraries/Resources/ps1079_adolescentliteracy_rev2012.pdf

Kamil, M. L. (2003). *Adolescents and literacy: Reading for the 21st century.* Washington, DC: Alliance for Excellent Education.

Kerr, N. H., & Picciotti, M. (2010). Linked composition courses: Effects on student performance. *Journal of Teaching Writing, 11*(1), 105–118.

Kipling, R. (1899). *White man's burden.* Retrieved from http://www.fordham.edu/halsall /mod/kipling.asp

Koch, C. (1996, March). The bright stuff: Interview with Howard Gardner. *CIO Magazine, 9*(100), 59–62.

Kovic, R. (1976). *Born on the fourth of July.* New York: Akashic Books.

Lesley, M., & Mathews, M. (2009). Place-based essay writing and content area literacy instruction for preservice secondary teachers. *Journal of Adolescent and Adult Literacy, 52*(6), 523–533.

Lesley, M., Watson, P., & Elliot, S. (2007). School reading and multiple texts: Examining the metacognitive development of secondary-level preservice teachers. *Journal of Adolescent & Adult Literacy, 51*(2), 150–162.

McGrath, A. G. (2005). *A new read on teen literacy.* Retrieved from http://www.usnews .com/usnews/culture/articles/050228/28literacy.htm

McKenna, M. C., & Robinson, R. D. (1990). Content literacy: A definition and implications. *Journal of Reading, 34*(3), 184–186.

National Governors Association Center for Best Practices (NGA Center)/Council of Chief State School Officers (CCSSO). (2010a). *About the standards.* Retrieved from http://www.corestandards.org/about-the-standards

National Governors Association Center for Best Practices (NGA Center)/Council of Chief State School Officers (CCSSO). (2010b). *Common core state standards for ELA, literacy in history/social studies, science, and technical subjects.* Retrieved from http:// www.corestandards.org/assets/CCSSI_ELA%20Standards.pdf

National Governors Association Center for Best Practices (NGA Center)/Council of Chief State School Officers (CCSSO). (2010c). *Common core state standards for ELA, literacy in history/social studies, science, and technical subjects. Appendix A.* Retrieved from http://www.corestandards.org/assets/Appendix_A.pdf

Neufeld, P. (2005). Comprehension instruction in content area classes. *The Reading Teacher, 59*(4), 302–312.

Nichols, W. D., Young, C. A., & Rickelman, R. J. (2007). Improving middle school professional development by examining middle school teachers' application of literacy strategies and instructional design. *Reading Psychology: Special Issue on Middle School Reading Instruction, 28*(1), 97–130.

O'Brien, D. (2006). Struggling adolescents' engagement in multimediating: Countering the institutional construction of incompetence. In D. A. Alvermann, K. A. Hinchman, D. W. Moore, S. F. Phelps, & D. R. Waff (Eds.), *Reconceptualizing the literacies in adolescent's lives* (pp. 29–46). New York: Routledge.

O'Brien, D. G., Moje, E. B., & Stewart, R. A. (2001). Exploring the context of secondary literacy: Literacy in people's everyday school lives. In E. B. Moje & D. G. O'Brien (Eds.), *Constructions of literacy: Studies of teaching and learning in and out of secondary classrooms* (pp. 27–48). Mahwah, NJ: Erlbaum.

O'Brien, T. (2009). *The things they carried.* New York: Mariner Books.

Olson, S., & Loucks-Housely, S. (2000). *Inquiry and the National Science Education Standards: A guide for teaching and learning.* Washington, DC: National Academy Press.

Palmer, L. (1987). *Shrapnel in the heart.* New York: Random House.

Pappas, T. (1993). *Fractals, googols, and other mathematical tales.* San Carlos, CA: Wide World.

Partnership for 21st Century Skills. (2006, October 2). *Most young people entering the U.S. workforce lack critical skills essential for success.* Retrieved from http://www.p21.org/index.php?option=com_content&task=view&id=250&Itemid=64

Pressley, M. (2002). *Reading instruction that works: The case for balanced teaching* (2nd ed.). New York: Guilford.

Pressley, M. (2004). Reflection on theory and current practice. In T. L. Jetton & J. A. Dole (Eds.), *Adolescent literacy research and practice* (pp. 415–432). New York: Guilford.

Project Based Learning. (n.d). What is project based learning? *Buck Institute for Education.* Retrieved from http://www.bie.org/about/what_is_pbl

Science/inquiry literature circles. (2011, December 19). Elementary Science Integration Project. Retrieved from http://www.esiponline.org/classroom/foundations/reading/science_lit_circle.html

Sejnost, R. L., & Thiese, S. (2007). *Reading and writing across content areas.* Thousand Oaks, CA: Corwin.

Shanahan, T., & Shanahan, C. (2008). Teaching disciplinary literacy to adolescents: Rethinking content area literacy. *Harvard Educational Review, 78*(1), 40–59.

Sohn, E. (2003, October 7). It's a math world for animals. *Science news for kids.* Retrieved from http://www.sciencenewsforkids.org/2003/10/its-a-math-world-for-animals-2/

Soven, M. I. (1999). *Teaching writing in middle and secondary schools: Theory, research, and practice.* Boston, MA: Allyn & Bacon.

State Educational Technology Directors Association. (2011). Transforming education to ensure all students are successful in the 21st century. *National Educational Technology Trends: 2011.* Retrieved from http://www.setda.org/c/document_library/get_file?folderId=6&name=DLFE-1302.pdf

The things they carry. (2006, November 20). *Time Magazine*, Retrieved from http://www.time.com/time/magazine/article/0,9171,1558328,00.html

Tomlinson, C. A., & McTighe, J. (2006). *Integrating differentiated instruction and understanding by design.* Alexandria, VA: Association for Supervision and Curriculum Development.

Top 50 cities in the U.S. by population and rank. (n.d.). Retrieved from http://www.infoplease.com/ipa/A0763098.html#ixzz2CvFEJxWI

Varlas, L. (2012, April). It's complicated: Common core state standards focus on text complexity. *Education Update, 54*(4), 1, 6–7.

Walker, K. (1985). *A piece of my heart: The stories of 26 American women who served in Vietnam.* New York: Presidio Press.

Wiggins, G. (2010). Why we should stop bashing tests. *Educational Leadership, 67*(6), 48–52.

Wiggins, G., & McTighe, J. (1998). *Understanding by design.* Alexandria, VA: Association for Supervision and Curriculum Development.

Wiggins, G., & McTighe, J. (2001). *Understanding by design.* Upper Saddle River, NJ: Merrill/Prentice Hall.

Wiggins, G., & McTighe, J. (2005). *Understanding by design (2nd ed.).* Alexandria, VA: Association for Supervision and Curriculum Development.

Wilson, J. T. (1996). Continental drift. *Colliers Encyclopedia CD-ROM (Vol. 7.)* Retrieved from http://www.platetectonics.com/article.asp?a=18

Wolpert-Gawron, H. (2011, November 1). Persuasive writing is a key focus in common core standards [Web log message]. Retrieved from http://www.edutopia.org/blog/common-core-standards-persuasive-writing-heather-wolpert-gawron

Yolen, J. (1992). *Briar rose.* New York: Tom Doherty.

Zumbrunn, S., & Krause, K. (2012). Conversations with leaders: Principles of effective writing instruction. *The Reading Teacher, 65*(5), 346–353.

Appendix

Lesson Plan Template

LESSON PLAN TEMPLATE

TOPIC (GRADE LEVEL):

TEXT TYPES AND PURPOSES:

CCSS STRAND:

TIMING:

BACKWARD DESIGN COMPONENTS:

DESIRED RESULTS/CCSS ADDRESSED:

Essential Understandings

Knowledge and Skills

ACCEPTABLE EVIDENCE:

LEARNING EXPERIENCES AND INSTRUCTION:

STRATEGIES (e.g., guidance and monitoring, modeling, cooperative learning, discussion, and writing process):

MATERIALS NEEDED:

SUPPLEMENTAL RESOURCES:

TECHNOLOGY/MEDIA OPPORTUNITIES:

SERVICE LEARNING LINKS:

VARIATIONS:

Index

CORWIN

A SAGE Company

The Corwin logo—a raven striding across an open book—represents the union of courage and learning. Corwin is committed to improving education for all learners by publishing books and other professional development resources for those serving the field of PreK–12 education. By providing practical, hands-on materials, Corwin continues to carry out the promise of its motto: **"Helping Educators Do Their Work Better."**